M

The
Cave Paintings
of
Baja California

Discovering the Great Murals of an Unknown People

Written and Photographed by

Harry W. Crosby

Additional Photographs by Enrique Hambleton

Illustrations by Harry Crosby and Joanne Haskell Crosby

Sunbelt Natural History Books
"Adventures in the Natural and Cultural History of the Californias"

A series edited by Lowell Lindsay

SUNBELT PUBLICATIONS

San Diego, California

Sunbelt Publications, Inc.
POB 191126
San Diego, California, 92159-1126

00 99 98 97   5 4 3 2 1

International Standard Book Number 0-932653-23-5
Library of Congress Catalog Card Number 97-14298

Photographs by the author and Enrique Hambleton
Interior design by Paul Slick
Cover design by Curt Boyer
Packaging by The Marino Group
Illustrations by Harry Crosby and Joanne Haskell Crosby
Introduction by Polly Schaafsma
Prepress work and cartography by ColorType, San Diego

"Sunbelt Natural History Books"
A series edited by Lowell Lindsay

Library of Congress Cataloging in Publication Data

Crosby, Harry, 1926
    The Cave Paintings of Baja California: Discovering the Great Murals of an
    Unknown People, written and photographed by Harry Crosby: additional
    photographs by Enrique Hambleton: illustrations by Harry Crosby and
    Joanne Haskell Crosby.
    Revised and expanded, 3rd ed.
        p.   cm.-- (Sunbelt natural history books)
    Includes bibliographical references and index.
    ISBN 0-932653-23-5 (hardcover: alk. paper)
    1. Indians of Mexico--Mexico--Baja California--Antiquities 2. Cave Paintings--
Mexico--Baja California. 3. Rock paintings--Mexico--Baja California. 4. Petro-
glyphs--Mexico--Baja California. 5. Baja California (Mexico)--Antiquities.
I. Hambleton, Enrique. II. title. III. Series.
F1219.1,B3C76 1997
972'.2--dc21   97-14298
                                                                       CIP

To the memory of Eustacio Arce Villavicencio, 1911–1986

That most intelligent communication network, the Baja California grapevine, led me to Tacho Arce. People I had come to trust recommended him, and he far outperformed their most confident expectations. When I met him, he was sixty years of age, rheumatic, diabetic, and suffering from bad teeth. Nevertheless, he responded with youthful enthusiasm to my request to visit his mountains and meet his people. During our ten years of close association, we spent a year riding together during which he acted as guide, packmaster, mule skinner, teacher, envoy, and diplomat. Through him, I met hundreds of people and visited dozens of sierra ranches. Because of him, I learned many things that others have missed. During the times we were not together, Tacho undertook to consult new sources and gather data that might further my fieldwork. Had I not had the advantages and pleasures of Tacho's friendship, guidance, and assistance, I would never have experienced Baja California's ancient art as I did, and this book would never have come to pass.

Beyond that, Tacho was a great man, one of the few I have known. He was poor in worldly goods all his life, but that did not make him small or bitter. He had the natural dignity of his people and a personal poise, wisdom, and egalitarian directness that allowed a poor and uneducated person to address everyone as a respected equal. He was both wit and philosopher in the oldest and best senses of those words. His vast fund of anecdotes and his spontaneous humor illuminated and reflected every aspect of life, but never demeaned it. From his little, he drew and gave much; to spend time in his company was to be enlightened, diverted, heartened, chastened, and, finally, inspired.

Memories of Tacho motivate me in my own later years. I try to approach each day as he did: to do the best I can, and to pass on what I have learned along my path. In the end, I hope that I will have justified his efforts with me and earned the right to have ridden by his side.

—Harry W. Crosby

The Great Mural Region
Of Baja California

PACIFIC OCEAN

GULF OF CALIFORNIA

Cataviña

Bahía de
los Angeles

SIERRA DE
SAN BORJA

Bahia de
Sebastian
Vizcaino

Isla
Tiburon

Guerrero
Negro

SIERRA DE
SAN JUAN

Scammon's
Lagoon

SIERRA DE
SAN FRANCISCO

Santa
Rosalía

San Ignacio

SIERRA DE
GUADALUPE

Mulegé

Loreto

N

MILES 0   10   20   30   40   50

KILOMETERS 0 10 20 30 40 50 60 70 80

29°

28°

27°

26°

115°   114°   113°   112°

Contents

Great Mural Art endures on the California peninsula at hundreds of sites in an area more than 300 miles long—but no two painted places are truly comparable. This small, well-protected rock shelter in the Sierra de Guadalupe displays paintings and rock carvings in a variety of styles. Ten other painted sites that differ greatly, physically and artistically, can be seen within a radius of 15 miles.

El Pilo

Foreword

The remark has been made that "There is no progress in art." This statement is borne out time and again by prehistoric rock art created by members of simple societies, from the artistically powerful Paleolithic cave paintings of Europe to the more recent elegant figures of elands and dancers in paintings of the southern San in Africa. Likewise, the Great Murals of Baja California are remarkable for their aesthetic content. Aside from its powerful appeal to contemporary observers, this visual imagery went far beyond mere aesthetic expression. Grounded in a cognitive system of beliefs, it is rich in metaphorical significance. This rock art played a primary role in communicating cultural values, and leaves us a tangible if enigmatic record of specific temporal, spatial, and social contexts.

Until rather recently, rock shelters in remote, rugged desert arroyos and cañadas in the central sierras of Baja California hid from the outside world their veritable treasure of grand painted murals. Not surprisingly, they were rediscovered by men who found themselves in the region for purposes quite apart from art or anthropology. A few painted caves were noticed and described in the annals of Jesuit missionaries in the mid-1700s. Well over 100 years later, Leon Diguet, an amateur anthropologist and naturalist, learned about the murals while working for a French mining company near the Great Mural area. Subsequently, in 1893–94, he led a French scientific expedition to Baja California and, in 1895, published the first report of specific rock art sites.

In the middle of the twentieth century these dramatic larger-than-life black and red painted images of people, deer, mountain sheep, and other fauna once again began to attract the attention of the occasional explorer into the rugged mountain back country. Dahlgren and Romero published an extensive article in Mexico in 1951. In the early 1960s, Erle Stanley Gardner, a longtime aficionado of Baja California, was guided to a few rock art sites. When he realized the scope and quality of the art, he brought in archaeologist Clement Meighan from the University of California at Los Angeles to validate the importance of his find. As a result, *Life Magazine* carried a major color spread and Meighan published an article in a scholarly journal. Still, however, only a handful of Great Mural sites had been reported to the outside world.

It remained for Harry Crosby in the 1970s to explore the central mountains by mule and pack burros in a systematic search for these rock paintings. Crosby's attention had been drawn to the paintings during an earlier expedition seeking the El Camino Real, the 18th century road that had once linked Baja California missions between Loreto and San Diego. Subsequently, covering hundreds of miles of rugged sierra trails, Crosby found and photographed over 200 open caves painted in the Great Mural style. By unrelenting persistence and dedication, he established that the paintings were not only a major and significant cultural artifact from the peninsula's prehistoric past, but probably the most distinctive art trove in North America. The scale of the paintings and the sensitive rendering of the animals is unmatched on this continent. Parallels are often cited between these works and the Paleolithic cave paintings of Europe.

Stories of discovery are, by their very nature, documents of unique moments in time. This volume is a personal account of the drama of finding and reaching these remote sites in the Baja California sierras. Motivated by his fascination with the murals, Crosby was assisted in his quest by Tacho Arce and relatives and friends from sierra ranches. Rough, brush-covered trails were negotiated into the deep arroyos to locate paintings in at times nearly inaccessible locations; paintings once seen but sometimes barely remembered by those in whose memories they resided. Crosby's narrative recreates the excitement of scrambling up steep talus slopes and seeing for the first time moving cavalcades of animals sweeping across rock surfaces, as well as the disappointment and frustration of finding wind-scoured walls bearing mere traces of paintings nearly erased.

Crosby's explorations and photo documentation of the Great Murals set the stage for continuing studies at a time when rock art research was coming into its own. The paintings have since been the subject of further inquiry by artists and archaeologists from Spain, Mexico, and the United States. In 1992, President Carlos Salinas de Gortari of Mexico inaugurated an archaeological program under the auspices of the Instituto Nacional de Antropología e Historia that included unprecedented research in Baja California and the largest project in Mexican history to deal with hunter-gatherer archaeology.

It is now hypothesized that these splendid murals were produced in the context of shamanic rituals among hunter-gatherers of the mid-peninsula. The murals are a significant statement of the ideological complexity of a people whose material culture was otherwise minimal. Importantly, some of the initial research in chronometric dating of the paint is in progress. In general, new archaeological data support earlier suggestions that the paintings are an artifact of the prehistoric Comondú culture. The Comondú were ancestors of the Cochimí, the Indians first encountered in this region by the Spanish in the 17th century.

In December 1993, the Sierra de San Francisco appeared on UNESCO's World Heritage List. Recently, INAH [Instituto Nacional de Antropología e Historia] placed informative signs on the Peninsula Highway at the turn-off where the rocky track leads to San Francisco de la Sierra. At this ranching community, guides to the paintings may be hired, and mules and burros for back country travel to the more accessible caves may be rented. But do not be misled. The trails are rough, steep, and long, and water is often scarce. The sierra guards its paintings with a rare tenacity.

After a lapse of years, this revised, enlarged edition of *The Cave Paintings of Baja California* is most welcome. Crosby's work has a special place in the investigative history of Baja California's rock art. In addition to his story of discovery, Crosby, who still has seen more of these particular murals than anyone alive, makes invaluable comparative observations between sites and between paintings in different sierras. In this edition, Crosby's fine collection of photographs is supplemented by those of photographer Enrique Hambleton from La Paz, Crosby's frequent companion in sierra explorations.

Polly Schaafsma, Archeologist and Research Associate

Museum of New Mexico, Museum of Indian Arts and Culture/Laboratory of Anthropology

CHAPTER *1*

A
Chance
Introduction

I*n the sierras of central Baja California, hidden in most forbidding terrain, thousands of brilliant paintings survive in caves and shelters. Here a prehistoric people created giant images, heroic assemblages of men and animals. The Painters' time passed, they laid down their brushes and disappeared, their art was lost to sight, and their existence was reduced to the breath of a legend. On these pages the Painters reappear. With their own works they make a place in our consciousness.*

On a slope about a mile north of Rancho La Candelaria, some 25 miles southeast of San Ignacio, a 50-foot boulder sits where it long ago rolled to a stop after being eroded from the face of a nearby volcanic mountain. Where the north side of this monster turns under, there is a series of Indian paintings in shades of ochre, brown, and red. I was guided to this spot in the spring of 1967. It was my first encounter with rock art in Baja California.

The subjects were various animals and birds. Most of the paintings were rather small and had been damaged by water seepage and rock deterioration. Two, however, caught my eye because of their greater size and the artistic skill with which they had been executed. One was a deer with a full set of antlers, the other a mountain sheep with characteristically curved and swollen horns. The pair were side by side, done in the same maroon paint and apparently by the same hand; each was about four feet in length. I photographed them and put the matter in the back of my mind. There things rested for several years.

Today, as I reinspect these photographs, I am surprised at my original nonchalance. The paintings are intrinsically beautiful and, to the best of my knowledge, had not been reported or published. Yet in those days I was consciously exploring; I was making maps and following trails and trying to observe and record all sorts of historical and archaeological data. Why was I so unimpressed by an encounter with prehistoric art?

I suppose the answer is contained in certain constants of human behavior. The more important we hold a subject to be, the more inclined we are to believe that it has been well studied and well reported. I have had a love of paintings all my life. I studied the history of cave art, and in earlier years I visited Lascaux, Altamira, and other celebrated paleolithic sites in Europe. I was enthralled by stories of their discovery and, I am sure, envious of those who first found these treasures of ancient art. Why then my total failure to comprehend the significance of what I saw at La Candelaria?

During the time of my first interest in Baja California, I was surprised and delighted by Erle Stanley Gardner's discovery of giant painted figures in the central part of the peninsula. Photographs showed artworks of a scope that could be called

2

murals in every sense of the word—the Great Murals of prehistoric Baja California. Gardner's story was spectacular; the works were found by flying helicopters into the farthest recesses of the remotest mountains. I envied Gardner his personal Altamira. I had read also that an archaeologist, Dr. Clement Meighan, accompanied Gardner and wrote a thorough study of his finds. My own studies revealed that at least some of the large rock paintings had been known since mission times. I also learned that a French naturalist named Leon Diguet visited dozens of such sites in 1894 and wrote a monograph on the subject. Those bits of knowledge must have conditioned my response. I naively supposed that the worlds of art and science had been alerted and that the phenomenon had been well studied. Further, La Candelaria was on a dirt auto road, and a local rancher directed me to the paintings. I assumed that he had pointed them out to others and that they were widely known.

Tacho Arce

In the early spring of 1971, I was determined to explore the Sierra de San Francisco north of San Ignacio. Rock art was a secondary objective at best. Principally, I hoped to scout for data on the isolated and old-fashioned people of the mountains. I planned to photograph significant aspects of their culture and to record folklore, oral history, and anecdotes. To this end I hired Eustacio "Tacho" Arce, a man born in the sierra and widely recommended for his character and unparalleled knowledge of the country. Selecting Tacho proved to be the most important of many decisions that I was to make in the long course of my studies in Baja California.

The itinerary and details of the ensuing trip are not important here. We rode mountain trails for nearly two weeks and visited a dozen ranches. I got my pictures and a great deal of information. It was a pleasant and rewarding time, and the last ranch on our itinerary seemed to cap the climax.

Rancho San Gregorio lies in an oven of an arroyo on the northeast corner of the sierra, the Gulf side. Here, some 40 years earlier, Loreto Arce Aguilar had founded a ranch based on a small but permanent spring. Tacho, as a very young man, got his first job from Loreto and labored at transporting supplies and building materials the 40 miles or so from San Ignacio or Santa Rosalía back to the ranch. When we rode in, Loreto and his family made us very welcome, and I had an especially rewarding time as I photographed and interviewed the family and eavesdropped on conversations between the old friends. The place itself was very compelling, with charming buildings and impressive groves spectacularly set in a narrow gorge. These, as well as the tidy condition in which all was kept, set it apart as the best of the places we had visited.

After two nights and a day, we sat at breakfast just before our planned departure. Tacho, however, was not quite satisfied to go. He and I had discussed paintings several times. We had even looked at a couple of minor specimens along the way. Here, he remembered, were others and he suggested a short detour to inspect them. Nothing about his manner implied anything out of the ordinary, and the

Loreto Arce Aguilar and wife

works we had seen previously were certainly not exciting. I weighed the probable loss of half a day and decided, on reflection, not to miss the experience. "After all," I remember thinking, "I will never come back all this way to San Gregorio."

Tacho led me up the canyon a few hundred yards and pointed up the steep west bank. There, perhaps 200 feet above us, was an unremarkable cave, fairly long but apparently only a few feet high. The rock face over the cave was stained in shades of red-brown and gray. As we toiled up a precipitous trail, our view was hampered by hillside brush and piles of fallen or tumbled rock. As a result, we were very close before we got our first real look at the place. Surprise is an inadequate word for my reaction.

Over the slitlike opening of a long shallow cave was a vast panel of fairly smooth rock. On it was painted a tumultuous procession of human and animal figures at perhaps double their life size. All the beasts seemed to form a herd in movement from right to left; huge red and black deer and an equally immense red mountain sheep dominated the surge. The successive figures were partially superimposed, creating a powerful sense of crowding, urgency, and motion—each animal in mad flight, treading on the heels of those ahead and straining to free itself from the crush behind. Scattered among the creatures of this bustling frieze were a variety of strangely static humans. Whereas the hurrying animals moved in profile across the stony canvas, the men faced us, frozen into identical erect postures with their arms upraised.

I was astonished and overwhelmed. The impact of that grand artistic statement at that moment was bewildering. Travel in Baja California certainly had conditioned me to expect Indian remains, to study them, and to appreciate their significance. I admit to viewing trails, rock circles, metates, arrowheads, and the like as mute and rather sad reminders of what is irrecoverably lost; it all seemed rather remote and impersonal. But the flamboyant painted scene at San Gregorio was alive and eloquent; the artists' work was an unforgettable message blazed across the ages. Nothing I had encountered before so put me in the presence of a supposedly unknowable people. Unconsciously, I began to think of them as the Painters in the same spirit that the Basketmakers of the American Southwest were named for their characteristic artifacts.

I was seized by one particularly powerful impression: This grand mural seemed entirely out of place. I realized as I stared up at it that I was carried back to paleolithic Europe. The art simply did not resemble anything I knew from the Americas, and it did indeed, in many ways, match that on the walls of Lascaux. True, the likes of San Gregorio's large, static human figures with their classic proportions have never been found in Ice Age art, but neither do they match the fantastic or grotesque man-figures common in New World rock art. Yet San Gregorio's animals hark back to ancient times in many ways. I found myself entertaining and rejecting wild associations. How could such resemblances be coincidental? How could any influence be felt across such spans of time and space?

Remnants *of a lost people*

In 1971, a rancher in a remote part of Baja California directed me to this impressive painted cave and said I was the first outsider to see it. At the time, the exciting discovery seems only a happy accident, a once-in-a-lifetime stroke of fortune— but there were stories of other such places. Pursuing one of these rumors led me on to El Batequi.

San Gregorio I

5

The rest of my visit was curiously anticlimactic. Tacho pointed out that the entire inner roof of the cave was decorated as well. We got down on our knees and inspected elegantly executed smaller animal figures: marvelous rabbits, birds, deer, and a snake, as well as some indeterminate beasts and others so overpainted as to be indecipherable. The riches were immense, but nothing for the moment could compete with the impact of my first impressions. I finally stopped poring over it all and made pictures.

Then followed a dreamlike sequence of events. Tacho led the way over a hill to another cave with other marvels. I remember a 10-foot whale and a brace of bighorn sheep, but it was really too much to take in after the other. I walked back to the ranch in a daze. The morning was gone and Loreto Arce insisted that we stay for lunch. I welcomed the offer as an opportunity to find out more about the paintings. We sat on the shaded porch of San Gregorio and our host threw more dry wood on the flames of my excitement. There were, he assured me, many more such works in the area and no one from the outside — Mexican or American — had ever visited any of them.

Those words rang in my thoughts day and night as we rode back toward San Ignacio. After a day of agonizing I made up my mind not to leave with so many unanswered questions. If what Loreto had said was true, a gold mine of lost art waited to be found and photographed. If he had exaggerated, all I could lose was time. As soon as I told Tacho my decision, I felt immensely relieved. We turned back into the sierra; despite the fatigue of two weeks on the trail, there was a fresh sense of adventure in the air.

That evening I explained my plans and hopes to Tacho, and I asked for his frank opinion. What did he suppose we might discover? Tacho was very honest about his knowledge. He had not spent much time in the sierra since his youth. Since then, he had married and worked in a number of lowland ranches, some far away. He recalled the men of the sierra who had known these caves well. Most of them now were dead, and he was unsure of the knowledge possessed by their sons. From his own memories, a few specific places stood out, one in particular that he had not seen in 30 years. I could go and evaluate that site — and with it the value of Tacho's memory. On that note, we set out.

After crossing the sierra's rugged heights, we began a descent into the upper reaches of Arroyo del Batequi. The steep, switchback grade had not been used for years and was heavily overgrown. We were tired and scratched by the time we finally reached the relative tranquility of the arroyo's rocky bed. We rode gratefully down to the west in the warm sun. Late in the afternoon, we came to the place remembered by Tacho, a large overhung cliff high on the northwest side of the arroyo. After such a tiring day, it would have been sensible to wait for morning before climbing up, but I was too keyed up to wait through a night of uncertainty. Tacho understood. We unloaded our worn-out mules and burros and the two of us crossed the wash and started up the steep slope. I will admit that I, too, was worn out. The little climb to the cave seemed like a major undertaking, but, by laboriously putting one foot in front of the other, I finally got to the cave level. Tacho had missed his mark a little; we were too far north, so we made our way along the top of the slope, inspecting the walls above us for signs of paintings. The first string of overhung places was completely blank. Then we rounded a corner and found ourselves in front of the objective that had been pointed out to me from the arroyo floor.

The open rock shelter at El Batequi consists of a vertical back wall, 12 to 16 feet in height, overhung by a short ceiling which represents the base of a massive stratum of volcanic rock that towers above. The material of the back wall is a soft, fine-grained rock in a pale beige tone. Both wall and ceiling are unusually flat and smooth.

My first glance at the back wall revealed that it had been heavily painted. There were vestiges of all sorts of handsomely delineated men and animals. Alas, vestiges, and nothing more. I hurried down the long wall and searched for a truly surviving picture. There was none. Without resort to exaggeration, that was one of the greatest disappointments I have ever experienced. The dream that began at San Gregorio came crashing down. I stood there dog-tired and grieved. The tragedy far transcended my personal disappointment. All around me was irrefutable evidence of a great center of primitive art; only enough of the substance survived to suggest the magnitude of the loss.

The cause of the terrible deterioration was not difficult to determine. That beautiful smooth rock, waiting like a ready-stretched canvas, has another, and tragic quality: Changes in temperature and humidity, and probably other erosive forces, cause the binder in that sandy stone to weaken and, thus weakened, to gradually release its particles a grain at a time. Exposure to water apparently contributed little to the destruction at El Batequi. The overhang is an excellent barrier against rain, even when wildly windblown, yet the highest and most sheltered places were almost as badly deteriorated as those most exposed.

As I wandered around in low spirits, Tacho went ahead around another corner. He returned and said that there was a similar display next door. Around I went, and found myself looking down an even longer gallery, with an even more inviting wall. On it I made out the familiar sad remains of fantastic men and graceful animals. Then I glanced at the ceiling. A miracle! There above me was the most beautiful rock art I had seen since Lascaux. In that instant, I was overwhelmed with emotions: admiration and thanksgiving. I looked for the cause of the survival. The back wall with its lost art is of the same soft rock as the shelter I had just left, but the ceiling is of another, somewhat different stuff. That ceiling rock is not perfect by any means; since it was painted, it has sloughed off enough fine surface material to weaken the colors. It also displays thousands of tiny pits. But the important thing is that this ceiling material had just enough structural integrity to support a great painting and bring it down through time. The gift seemed magnified in a place where so much had been lost.

7

A unified masterwork from many hands

This grand cavalcade is one of very few
Great Murals that gives a sense of organized
composition. Even successive layers of
painting did minimal damage to the overall
design and helped to create the impression
of a herd pressing across some ancient tableau.
The implicit cooperation among successive
generations of artists would be impressive in
any context, but it is astounding among the
Painters, whose hallmark was the artistically
destructive practice of overpainting without
regard to size, color, line, or flow of older
images.

El Batequi

I stood dazzled. It was several minutes before I could look around. In front of
me on my right was a loose pile of large stone chunks. They had fallen from a
natural column which divides this gallery from the other. The painted ceiling is
about 15 feet above the floor of the shelter for most of its length, and then, at the
far end, curves down almost to the floor. The entire length was covered with an
incredible cavalcade of animals and men, a procession longer, larger, and more
stylized than that at San Gregorio.

Surprise and delight soared as I walked the length of the area looking at the
work overhead. I went through stages of mounting excitement as I realized the
quality and significance of what I was seeing. At first I was attracted to the artistry
and finesse of a grouping of deer at the right end of the procession. That for me
had the air of highly formal, sophisticated primitive art. Then I was impressed by
the power and motion of some great dark animals at the left end, figures in quite a
different style.

At last, after I had examined the mural figure by figure, it dawned on me that unity and composition were its greatest glories. The mural is clearly not the work of a single artist; that is demonstrated by distinctly different styles, techniques, and materials used as well as differences in aging. It is certainly the product of many generations. Some of the figures are much older than others. In places the work displays four or five layers of superimposed painting, the newest relatively fresh, the oldest quite eroded. The wonder is that all the artists who contributed the animal figures responded to an urge to preserve the movement of the herd. All figures, with trivial exceptions, run from left to right in one long sweep.

Again, as at San Gregorio, the human figures seemed curiously detached. Even though some are deeply entangled in the confused overpainting, they stand apart in spirit, no sense of participation emanates from them. The combined effect of the active and static is powerful. The inexorable force of the galloping beasts is countered by the inertia of the men. This impression is heightened by an unusual

A Chance Introduction

A classic gallery set me on a new course

This isolated mural inspired me to search for works of the prehistoric Painters of central Baja California. After visiting San Gregorio and El Batequi, I became convinced that the Sierra de San Francisco concealed a treasury of primitive art. The hunt was on.

El Batequi

device used in depicting several of the human figures. They were painted facing the front, but the vertical division was made so that the darker half of each looks like a man in profile, facing the deer. Thus the herd appears to be encountered by several men with arms upraised as if to halt the procession. Whether intended or not, the device undeniably adds tension to the scene. All the man-figures so treated seem to be from the hand of one artist. The technique used to create the combined head-on and profile effect is very unusual and may even prove to be unique.

Gradually my first shock from the encounter at El Batequi wore off and was replaced by a proud and proprietorial mood; now I had the acute desire to share the experience. In those moments, I knew the loneliness of private art collectors and I understood why so many donate their treasures to society. While the sun set and Tacho went down the hill to ready the animals, I paced back and forth under that great cavalcade, trying to commit every detail to memory.

Finally I turned away and stumbled down the slope. We rode quietly in the dusk to Rancho El Batequi, which had water and pasture for our animals. We made our camp that night under a wide-spreading mezquite. I placed my sleeping bag in a natural garden of handsome plants with lush green foliage. As the moon rose, large trumpet-shaped flowers of the purest white opened all around me and the air was filled with heavy perfume. It was the wild datura, which the Indians of northern and central Mexico called *toloache* and used as a drug to create the dreams of their rituals. I spent a fitful night haunted by the beauty around me and by what I had seen that day.

Once again, as at San Gregorio, I was overwhelmed by the sense of a people, a living culture, expressing itself to me in powerful terms. In my mind, those silent arroyos once again echoed with voices. I pictured the caves alive with people practicing the many skills that put the Great Murals on the walls. I imagined paint making and scaffold building before the artists could begin, and then the processes of sketching and painting. I wondered what special people the actual Painters might have been. Priests? And was the painting or its completion accompanied by ceremony? Were these places visited by all members of the band? Were they places of worship? Or were they hidden places where shamans worked out the tribal destiny alone with their magic?

Over and over during that night I opened my eyes and the unblinking moon brought me back to the quiet and empty arroyo. But not even the light of morning could completely break the spell. All around me at dawn were still the white faces and fragrance of toloache and a sense of the powerful reality of what was painted a short distance away.

The trip continued and, before its momentous three weeks were done, I visited the great sites near San Francisco, previously reported by Diguet, Gardner, and Meighan, and I was taken to other new ones as well. But nothing changed the conviction and resolve created by the Great Mural of El Batequi. I no longer had the slightest doubt about what I was going to do. If Tacho could produce such a place from a 30-year-old memory, I knew that there must be other men and other memories.

A painted cave known to Jesuit missionaries by 1767.

San Borjitas

CHAPTER 2

The First to Find Them

California began as a geographic myth, an insular place on the right hand of the Indies. Then it became the line of misty peaks scarring the sunsets as Conquistadors looked west. In the mid-18th century, California still meant only the peninsula, and many thought of that as an island. Two or three Jesuit missionaries, toiling in this most rocky of vineyards, made surprising finds of ancient art. During two centuries, their little-known accomplishment was augmented at long intervals by the efforts of a French chemist and an American writer of detective fiction. This oddly assorted group carries the flag, beats the drum, and sounds the fife for a slowly gathering parade back to the places and times of the Painters.

During the last thirty years of the 18th century, the university city of Bologna, Italy, was the seat of a strange little colony of frustrated men. Spain's expulsion of the Society of Jesus in the late 1760s had returned most non-Spanish Jesuit missionaries to their homelands, but Spain and all her possessions were barred to them. Those of Spanish extraction were placed under papal care, and many were assigned to a Catholic institution in Bologna. These had recently been the most active of men, movers and shakers along the frontiers of Catholic Christianity. Their new idleness must have been a trial, coupled as it was with little hope for any return to the labors in which their lives had been immersed. One of many crosses these missionaries had to bear in their banishment was an almost total ignorance among Europeans about the lands in which they had worked. The California group was especially incensed. The only available account of their mission field was by a Jesuit who had never seen the peninsula. That compiler, Miguel Venegas, had worked from reports and letters of missionaries who had served on the ground, but he had not been content with an editor's role. Venegas' text was filled with his own interpretation and judgments, and with insertions intended to defend and fortify the Jesuit position. The published form of Venegas's already secondhand account was then heavily edited and revised prior to printing. This work, now known as *Noticia de la California*, became widely popular and was soon translated into several languages. The resulting spread of misinformation and half-truths distressed the few men who knew California.

The unusual circumstances proved to be a boon to peninsular history. Had the California missionaries remained at their posts, they would not have been so aware of the poor material in circulation and its impact, nor would they have had time to reflect and respond. But in exile they had time to read and react. Padres Johann Jakob Baegert and Benno Ducrue published works of reaction in their native Germany.

At Bologna, another exiled California missionary, the Spaniard Padre Miguel del Barco, planned an ambitious tome of "corrections and additions" to the Venegas text. This huge work, over 1,000 handwritten pages, was destined to have a curious history. Another Bologna exile, Francisco Clavijero, a young Mexican Jesuit who had not served in California, was nevertheless an intimate of the California group. He was intelligent and literate, had participated in years of discussions and reminiscences, and eventually wrote a book, *The Story of California*. His work drew heavily on that of Miguel del Barco, but it had the graceful form of a complete text whereas the old missionary's writing was an earnest set of point-by-point refutations and clarifications. Clavijero was published in 1785, and his book became a standard history for nearly two centuries. Barco's manuscript, which never had a public airing, was shelved and virtually lost, even to scholarship. Finally, in 1972, the noted Mexican historian, Miguel León-Portilla, published an annotated transcript of Barco's work as *Historia Natural y Crónica de la Antigua California*. What a treasure it is! Barco proves to have been an admirable reporter—thorough, observant, and amazingly unbiased. With one stroke, the reappearance of his text virtually doubled our firsthand knowledge of early historic California. Here are lengthy accounts of missionary labors, Indian languages, legends, customs, dress, and crafts; a virtual ethnography focusing on the mid-peninsula where most of the Bologna expatriates had worked. And in it we find the first concrete references to the Great Murals.

During the Bologna years, the exiles discussed the Indians' own beliefs and prehistory, and there was much interest in a persistent legend about giants on the peninsula. This was the subject that brought cave painting into Miguel del Barco's book. For a written account, he turned to one of the group who had been an eyewitness. Joseph Mariano Rothea—the missionary at San Ignacio from late 1759 until the expulsion in 1768—responded to Barco's request with a few priceless paragraphs. Thanks to the survival of Barco's manuscript, we have Rothea's historic account "copied," as Barco assures us, "to the letter . . . without any alteration."

> The propositions arguing that there were giants in California can be reduced to three. First, the bones that are encountered in various places. Second, the painted caves, and third, the general belief of the elders. [Rothea then offered an extended account of digging up giant human bones near San Joaquín, a *visita*, or visiting station of his mission, before he returned to the matter of our direct interest.]
>
> . . . I happened to investigate several painted caves but I will only talk about one which is the most noteworthy. This one would be about 30 to 35 feetlong and about 18 feet wide. Its form was like half a vault that rested on a pavement of the same material. From top to bottom it was all painted with various figures of men, women, and animals. The men had loose shirts with sleeves; beyond this a greatcoat and breeches but no shoes. They had their hands open and somewhat raised with extended arms. Among the women was one with loose hair arranged on the head and a dress of a native Mexican type called *huipil*. The paintings of the animals represented all those now known in the land, like deer, jack rabbits, etc., and others now unknown like the wolf and the pig. The colors were those found in the volcanos of the Tres Vírgenes:

green, black, yellow, and flesh-colored. The durability of these colors seemed notable to me; being there on the exposed rock in the inclemencies of sun and water where they are no doubt struck by rain, strong wind or water that filters through these same rocks from the hill above, with all this, after much time, they remain highly visible.

Finally, with these preliminaries, I gathered the oldest Indians of the mission to ascertain what information they had among them relating to this legend about giants. I asked that the same be done at the missions of Guadalupe and Santa Rosalía whose missionaries then were Father Benno Ducrue at the first, and Father Francisco Escalante at the second. And, as I remember, there chanced the coincidence that this said inquiry was made, or one of them at least, on the same day that I carried it out with my people.

All agreed in essence; it was known that knowledge had passed from fathers to sons concerning a group of men and women of extraordinary stature that had come from the north in very ancient times, and that they came fleeing from one another. Part of them directed their course along the coast of the Southern Sea, and of these, they told me, are still seen the capes that they fashioned and that are like those that the present Californians wear, but very large by comparison. I was not able to investigate with my own eyes these memories which are the only things that remain of these first people. The other part of them directed their course to the rugged portion of the sierra, and they are the authors of said paintings. In truth, those that I saw are convincing because, without scaffolds or other implements suitable for the purpose, only giant men would have been able to paint at so much height.

They told, lastly, that part of them [the giants] died at each others hands, and part also were killed by the self-same Californians [the tellers' ancestors] who would not tolerate such strange residents in their land.

IHS

Joseph Mariáno Rothea

Miguel del Barco also gives us a second account in which he relates what was told to him by Padre Francisco Escalante:

The missionary at Santa Rosalía [de Mulegé] says that, among his Indians survives the same knowledge of giants that came from a place in the north, who painted, in the territory of his mission, a cave which the same missionary went to see and which is almost as large as the other near the mission at San Ignacio [i.e., the one described by Rothea above]. This one is about 35 feet long, 16 feet or more wide and 16 high with little difference [from Rothea's cave]; this one is not in the form of a vault but rather of a flat ceiling formed of one [layer of] rock thick and strong enough to support a high mountain. This flat ceiling is painted and full of figures now of animals and now of men armed with bows and arrows representing the hunts of the Indians. These paintings are well preserved, clear and perceivable, not withstanding being on naked rock without other protection, and that in wet times and in fogs the air of the cave cannot help but be damp. Apart from this, he says that it is untutored painting, that it is very far from the niceties of this art. Nevertheless, he gives us to understand that its authors had more application, more talent and more understanding than the [present] natives of that country.

Some salient points emerge in these accounts. The Cochimí, who peopled the missions in the area of the Great Murals, had widely known legends which dissociated them and their ancestors from the Painters, and the paintings were already impressively old, at least in the missionaries' opinions. As far as the actual belief in giants was concerned, we can remain skeptical. There is no need to doubt Rothea's discovery of huge bones; the remains of outsized individuals are encountered here and there all over the world. Immediately after quoting Rothea, Barco expressed his own doubts about reports of giants.

Like the rumor, the more it is spread, the more things are magnified. The memory which remained of the stature of these giants, communicated from father to son in the passage of many centuries (though we do not know how many, nor is it possible to ascertain among the Indians), this memory, I say, has grown to the point that the people of this land say that the giants were so large that, when they painted the ceiling of a cave, they lay on their backs on the ground and that even thus they were able to paint the highest part. An enormous fable that, for its verification would necessitate those men to have a height of at least 30 feet, unless we imagine extremely long paint brushes in their hands! Besides, even if they said that, standing on the floor of the cave, they painted the highest parts of it, it seems difficult to believe. It is simpler to persuade oneself that, for this work, they found and conveyed to the cave, or caves, some wood with which to form a scaffold, which, with the little height that it could have, was enough that the giants could have painted comfortably, nor for this did they lack sufficient wood. What is certain is that these pictures represented clothed people and animals that were not found in California. One can well believe that their creators were not natives of that land but came to it from other regions.

Not long after this activity in Bologna, the erudite Spanish Viceroy of New Spain, the second Conde de Revillagigedo, requested the formation of a thorough collection of documents relative to discoveries and missionary activity in the area for which he was responsible. In 1792, a compilation was ready and it contained a considerable natural history of Baja California which has been traced tentatively to a report penned by a Jesuit before their expulsion in 1768. If the attribution is correct, this work contains the oldest known reference to rock art on the peninsula, if not to the Great Murals specifically:

In all of civilized California, from south to north, and particularly in the caves and smooth cliffs, rustic paintings can be seen. Notwithstanding their disproportion and lack of art, there can be easily distinguished the likenesses of men, fish, bows and arrows, and diversely assembled lines in the fashion of written characters. The colors of these paintings are four: yellow, red, green and black. The majority of the images are painted in very high places, and from this, some infer that there is truth in the constant tradition of giants among the ancient Californians. Be that as it may, at the Mission of Santiago, which is located in the south, there is exposed to view on a very high, smooth cliff a series of stamped red hands. In the tall boulders near the beach, fish of different shapes and sizes, bows and arrows, and some obscure characters can be seen. In other places, there are Indians armed with bows and arrows, and at their feet various species of insects, snakes and mice, with lines and characters of a different form.

It has been impossible to ascertain what these figures, lines and characters mean, despite extensive questioning of the California Indians. The only thing which has been determined from what they say, is that they are from their ancestors, and that they have absolutely no knowledge of their significance. One could infer from the paintings and lines of the Californios that they are symbols and meaningful signals with which they attempted to leave a memory for posterity or of their settlement in that place, or of some wars or other political or natural events. These paintings are not like the [mainland] Mexican ones, but must have been [independently] developed.

Several interesting items emerge from this entry. It covers a greater geographical area than did the previously cited references. It seems to show a knowledge of the Great Murals, but focuses more sharply and accurately on smaller works in the Santiago area near the cape. Red hands, fish, and "diversely assembled lines" are indeed characteristic of rock art in that region. The casual reference to the giant legend suggests that its association with rock painting was widespread among missionaries and presumably among California natives.

After the decade of Barco, Clavijero, and the Revillagigedo collection, nearly a century passed without any notice of peninsular rock art. This long dry spell was broken when, in 1882 and 1883, a Dutch physician, Herman Frederik Carel Ten Kate, pursued his interest in anthropology with a long journey through the American Southwest and northern Mexico. He visited the Cape Region of Baja California, dug up ancient burials, collected artifacts, and noted a few rock paintings. Ten Kate published several accounts of these activities.

Meanwhile, in the mid-peninsula, some events occurred which would soon affect the history of the Great Murals. José Rosas Villavicencio, scion of one of California's first Hispanic families and a rancher at Santa Agueda, discovered copper deposits near what is now Santa Rosalía. After some small-scale efforts showed the magnitude of the find, a French corporation financed by Rothschild banking interests acquired all the pertinent mining claims. The corporation, popularly known as El Boleo, negotiated agreements with the Díaz regime of Mexico, under which they got mining and export rights and also virtual control of 2,000 square miles of adjacent territory and, tacitly at least, the people within it.

By 1889, the French concern had installed and manned mines and mills and created the company town of Santa Rosalía. Among the personnel imported for this enterprise was a French industrial chemist named Leon Diguet. Diguet, born in Le Havre in 1859, seems to have taken a broad interest in the region's naturalism. He knew Ten Kate's published papers and they may have served as a basis for his inquiries. At any rate, Diguet explored and collected in the area during his three-year stint with the company and, on his return to France in 1892, he was able to give extensive collections to the Museum of Natural History and the Museum of Man in Paris.

The quality of these collections and Diguet's enthusiasm attracted attention. Shortly after returning to France, he was authorized and financed to lead an expedition to observe and collect in Baja California. This proved to be the beginning of a series of five such ventures in various parts of Mexico.

Diguet's Baja California exploration of 1893–94 appears to have produced most of his contacts with rock art and is the basis of his important paper, "Notes on the Pictographs of Baja California" (1895). Diguet's work and especially this article and its photographs and drawings entitle him to be considered the first serious student of the Great Murals. Through him, the outstanding sites of San Borjitas, San Juan, and Cuesta de Palmarito were disclosed to the world and, indeed, the phenomenon of rock painting on the peninsula was rediscovered. It is noteworthy that, despite extended travels, Diguet managed to visit only a fraction of the sites now known to exist, and he missed the greatest concentration altogether—a complex of exquisitely painted caves and shelters in the heart of the Sierra de San Francisco. This first aficionado was quite aware of the problems that kept him from even greater discoveries. The final words of his 1895 paper are eloquent on this point and, incidentally, were almost as true 75 years later: "The inhabitants of the villages and towns often know them only through hearsay, and it is with difficulty that the ranchers of the interior are induced to direct a stranger to them."

After Diguet there was a hiatus of over 50 years before the Great Murals again became a topic of remark or study. In 1951, Barbro Dahlgren and Javier Romero came to San Borjitas cave under the aegis of Mexico's prestigious Instituto Nacional de Antropología e Historia. Their findings were reported in a paper and illustrated in a 1954 issue of *Artes de México*.

None of the discoveries or publications prior to that time, although they covered a period of nearly 200 years, had made any impression on the public in the larger world, but the next adventurer on the Great Mural horizon was to change all that. Beginning in the mid-1940s, Erle Stanley Gardner, the writer of detective stories, made a hobby of Baja California exploration. His trips were recorded in a

El Zotolar, Sierra de Guadalupe

series of rambling adventure books, and he developed a coterie of friends and helpers for his elaborately mounted assaults on the peninsula's more remote terrain. He also met and befriended a number of people from Baja California's formidable outback. Around 1960, one of them, José Rosas Villavicencio (grandson of the man who discovered the copper deposits that formed the basis of El Boleo and the town of Santa Rosalía) informed Gardner of huge paintings near his childhood home in the Sierra de San Francisco. The mystery novelist was getting on in years, but he had the enthusiasm and imagination as well as the financial resources required for an exploration of the sierra. In 1962, he arranged for the use of helicopters and, with Villavicencio's help, was able to visit the tiny village of San Francisco in the heart of the sierra and a group of caves in the nearby but rather inaccessible Arroyo de San Pablo.

When Gardner saw the size and character of the artwork, he realized that he had uncovered a major archaeological site that would create great interest in the outside world. To his credit, Gardner used his influence and resources not only to publicize his find, but also to study it. Very shortly after his first trip to the painted caves he returned with a qualified archaeologist, Dr. Clement Meighan of the University of California at Los Angeles.

The results of these two explorations were reported by Gardner in a sensational spread in *Life Magazine* and in his book, *The Hidden Heart of Baja*—the latter in the unstructured, highly subjective style of his other Baja California books. Gardner depended on no research whatsoever, and his book abounds in quaint and fanciful observations, interpretations, and homemade myths. Dr. Meighan's report was another matter. "Prehistoric Rock Paintings in Baja California," 20 terse pages in *American Antiquity* in 1966, demonstrates admirably what a professional could accomplish on the basis of fieldwork carried out in three days at a site. The sheer volume of his collections and recorded data is impressive, and it is combined with analysis and comparative observations made possible by the author's wide experience with Southwest Indian cultures. The accomplishment inevitably stirs regret that Dr. Meighan could not have followed with a thorough study, an effort which might have shed light on some of the many mysteries surrounding the Great Murals.

However, in keeping with its past, it seems appropriate that Baja California's noble rock art gives up its secrets in grudging increments and only to those who persevere.

Arroyo de San Pablo

Aerial view looking
south-southeast

CHAPTER 3

The
*Sierra
de San Francisco*

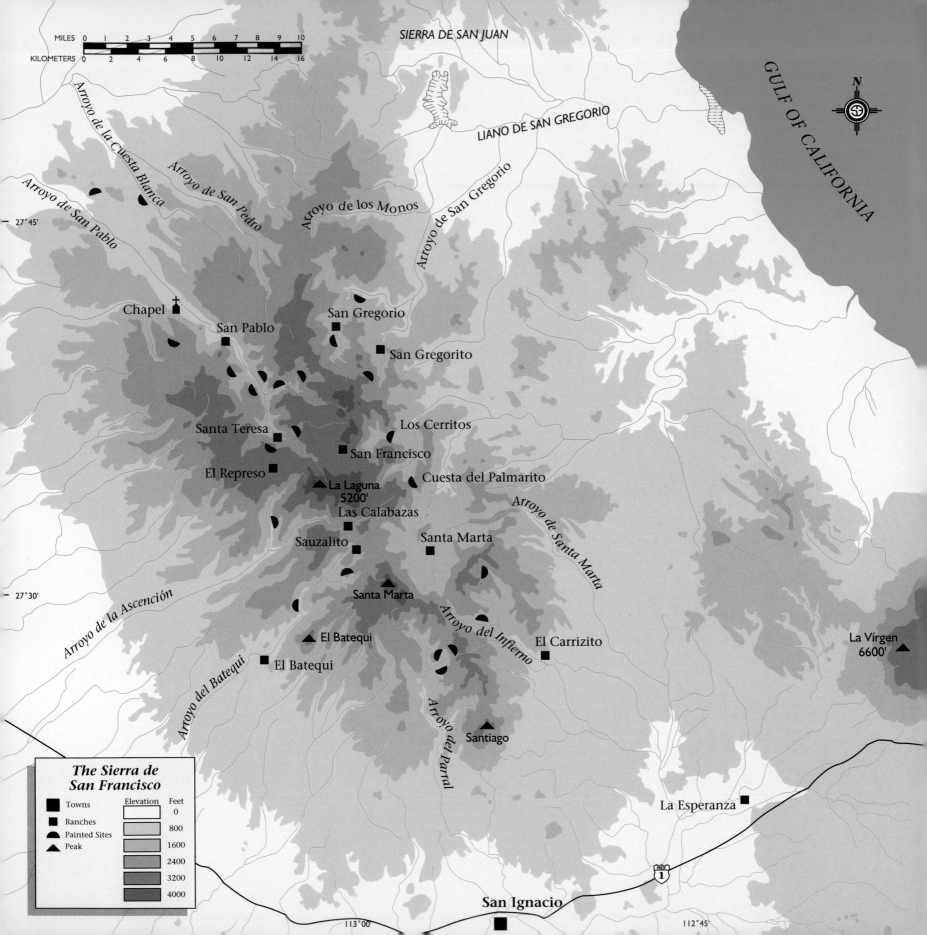

SIERRA DE SAN JUAN

GULF OF CALIFORNIA

LIANO DE SAN GREGORIO

Arroyo de la Cuesta Blanca

Arroyo de San Pedro

Arroyo de los Monos

Arroyo de San Gregorio

Arroyo de San Pablo

27°45'

Chapel

San Pablo

San Gregorio

San Gregorito

Santa Teresa

Los Cerritos

San Francisco

El Represo

Cuesta del Palmarito

La Laguna
5200'

Arroyo de Santa Marta

Las Calabazas

Sauzalito

Santa Marta

Arroyo de la Ascención

27°30'

Santa Marta

Arroyo del Infierno

El Carrizito

La Vírgen
6600'

El Batequi

Arroyo del Batequi

El Batequi

Santiago

Arroyo del Paral

The Sierra de San Francisco

■ Towns

■ Ranches

◖ Painted Sites

▲ Peak

Elevation   Feet
0
800
1600
2400
3200
4000

La Esperanza

San Ignacio

113°00'   112°45'

N orth of San Ignacio lies a mountain wilderness, the deeply eroded remains of layer upon layer of volcanic outpourings. This rugged mass rises from the surrounding desert to heights of more than 5,000 feet and covers an area 35 miles from north to south and half of that from east to west. From its uplands, there are views west to Scammon's Lagoon and the Vizcaíno Desert, northwest to the even taller Sierra de San Borja, and east to the abrupt eminences of Las Tres Vírgenes, taller and more recent volcanos that tower in front of the Gulf. The sierra embraces a world that would never be suspected from the low, barren lands outside. Groves of palms and pools of water are set between walls of vertical grandeur water-carved from rich-colored rock. A few ranches, built by rustic and hospitable people, nestle near the few water sources. Here also are the grandest reminders of the Painters, corridors decorated by their hands and haunted by their spirits.

My first experiences in the Sierra de San Francisco revealed it as a gallery of ancient art. I also learned that the Painters contrived to hide their art in a labyrinth that would have gladdened the heart of Minos of Crete. When I reviewed the literature of the two centuries in which outsiders were aware of the art's existence, I concluded that previous efforts to find and know these works had been sporadic and haphazard. It stood to reason that the findings to that point represented only a fraction of the potential. The problems for field researchers were complex; a number of factors quite beyond the actions of the Painters helped to hide and guard their secrets.

Rugged topography has been the greatest single deterrent to anyone attempting to enter and know the Painters' realm. Although the area most involved is no more than 300 or 400 square miles, it is a maze of deep-cut water courses with towering walls. The terrain is difficult to learn or to find one's way through; any part of it is physically demanding to traverse. Distance in air line miles cannot serve as a measure of the difficulties; it does no good to think of this sierra as 35 miles long unless you plan to fly over it. On the ground, trails are forced into tortured horizontal and vertical courses which multiply the miles and tax the muscles of men and beasts of burden.

There are other obstacles. Water is scarce or absent in most parts of the sierra. The complexity of the landform insures that no one can know it all; each rancher knew a part of it as it suited his needs. Further, these people felt little curiosity as far as Indian remains were concerned; such things formed no part of their cultural heritage. The aboriginal peoples and their cultures perished or were assimilated two centuries ago, and mission life diminished or extinguished their power to leave behind legends or to impart a sense of spirits, magic, or fervor. Beyond finding the occasional conveniently sized metate or mano and taking it home for use in their kitchens, the profoundly practical Hispanic people of the mountains viewed the works of former inhabitants as useless artifacts found on every side. With so little demand, the supply was largely uninventoried.

Tacho Arce

Once the decision was made to find the Painters' work, a system was needed, a modus operandi to take advantage of local knowledge and avoid time-consuming repetition during what would necessarily be a number of expeditions. First, I looked for a local man who could advise me. I quickly found Tacho Arce and the answers to all my questions. Here was a man privy to the secrets of trails and water supplies, adept at the lore and skills surrounding the use of animals, and known as the friend or relative of every sierra family. The last was the most crucial. In Tacho's company there were no closed doors; he was the key to the people and their memories.

The Arce name is among the oldest in the Californias. The first to bring it to the peninsula was Juan de Arce, a man of English birth who served as a soldier in California's first presidio. Juan came to Loreto in 1698, then, in 1701, returned to his home in Villa de Sinaloa in the province of Sinaloa, just across the Gulf of California. The first Arces to raise families in California were José Gabriel de Arce and Sebastián Constantino de Arce, brothers who arrived at Loreto in the 1740s. They cannot be positively linked to Juan de Arce, although they were born in Villa de Sinaloa. Tacho's great-great grandfather, Buenaventura Arce, was a grandson of Sebastián Constantino de Arce. Buenaventura was the benevolent despot of the San Ignacio region, a man who claimed the first ranch titles from independent Mexico and who served from the 1820s to the 1870s as formal or informal *alcalde,* a sort of mayor-judge of the village and its environs.

Tacho was born in 1911 at Rancho San Francisco in the heart of the sierra. As a child he herded goats at nearby Rancho San Antonio, then grew to the estate of a boy capable of handling the mules and burros that took cheese down from the mountains and returned with supplies. Most significantly for me, Tacho next essayed a career as a *falluquero,* a mounted dry goods salesman who hawked his wares all over the sierra. In this way, Tacho not only learned the paths and water holes, but also came to know the people. Alas, he tried to extend credit to his customers and, in the depths of the depression, found it difficult to collect from needy friends. Next, he left the sierra for long stints as a *vaquero,* or cowboy, and tenant cattle rancher. In time, he helped to support his family by sharpening his considerable skills as a hunter, an asset that led to becoming a professional guide for those who came after the trophy of a *borrego,* or bighorn sheep.

In 1971, Tacho helped me to devise a plan that eventually took me and various companions to every ranch in the sierra and involved most of their people in our search. We used Tacho's ranch at La Esperanza, 15 miles northeast of San Ignacio, as a headquarters. I notified him of impending trips and he was responsible for acquiring an assistant and the needed animals and their gear. Camping equipment and supplies were stored at his place and, between trips, he collected information from his many friends as they passed on their way in and out of the mountains. In practice, his listening station provided clues from far beyond San Francisco, data that led us to rock art sites as far afield as the regions of San Borja and Mulegé.

But all of this only implemented the basic idea: to ride into the sierra, question all the ranchers of successive regions, and follow up their suggestions. Eventually that enterprise consumed parts of seven years and included expeditions into four different mountain ranges, including eight extended trips into just the Sierra de San Francisco. And while Tacho and his son Ramón were nearly constant figures as guides, various friends and family members joined me on different trips. An account of our first long expedition, 45 days in 1972, will serve to show how it went. For the rest, I will concentrate on the mountains, the caves, the paintings, and the shadowy presence of the Painters.

Arroyo del Parral

The largest arroyo on the southern end of the Sierra de San Francisco is called El Parral. It was born (as they say in the sierra) on the southern slopes of Cerro de Santa Marta, a 4,600 foot peak, and it carries periodic deluges out of the mountains and across the mesas to dump tempestuous floods into the arroyo of San Ignacio just east of the town. La Muralla, a three-mile-long dike of rock and rubble, was erected in Jesuit times to keep the marauding waters of El Parral from devastating vital fields and orchards of the mission. Since far earlier times, this waterway has served as the principal avenue between the oasis of San Ignacio and the seasonal food resources of the uplands.

In 1972, there was no inhabited ranch in the entire drainage of El Parral; indeed, no one may ever have lived there for longer than a season. For information, Tacho and I went to San Lino on the north side of Arroyo de San Ignacio to see Jorge Espinosa, a man nearing 80. He, his father, and his grandfather before him had run cattle in El Parral. Jorge did know the whereabouts of several paintings and he provided minute directions. His son, José María "Chato" Espinosa, could be of more direct help. He had guided a helicopter-borne Erle Stanley Gardner group to an outstanding site called The Serpent Cave for its unique painted representation of a giant snake. He could take us there and to many of the places his father knew. At San Lino we also picked up Tránsito Quintero, an ancient mule skinner who could help Tacho. Thus informed and assisted, we set out on the second day of November.

Our packtrain climbed from the arroyo to the mesa by way of one of those steep, zigzag trails called *cuestas*. For a few moments, from the rim, we could look back over the tops of thousands of date palms to the pueblo with its stately mission church. Then it was gone and we were alone on the mesa.

To the southeast, the lost view was replaced at a greater distance by the misty profile of the Sierra de Guadalupe dropping down to Laguna de San Ignacio and the Pacific. To the east rose the highest mountain in the region, the solitary volcanic form of Cerro de la Vírgen. To the west the phantomlike Picachos de Santa Clara pierced the morning fog that had ventured off the ocean overnight.

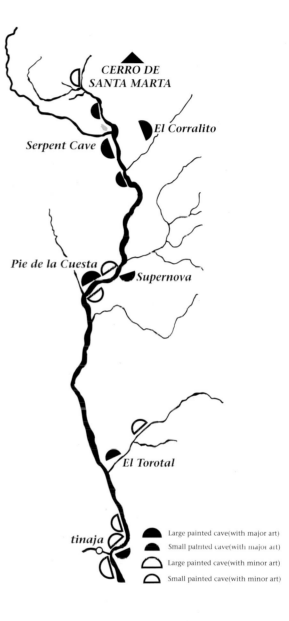

The Sierra de San Francisco

27

Arroyo del Parral

My attention, however, was soon riveted on the mountains to the north and the trail leading into them, a scene dominated by two peaks. On the left, the more distant was the abrupt and jagged Cerro del Batequi; nearby on the right was the odd, toothlike *picacho* of Cerro de Santiago. The foreground appeared to be one vast mesa gently sloping upward to blend with the foothills of the sierra.

Stretching ahead was a broad old trail with the familiar character of a Jesuit road, surveyor-straight and carefully made. The builders laid it out about 16 feet wide with stakes or string and then removed all the rock between the boundaries. The shifted stones were piled in neat rows as borders along either side. As we rode along, the better stretches of this onetime principal route, or *camino real,* imparted a strong presence of history and romance. The instigator and architect of the construction may well have been Padre Fernando Consag, who encouraged the chiefs of all his neophyte tribes to build roads to connect their *rancherías,* or seasonal encampment areas, with Misión de San Ignacio.

All around us was a great mesa, surprisingly green and blooming from recent rains. In every direction the wild and exotic character of Baja California was evident; we could have felt like pioneers if we had not had this incredible road underfoot and stretching as far ahead and behind as the eye could see. It seemed to me so mighty a labor that, despite the toll of time and the elements, it had become a permanent feature of the landscape. To test the sense of isolation, I stopped and got out my binoculars. It was true. No other trace of civilization was visible in any direction, not pole or wire, not ranch or town, not mine or mill. We were alone with the lively spirits of the old road builders.

Our experience on the mesa ended as suddenly as it began. The great Arroyo del Parral bore down on us from its origin in the sierra to the north and, at about that point, swung off to the southeast, behind us on our right. At this point, the arroyo had cut down almost 100 feet below the mesa and lay before us as a broad sandy wash between vertical walls of lava. We came upon it quite abruptly, hidden as it was by the flatness of the mesa. Our trail immediately took us down into it by a well-made switchback cuesta, probably as old as the road itself. What a change! After over two hours of open mesa with panoramic views of 50 miles or more, we were suddenly enclosed by red rock walls. The boxed-in feeling was enhanced by windings of the arroyo; we rode toward apparent barriers that became turns as we drew near.

I became aware of a growing contrast between what I saw on my map and what I experienced on the ground. As seen from the air, the general plan of the sierra is roughly elliptical, with its axis running from southeast to northwest. The silhouette of the sierra is also rather simple: a regular volcanic mound interrupted only by the somewhat eccentric distribution of a few peaks. But on close inspection, the apparently simple overall form of the sierra is obscured by a fantastically complex pattern of water erosion. The basic structure of the range is made up of successive flows of harder and softer volcanic rocks; indeed, these components range from very hard basalt to very soft agglomerated ash. Within the sierra, water courses cut down through these layers to great depths. Since hard basalt tends to remain and cap softer tuffs, the erosion produced a generally steplike pattern as it plunged to depths as great as 1,200 feet below the high mesas. Typically, the walls of these steps are perpendicular. When one flies low over the range, it is difficult to imagine any sort of surface travel.

On either side of the arroyo, we saw petroglyphs pecked into the vertical rock faces and on large fallen boulders. They were not particularly noteworthy for artistic merit, but the numbers and variety augured well for the arroyo's reputed richness in old rock paintings and engravings.

Just three hours out of San Ignacio, Chato reined up, pointed to an unusually steep *cañada,* or side canyon, on our left, and indicated that it contains a beautiful and seldom visited *tinaja,* a catchment pool worn into the bedrock. We knew from experience that artifacts of all sorts are particularly likely to be encountered in such places, so we stripped our animals of saddles and burdens and climbed the hillside. Tumbling waters of the millennia have scoured this steep cañada out of solid rock and it is free of debris — an oddity, since these side canyons are usually littered with boulders. The tinaja proved to be a classic, beautifully carved and perfectly round; it measures about 20 feet across and over six feet deep.

As I returned to the floor of the arroyo my eye was caught by a small cave on the opposite or east side. Its ceiling, though heavily shaded, glowed with a rich red hue. I crossed the wash and climbed up a steep bank. There above me was the first painted cave of the trip, and it was a curious sight.

The entire roof of the cave, an area of perhaps 200 or 300 square feet, is covered with layer upon layer of painted figures, mostly human, as large or larger than life judging from those that can be distinguished. I had seen overpainting before, indeed, it is a feature of most sites displaying Great Mural works, but never had I seen such an incredible exhibition. I could not count, or even imagine, how many

Profile of a respaldo,
the Painters' typical canvas

A dynamic process of erosion
created overhung walls which
attracted the Painters and
sustained their art. Here we see
the aftermath of erosion in a soft
layer of bedded volcanic ash at
the base of the formation. When
sufficiently undermined, the
harder layer above suffered
stress fractures from its own
weight, and great sheets of stone
dropped into the void left by
the erosion. The Painters created
their art on the fresh surface
thus exposed.

Cueva Pintada

figures had been depicted, nor in how many layers. The entire ceiling is absolutely covered with paint, some black but largely red. If I half-closed my eyes the cave resembled the mouth of a fireplace with darting tongues of flame.

Tacho had noted my preoccupation with the little cave and he came over for a look at the flaming ceiling. *"¡Que tantas manos de monos!"* was his remark. That translated literally as, "What a lot of layers of human caricatures!", and it raises the question of a controversial word. In standard Spanish, *mono* means a monkey or a person who apes or mimics the actions of others. In Mexico, mono is also applied to the king, queen, and jack on playing cards and to cartoon figures in comic strips, probably because they depict humans with the exaggerated antics associated with mimes and monkeys. The rural folk in many parts of Mexico apply the name mono to any pictograph of a human figure, including those drawn by their small children. In the sierras of Baja California, this is the only specific term applied to the human forms painted by the ancients. Some educated Spanish-speaking people are offended by the use of this word in the rock painting context. No doubt they view it as a form of slang beneath the dignity of the subject. I feel otherwise. The word is short and simple and it substitutes neatly for such awkward phrases as "human figures," "man forms," "representations of humans," etc. A final argument is more compelling. The word is used and understood by a large number of people including all those who find these works and guide us to them.

Just upstream from our stopping place we passed through an impressive *angostura,* or narrows, where the walls of the arroyo seem to lean almost together. Lodged in crevices 20 feet or more above the floor were bits of flotsam from a recent *chubasco,* or cyclonic summer storm, reminders of the dangers in such a place during the rainy season. After traversing these narrows and a series of bends, we came to the first great fork in the arroyo. To the right was a huge cañada called *Torotal,* which means a stand of *torote,* or so-called elephant trees. We bore on to the left into deeper and more massive ravines of El Parral. Clearly, the sierra gains altitude at this point more rapidly than the arroyo and the gorges here become really impressive.

We continued to see occasional petroglyphs and small paintings along our way, most of no great interest because of their faded condition. As we rode along and discussed rock art and the terrain, the word *respaldo* cropped up repeatedly. In answer to my query, Tacho explained that a respaldo is an overhung rock face. He pointed out a number, and they invariably proved to be broken edges where bedded layers of volcanic agglomerates had been cut through by water courses. (These successive strata of dissimilar pyroclastic materials typically have thicknesses ranging from four feet to 60 feet.) The genesis of the typical respaldo, particularly those that attracted the Painters, can be easily observed. Such formations occur where a relatively thick layer of a harder agglomerate overlies a thinner layer of softer material. The exposed face of the softer stratum disintegrates continuously due to heating and cooling, hydrating and dehydrating, and direct actions of water and wind. After 20 or 30 horizontal feet of the soft layer have been eroded out, the harder stratum above no longer has the mechanical strength to sustain the part of its mass that is now cantilevered. In a typical instance, a great piece breaks away after a conchoidal stress fracture — "conchoidal," or shell-like, describes the form of the piece that falls away. Thus a respaldo resembles half of a clam shell seen from the open side and with the hinged edge downward. This form attracted the Painters because the fracture left a clean, rather smooth, recessed surface, the top overhanging the lower part. Most of our future exertions were to be expended in investigating poorly accessible but promising respaldos.

A few other terms useful in rock art pursuits in Baja California are *falda*, the steeply sloped sides of a watercourse formed from detritus sloughed off from cliffs above; *caja* for the bed or wash of a watercourse; and *ancón*, for any level surface or bank higher than the caja. Arroyos are unusually dynamic features of the landscape, constantly being deepened by runoff from rains, and particularly by flash floods resulting from passing chubascos. Thus, the ancón of today was the caja of yesteryear, a transitional formation that eventually disappears as the arroyo widens and deepens. Most arroyo trails, including the one on which we rode, are located on the generally smooth ancón; only at an angostura between vertical rock walls is it necessary to ride in a boulder-strewn wash.

By now we rode entirely in the deep shadows cast by our towering surroundings. Occasional vistas to the east showed dazzling afternoon light on layer after layer of rich red volcanic rock. Before dusk we came to a second great fork in the arroyo and saw before us the steep Cuesta de la Higuerita leading up out of the arroyo to the mesa above. It was time to camp; we rode up onto the ancón and broke down the mule packs to get at our camping gear.

I climbed a little knoll just above our camp and looked around. To the east lay Cañada del Corralito where we would go to see the painting of the serpent. To the north, El Parral wound inexorably on into the sierra. Chato saw me surveying his world and climbed up to give me a few proprietary pointers. He indicated a cave near the cuesta, high above us and on the north side of the mouth of Corralito. I put the glasses on it. A huge red figure of a man with upraised arms seemed in the act of springing from his lair. Other smaller but significant figures showed below. I was suitably impressed. Nothing we had seen during the day was nearly so large or well preserved.

The next morning Chato explained his plan. The Serpent Cave — which Chato called *Cueva de la Serpiente* as I shall do hereinafter — and one or two other painted places were located up Cañada del Corralito, so our visit would be a round trip, returning to our camp at the foot of the cuesta. We passed the nearby painted caves without a stop because Tacho remembered that Cueva de la Serpiente is best lighted in the morning. For a while we made fairly good time; the trail was open and there were few temptations to pause. An hour or so after we left camp, Chato

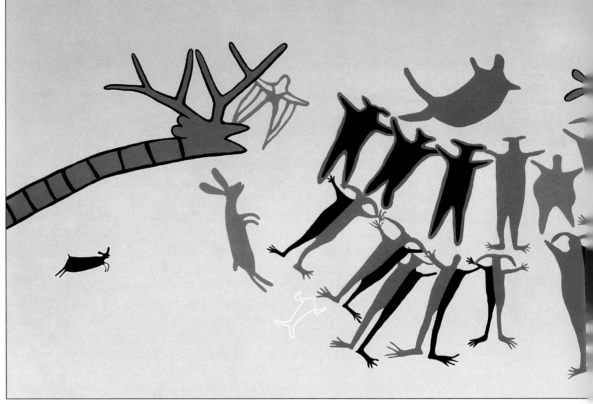

A *singular work from a single hand*

The most extraordinary composition in
the Great Mural area is this 26-foot-long
panel, apparently painted by one artist.
No other site displays fanciful creatures
like these deer-headed serpents, nor do
others show large groups of interrelated
figures like those clustering around the
sinuous body of the snake-monster on
the right. As if to heighten the mystery of
this unique conception, the smaller
figures *do* closely resemble the work of
Painters at other sites. The photograph of
the area between the serpents shows the
rough surface on which this great work
was rendered—and attests to the fidelity
of Joanne Crosby's recreation of the entire
panel.

Cueva de la Serpiente

32

Chapter 3

pulled up in a clearing at a fork in the cañada, and pointed at the sheer wall just
above us to the west.

Cueva de la Serpiente   We looked up and saw a small, shallow cave not more
than 30 or 40 feet above the wash. The entire wall including the cave is composed
of a sort of pudding stone, a rough, broken conglomerate. The colors are speckled—dark stones set in a warm sandy matrix. I could see a rather formless painting on this unpromising surface, and I was disappointed. The fame of the place
had led me to expect a more impressive cave, a better working surface, and a larger
painting. With Chato's feelings in mind, I gave no sign of my thoughts. It was just
as well.

   In a few moments I untied my camera bags and scrambled with them up to
the cave. Closer inspection of the paintings reversed my preliminary judgment. I
crawled along the ledge below the work with a growing sense of wonder.

   The whole painting is in exceptionally fine condition. The uneven rock is
apparently hard and resistant to weathering. As a result, the colors are still vivid
and the outlines sharp. The scale is impressive: The total length of the mural is
26 feet. My first estimate of its size was badly in error due to the viewing distance
and the absence of real masses of color or form.

The composition of the work, when seen close at hand, is striking as a whole and full of fascinating details. A serpentine figure forms the literal spine of an assemblage fleshed out with over 50 doll-like human and animal figures. The sinuous form of the serpent and these lesser bodies were conceived and executed as a unit. The small figures do not interfere with the movement of the large one; indeed, their placement creates an odd, rocking effect that enhances the apparent weaving of the serpent.

This painting would prove to be unique in several ways. In my eventual travels in Baja California, I have seen over 50 groupings of painted figures that could loosely be called compositions. None of them is so obviously intentional, so homogeneous, so literally tied together as is this one. The feeling of oneness goes far beyond the basic composition. The colors are consistent throughout. The degree of weathering is more or less equal on all parts. To my eye, the entire work belongs to one school and looks like the work of a single artist.

I gradually became aware of other intriguing features. The wall actually bears two orange-red snake forms separated by a gap of about five feet. The right snake is complete. Its head sports ears and antlers, its long body is ringed with black stripes and drawn as if in sinuous motion, and its tail is plainly bifurcated. The left snake form also has an elaborate set of antlers, but most of its body disappeared

33

The Sierra de San Francisco

at some earlier time when a section of the rock surface fell away. The left serpent lacks the small figures around it, but perhaps it was never completed; nearby, small figures were sketched in chalk but left unpainted.

The conception of the serpents is astonishing. In any context those eared, antlered, and fork-tailed monsters would seemed bizarre and fanciful concoctions. In the land of the Great Murals, where animals regularly have literal outlines, they are downright iconoclastic.

For half an hour I studied the mural, looking at it from every feasible angle and using the camera to try tentative compositions, but for a time photographs could not be made. The morning sun burned on the front of the cave so close to the painting that no film could cope with such contrast. I needed to wait for a shadow from the overhanging rock.

Chato had mentioned a large stone corral in the vicinity, so we set off to look at it while waiting on the sun. In front of Cueva de la Serpiente, the wash of the arroyo turns sharply east then makes a second turn in two hundred yards and continues northward to its origin on the flanks of Cerro de Santa Marta. At the second of these turns, on the west bank, there is a boulder-strewn promontory on top of which was Chato's old corral. The structure proved to be about 40 feet square and made of really large dry-laid stones. It is so old that even Chato's grandfather knew it only as an ancient work; he had supposed it dated from Indian times. No tradition survives to tell us if it once served a ranch, or whether it was a stopping place for animals driven between the high and low country. Unless someone stumbles on records now unknown, hundreds of such puzzling monuments wait in odd places as venerable question marks to confound their rare visitors.

After examining the corral for a quarter of an hour, I could see that the serpent was in shadow; it was time to make photographs. As we returned, the painting once again looked insignificant; the slim figure of the serpent and small images of his entourage simply do not "read" from the bed of the arroyo, over 100 feet away. I climbed up and photographed it as well as possible but it would have gone a whole lot better with a 20-foot stepladder. Anyone who visits Baja California cave painting sites will understand this perfectly. It is frequently impossible to get far enough back to compose a picture without falling down the mountainside. Between working and musing over the art, an hour passed.

I climbed down from the cave shelf and started to the right along the cliff face, an apparently easier descent than the one used before. Just south of the cave is a prominent rock. The legend "Oregon Archaeological Expedition" was printed large upon it in oil paint. Beneath that line, all the members of the group were listed.

I felt ashamed that my countrymen had come and defaced a place that had been known and visited for so long. Chato's grandfather knew the place of the Serpent and probably knowledge of it among the sierra folk has never been lost since ancient times. True, Chato and Tacho guided those people into the site and were included as members of the offending group, but that does not in any way

excuse the act. The Mexicans were provincial folk with little worldly experience.
It is not the way of their culture to interfere in the apparently well-intentioned acts
of visitors.

In an old mural painted on the wall high above this modern sign painting, a
faint row of giant men with arms uplifted keep an ancient vigil. It was a touching
sight. In my mind I saluted the Painters' grave images and resolved
afresh to find and record them and their cryptic messages. Across
the arroyo, Chato was motioning toward another find, a variety of
small paintings in a low cave with a partially fallen roof. The
prize was a pair of black deer in full flight across a ceiling so
low it is seen best from a reclining position.

Halfway back to our camp, we stopped at a cave left behind in the morning's
rush. On the east side of the wash and not far above it is a long overhang with a
flat roof like a miniature El Batequi. On its smooth ceiling is a striking pair of deer
in marvelous condition. The smaller deer on the left was rendered in a rich brick
red. Painted over that ground color is a grid of black lines dividing the internal
space like a checkerboard. In addition, parts of the body and legs were firmly outlined in black, and the head was depicted as if pierced or struck by a short, stout
stick of wood. The larger deer on the right is even more elaborate. First, it was
chalked in white, then strongly outlined in red-brown. The interior space was
divided lengthwise into three broad bands of color, the outer two black and the
central band in the same red-brown. This deer was depicted with a showy set of
antlers and an arrow or spear piercing its back and emerging, with a well-drawn
stone point, from the belly.

Elsewhere in the shelter are a group of three fish or dolphins divided half red
and half black; a pair of large monos, one red, the other divided red and black;
and numerous small paintings. Among the latter are some carefully wrought
monos, some badly eroded fishlike forms, and a pair of symbols that immediately
struck me with their novelty and possible significance. On the rear central area of
the ceiling is a circle perhaps 10 inches in diameter, outlined neatly in red-brown
and divided into halves, one unpainted and the other filled in with the same red-
brown paint. This unique figure suggests a representation of the half moon, and its
associated symbol makes the suggestion stronger. Almost tangent to it is a much
smaller circle depicted as having rays like a conventional sun symbol. At the time,
I imagined that the painting might represent the beginning or ending of an eclipse.
Later, this painting would figure in speculation—and may have special significance for students of the Great Murals and the Painters who made them.[*]

Beneath all the paintings is the usual thick layer of soft tuff, the material that
weathered away to form the shelter. Its exposed surface is heavily engraved with

*See pages 226-228 in Chapter VII, "The Practices and Puzzles of Painters."

Realism and symbolism merge in the Painters' traditional art

This pair of deer provides an illustration of a paradox in the realism of the Painters' style: Outlines of these and most other figures were drawn as recognizable animal forms—but then infilled with arbitrary and fanciful patterns.

El Parral XIV

A record of a supernova sighting?

This design with its two suggestive forms may be one of the most important of the Painters' works, despite its modest scale, limited palette, and mediocre condition. It could represent the night and day show provided by the supernova that formed the Crab Nebula. The light from this event reached Earth in 1054 A.D.

EL PARRAL XIV

36

lines, symbols and patterns of drillings, a phenomenon I later would note at most of the painted caves that offered this invitingly workable rock.

We mounted our mules and I had a decision to make as we rode below Pie de la Cuesta de la Higuerita, the cave with the gigantic red human figure gesturing from its ceiling. We were ready to leave El Parral and there was enough time left in the day to go up the cuesta to a stopping place with food and water for the animals. If we visited this cave, we would have to spend another night in the arroyo. I looked up at the red phantom in his den. I thought of all the Indian art we had seen that day, and all that yet to come, and decided to go on. That was a mistake, and I paid dearly for it. Almost as soon as I left, I could feel a tugging at my mind. Long after, far away in time and distance, I was troubled by recurrent thoughts of the monster and those figures seen dimly at his feet. If I had just climbed up and taken a quick look. . . .

That experience ended my first exploration of El Parral. The trip continued to Arroyo del Batequi, as will be told shortly, but there is more to the Parral story. Exactly three years later, I returned with Tacho and my friend, Dr. Ray F. Weiss, a geochemist at Scripps Institution of Oceanography in La Jolla, California. As an assistant, we had Tacho's youngest son, Ramón, a man who figured prominently in many of my rock art searches. My second Parral trip followed exactly in the steps of the first as far as the large and hidden tinaja. Then began a series of curious and revealing occurrences. I took Ray up to see the water catchment and, while we examined and photographed that place, Ramón made his way to the south along the base of a cliff. When he had gone 100 yards he returned to tell us he had found a large painted site. We followed him back and saw an overhung rock face painted with dozens of monos and a number of animal representations. The rock is a coarse, rough conglomerate and the paintings are in poor condition. Nevertheless, the experience was astonishing. Three years before we passed in plain sight of those works at a distance of less than 50 yards—and had no inkling of their existence. To make matters even more embarrassing, the paintings proved to be quite noticeable from the bed of the arroyo where we dismounted on both occasions. In particular, the image of a rabbit overlaid by an arrow, skillfully painted on a smooth included rock, was quite visible from our stopping place—once we knew where to look.

The comedy played on as we rode up the arroyo. In the first quarter of a mile we took turns discovering new paintings in three separate small caves. We reached the climax of this experience at the mouth of Cañada del Torotal. The day was ending and the low sun shone on the north side of the cañada. Our first cursory inspection revealed a large and important group of painted figures high on the wall a quarter of a mile away. Tacho and I were astonished that we both missed all these things before. The experience provided a measure of what we had learned in three years.

A nasty climb on a crumbling and steeply inclined approach made possible a close inspection of the painted site. We found a generally rough respaldo with one smooth area in the form of an arch superimposed above the entrance of a small cave. On this flat surface awaited seven or eight stately monos, with their usual appearance of a solemn ceremonial group. The mural also displays three large deer and several smaller animal forms, but all are difficult to distinguish, so obscured are they by the confusion of overpainting.

We next stopped at the foot of Cuesta de la Higuerita, at the cave of the red giant that I had spurned three years before. When we climbed up and stood at his feet, my earlier fears were justified. The large mono seen from afar is less interesting than the dozens of vividly colored red and black deer and monos we now saw painted on the wall below and extending into a narrow cave opening off the larger shelter. The site is felicitous in several ways. From its ample "porch" there is a fine view of handsome canyon scenery. Visitors can enjoy the balcony panorama and then turn to the choice collection of paintings that more than repay them for the climb. And all the while the great red figure above stands with arms outstretched as if he were the messiah or protector of El Parral.

The Sierra de San Francisco

We planned to quit the arroyo and go to Santa Marta by way of the ancient cuesta, perhaps built by Consag in the 1740s. Tacho volunteered to clear brush off the little-used grade with his long belt-knife while Ramón, Ray Weiss, and I went to see Cueva de la Serpiente. No sooner had we left him and rounded a turn in the cañada than we once again discovered a painted site in full view of the trail. Numerous figures, although not well defined or colorful, were evident on a smooth, light-colored respaldo about 60 feet above the caja on the west wall of the watercourse. We climbed to the painted respaldo over a crumbling bedrock incline—had it been steeper, it could not have been scaled without special equipment.

Despite severe weathering, the figures at this site were well worth the effort needed to inspect and record them. We found several deer, two borregos, one large mono, and a pair of smaller figures that appear to represent coyotes. Many of these are involved in complicated overpainting that reduces their stature as artworks by making it difficult to distinguish their separate outlines. Nevertheless, two of the deer and both the borregos are beautiful. One of each had its outline infilled in an unusual fashion. A deer was depicted in black except for a pair of large red patches on the body, patches with rounded rectangular forms. One of the borregos reversed this pattern, being painted red and having two black patches. It is a shame that the apparent coyote figures are not clearer and more complete. They seem to have been skillfully depicted and would be especially welcome since most paintings assumed to be of coyotes are rather crude and graceless.

We proceeded to Cueva de la Serpiente about 400 yards to the north and devoted an hour to mapping its large and complicated mural. Our technique involved making nine overlapping photos with the camera exactly six feet from, and perpendicular to, the painted surface. The facsimile in this book was derived from our results.

Meanwhile Ramón was off exploring, and when we were almost finished he returned to tell us of a discovery. We followed him for a quarter of a mile up the more northerly fork of the cañada to reach a large respaldo low on the west wall. There in very faded condition are six beautiful deer in a graceful running frieze. Some are black, others red and, although erosion has left the paint rather faint and incomplete, the group retains much charm. I photographed such disappearing art because I hoped to record enough to make facsimile restorations possible. It must be said, however, that photography is not the ideal medium. An artist working at the site could detect vestiges that simply do not appear in the best photographs.

Across the wash from the ancient stone corral (described on page 34), is a steep falda covered with volcanic boulders slid and tumbled from layers of cantil above. Near the top is a rock art site—a long, low cave shelter containing many paintings, to date, the only large group found in the drainage of El Parral. This shelter is so curiously hidden and is so high above any observation point that it went unnoticed until 1975, when Tacho López (a Santa Marta resident and one of

Tacho Arce's many nephews) discovered it while rounding up a herd of strayed goats. In deference to the ancient corral in the cañada below, local people call the place El Corralito.

Cueva del Corralito   The painted shelter at Corralito is about 200 feet long, a respaldo from which many huge fragments have fallen in relatively recent times. These pieces of the overlying rock stratum choke much of the entrance to the shelter and provided the Painters with useful stairs by which to approach the newly exposed rock surface. Farther from the entrance sits a jumble of material that slid down from the steep slopes above, overshot the cave itself, but piled up in front to block any distant view of the cave. Talus piled in front of caves is common in the greater area, but it seldom leaves the opening as hidden as the one at Corralito. Tacho López must have climbed this embankment and hiked close to the respaldo in order to have found the virtually buried cave.

As a rock art site, Corralito is interesting and disappointing. Most of its figures are on a grand scale. One 13-foot deer may be the biggest Great Mural representation of this most often painted animal. However, these larger-than-life figures were delineated in a familiar style that I consider decadent and representative of the last stage of the Painters' work. Little paint was used; even the outlines were drawn in a stingy dry-brush technique. And infills, where attempted at all, consisted of a few swipes at the rock which left lines that look as if a giant piece of chalk had been carelessly scratched over the rough surface. Most of these large figures exhibit little artistry; they look as if someone was in a hurry to create the trappings of an important ceremonial center. This low standard contrasts strikingly with the elegance of the nearby serpent and its attendants.

The generally poor condition of Corralito's earlier and more classical works detracts from a visitor's enjoyment of the place. The rock surface has sloughed away to such a degree that, in some cases, only patches of large figures remain or, at best, significant parts are missing. For example, there is a large red *león*, a mountain lion, richly painted and outlined in black but now missing head, paws, and part of its tail. Not far away, you must look closely to perceive all the parts of a handsome red mono with its upper torso and head infilled with vertical parallel stripes in contrasting black.

On a positive note, some of the better preserved figures are unusual and deserve attention. One large red and black mono has a unique, pale red, spherical headdress and a pair of foot-tall, lobsterlike devices painted one over either shoulder. The latter must have had some traditional, ritual meaning because almost identical juxtapositions can be seen between large monos and small figures at nearby Cueva de las Flechas and at El Carrizo, 40 miles to the southeast in the Sierra de Guadalupe.

A much cruder but prominent red mono is flanked at its feet by rarely seen figures: a snake on the left, its sinuosity emphasized, and an apparent moray eel

on the right. Each creature is depicted in red with black lines running down both back and belly.

On the ground directly in front of this group is a pile of broken stone, pieces small enough that men might have carried or rolled them into place. These form a rude semicircle and seem likely to have been used as seats. At the focus of this arrangement is a naturally formed stone pedestal about four feet high, clearly selected and embedded here because of its columnar form. The top and upper sides have been heavily painted in red—the same paint used to delineate the figures on the wall. More remarkably, portions of the pedestal are exceedingly smooth, and the top especially has been worn smooth by long use as a seat or standing place. Single large polished rocks of this sort are found at half a dozen other Great Mural sites, but none of the others is painted, nor are any so suggestive of ceremonial use. This extraordinary and tantalizing artifact alone justifies the difficult 30-minute climb from Cueva de la Serpiente.

El Parral clearly has been an important avenue into the heart of the sierra since prehistoric times, and it provided a convenient place to begin my itinerary. However, the rock art of El Parral is by no means typical of similar areas elsewhere in these mountains. The principal differences should be noted so the reader is not misled. Twenty or more painted caves or shelters is a large number even for a major access arroyo. Nevertheless, other than Corralito, these artistic sites are quite small both in physical extent and in numbers of painted figures. Most arroyos displaying this number of sites would include more large, extensively painted locations that would suggest meeting places for ritual purposes. Further, the artwork of El Parral is unusually diverse in style, even apart from Cueva de la Serpiente—that assemblage, to me, is the most surprising and unique work among all the Great Murals. Perhaps the variety of artistic expressions found in El Parral can be explained by its location at the southern extreme of the sierra.

The San Francisco range was once a rather simple shield volcano, roughly oval in outline, rising as a low spreading cone to an apex near today's highest peak, Cerro de la Laguna. During roughly 20 million years, rainfall running down from the central heights have cut an arrangement of arroyos that, from the air, despite these waterways' far from straight courses, looks like the pattern formed by spokes of a wheel. This erosion has been so extensive that today the beds and slopes of the arroyos make up more of the sierra's area than do the peaks and mesas, the surviving parts of the original surface. The steeply tiered sides of the watercourses produced virtually all of the caves that came to contain aboriginal art. All available evidence suggests that the beds of the arroyos were the avenues by which people made their way into the heart of the mountains.

The arroyos vary considerably in the amount of art they exhibit. A few appear to lack paintings altogether, while in others they abound. Reasons are not difficult to deduce. Some arroyos are much more transitable than others; some contain springs; others lead to areas once rich in food; and some relate to natural routes leading from ocean to gulf. Those used most by people of the Painters' time apparently received the majority of their artistic and ceremonial attention. For this reason, the account given here of San Francisco art is divided into arroyos. Ten of these are named and discussed because they have been found to contain significant art, but it is also important to note that 10 is less than half the total number of large drainages.

We know from accounts written early in the period of European contact that the mid-peninsular Cochimí lived in bands of about 40 to 80 people each. Typically, two to four related bands roamed and collected food in an area of several hundred square miles that was tacitly recognized as their domain. However, a few oases, of which San Ignacio was perhaps the foremost example, produced such a large and secure supply of water and associated fruit and game that they were visited at least annually by many bands and served as meeting places important in cultural interchange. Thus El Parral, as the nearest arroyo to San Ignacio, must have served more different groups as a path than did any other of San Francisco's watercourses. During the Painters' era, most arroyos probably were used by bands that frequented the adjacent lowlands or, seasonally, the mountains themselves. These annual visitors, each occupying a somewhat proprietary area, may have been the creators of typical San Francisco art. But El Parral's more diverse art seems to indicate that it was used as an avenue by many of the far-ranging bands that met at San Ignacio. The absence of large ceremonial sites in El Parral (with the exception of El Corralito) could be attributed to the same phenomenon—each group of related bands may have preferred a principal ceremonial center in its own area rather than in a corridor much frequented by competitive and unsympathetic strangers.

As speculative as it is (and as all explanations of the Painters' work must be), this discussion of arroyos will be meaningful to any student of San Francisco art, especially if this person visits the works themselves. Each of these great watercourses seems to have a character of its own, and each dictates routes of travel as well as sites for human occupation, ancient or modern. The local people clearly think of their geography on an arroyo-by-arroyo basis, and a visitor almost certainly will carry away memories divided and packaged in much the same way.

Arroyo del Batequi

Cerro de Santa Marta, whose southern drainage formed Arroyo del Parral, gives rise on the west to the very different Arroyo del Batequi. Whereas El Parral is deep and narrow with many convolutions, El Batequi is wide and makes its way into the desert to the west with only a few curves. The heads of the two watercourses are separated by the Mesa de la Higuera's 3,000-foot elevation and from that vantage point most of El Batequi can be seen. The panorama is reminiscent of the Grand Canyon in form and color, although at only a quarter of the scale.

Near El Batequi's origin on the spine of the sierra, two cañadas come together to form the single arroyo that makes its way westward. The more northerly of these tributary cañadas is called La Higuerilla; during my search for the Great Murals, it contained a ranch inhabited by two families. The south fork is called La Natividad and its only ranch had been abandoned for two generations. Both cañadas have permanent springs that must have attracted Indians.

Tacho took me to La Natividad in 1972. He had visited the ranch back in the 1930s and, at the time, one of the sons of Vérulo Ojeda, the founder, had taken him a short distance to see Indian remains. Tacho remembered only that the place was vast and had paintings—which he now proposed to show to me. We parked our animals at the now-deserted ranch site and set off on foot, approaching the cave from the east down a shallow slope. When this suddenly deepened, we dropped to the floor of the canyon and started downstream, Tacho striding ahead. In a moment we turned a little corner and he pointed up.

Cueva de la Natividad Tacho and I looked up a steep falda and saw, high above that, an immense, overhung respaldo, the upper part of the cave we were seeking. It was quite a scramble up the steep bank but in a few minutes my guide and I were standing on the floor of what is probably the largest painted rock shelter in Baja California.

The basic natural formation is an overhung rock face about 500 feet long and about 100 feet high. The extent of the overhang varies from a few feet to as much

● Large painted cave(with major art)

▲ Small painted cave(with major art)

◓ Large painted cave(with minor art)

◒ Small painted cave(with minor art)

R Ranch

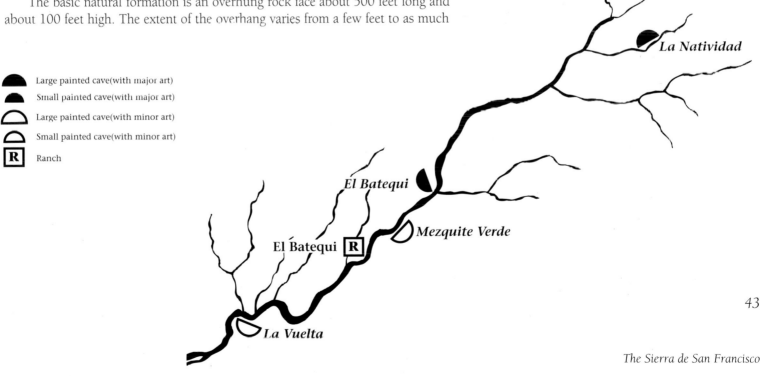

Sauzalito
R

La Natividad

El Batequi

Mezquite Verde

El Batequi R

La Vuelta

43

The Sierra de San Francisco

as 40 or 50. The covered area gives the impression of being arched over. People familiar with the great caves of Betatakin, Keet Seal, and Inscription House in Navajo National Monument will know what I experienced in La Natividad. At the west end of the shelter, an enormous pile of fallen rock chokes the floor area and makes passage difficult, but the rest of the floor is quite clear. Retaining walls have been built from large pieces of the fallen rock and laboriously backfilled with earth to provide a broader and more level floor. Such stone and earth work is rare in Baja California, although it is common in Sonora in such places as Las Trincheras.

In addition and equally unusual, walls of rock have been erected perpendicular to the back wall of the cave to form either animal pens or human dwellings. The work is sturdy and reasonably neat but not up to the craftsmanship of the cliff dwellings at the Arizona caves mentioned previously. My first thought was that the rancher who had lived below had built these as goat pens, but Tacho insisted that no one would have done such a monumental amount work for that purpose.

A further oddity also involved wall building: For a stretch of many feet, the soft floor-level layer of rock has eroded to form a sub-cave within the larger one. Its ceiling height ranges from three or four feet to almost nothing, yet walled-in shelters a few feet wide have been built with headroom down to as little as two feet. These small pens may have been used as sleeping quarters with the entrances closed by piling rocks for protection.

At one time the entire 500 linear feet of wall has been more or less heavily painted. Along that great length, hundreds of figures can be made out, the vast majority being deer. Some were painted on an enormous scale, larger than any at El Batequi. Sadly, most are in bad or very bad condition. It is frustrating to stand below a gigantic mural of a rampant borrego and barely be able to make out the outlines and detect the color.

In one small area near the west end, at about eye level, there is a myriad of tiny figures painted with amazingly fine lines. The usual subjects are represented, but each figure is no more than four to eight inches tall. Later, I found similar work in Arroyo de San Pablo and far south in Arroyo de Guajademí of the Sierra de Guadalupe—but this was my first encounter with a large group of such miniatures.

Providentially, as at El Batequi, part of the painted display survives almost intact. At the west end, in the vicinity of the fallen debris, the wall is sprinkled with rather sketchy paintings of deer. These were all done using the equivalent of a dry-brush technique which produced less firm outlines than were usual to the Great Murals. They were also filled in with color in a very sparing fashion, each one either black or maroon. So similar are all these well-preserved figures that they could have come from one hand, and certainly from a single period. The art is competent and attractive but it did not impart the excitement that I sensed at El Batequi. However, close inspection of the older, more deteriorated work at the east end of La Natividad did suggest a relationship to the great black deer of the

Batequi mural. Objective comparisons will be difficult because the comparable figures at La Natividad are so heavily overpainted and in such bad condition.

Art is not the only attraction at the grand old site of La Natividad. From the "front porch" created by the retaining wall there is a fine view down the arroyo system to the west and, in the other direction, of the more open space by which we had entered. The bank opposite the cave is composed of an abrupt series of grand rock faces tiered up like the layers of a wedding cake. I measured the elevation of the place at 2,600 feet, stood a little longer scanning that panorama, and then turned and had a last look at the cave. Its sheer size is awesome; turning away for a moment brought it back into perspective. My eyes scaled its 100-foot height and then returned to features like the retaining walls, pens, and low shelters. I can say now what I could only guess then: the amount of human labor expended there is unique in the painted caves of Baja California. Probably no other site so strongly suggests human habitation. I wonder now, as I did then, if that was all aboriginal work or whether some was done in historic times. As if to underscore the latter possibility, a three-foot rock protruding from the wall of the cave over 10 feet from the floor displays a pair of unmistakable Christian crosses painted in bright ochre yellow, the only glint of that color in the cave.

Rancho Sauzalito is located in Cañada de la Higuerilla, parallel to and less than a mile north of Cañada de la Natividad. Jorge Arce, a resident rancher, responded to questions about ancient paintings at Sauzalito by pointing up the north wall of the cañada less than 200 yards from his home. There, he informed us, were many paintings, but *muy borradas*. This description, meaning very worn or erased, was unwelcome at the time, and later I would hear it with depressing regularity throughout the Great Mural area.

Looking up at the steep canyon wall, it was easy to imagine many examples of rock art. Tier after tier of respaldos are piled one on another and each seems to overhang a slit cave several hundred feet long. Jorge volunteered to show us how to get around on the precarious cliff.

On the first level, the long shelter has weathered from a very soft, powdery rock, and most of it is smoke-blackened. A few fragments of paintings indicate what once must have been many works. The second level is similar, but the third and fourth are considerably more rewarding. Despite deterioration, their long galleries still reveal unmistakable evidence of dozens of large paintings, mostly groupings of red and black monos. We ranged along these open passages feeling both fascinated and frustrated by the painted remains. In spite of large numbers of figures, not one is clear enough to promise a decent photographic image.

Finally Jorge conducted us to this area's last and most distant bastion. At the east end of the top level, at an elevation close to 3,000 feet, we entered a large open cave where, at last, we found a few appreciable paintings, notably of deer and birds. A single hard rock about six feet long is embedded as part of the cave wall in the painted area, and that durable surface has held the paint extremely well; the figures there, or the parts of figures that extended onto it, are unusually clear and brightly colored.

A few hundred yards west and downstream from Sauzalito, the cañada makes a sudden drop of 100 feet creating what, during a summer storm, must be a spectacular falls. For an hour's ride below the falls, the canyon remains narrow and deep and the trail, while beautiful, is slow because it winds through a rocky defile picturesquely planted with fruit trees by the ranchers above. Then La Higuerilla joins La Natividad to form the broad Arroyo del Batequi. It is another two-hour ride to its foremost painted place, the cave of El Batequi.

My second visit came a few months after the first. We arrived late and passed the night at the great bend of the arroyo just below the cave. At dawn I rolled out and started the climb to the murals. All sorts of thoughts and feelings raced through my head as I labored up the hill, and not the least of them was fear—fear that El Batequi could not possibly measure up to my idealized memories.

Cueva del Batequi   The sun rose for all the higher parts of the sierra. Cerro del Batequi, just to the south, was rimmed with gold on its east face, but the depths of the arroyo were still wrapped in the blue-gray light of dawn. When I arrived at the great painted rock shelter, its mural ceiling was shadowed and dim. I felt as if I had been admitted to the Louvre before the lights were turned on.

While awaiting the sun, I read my altimeter and recorded an elevation of 1,800 feet; then I fell to examining the lower parts of the shelter. I had remembered that the soft tuff of the back wall bore engravings, but I was astonished, during a real inventory, to see their number and complexity. The first identifiable figures were vulva symbols, a puzzlingly universal image both geographically and temporally. Over the course of 15,000 or more years throughout at least four continents, vulva depictions have been engraved and painted by hunting and gathering people. Did that image evolve with each culture as a separate if obvious inspiration, or was it used to represent procreation so early in our history that humans were able to take it with them on all their roamings of the earth?

On the back wall of the shelter, dozens of such symbols were worked deeply into the soft rock. Above, on the ceiling, a number of vulva symbols had been painted in white, much rarer artifacts than engravings of the same theme. We also noted innumerable drilled holes, perhaps a half inch in diameter, which at first appeared to be natural occurrences. I soon found, however, that they formed lines and patterns too perfect for chance, and I also noticed that numerous sets of slightly divergent lines were carved into the same material. Some of these hundreds of figures are sharp and clear, but most are so weathered that their engraved lines became softened and rounded. A few are so eroded they can be detected only when the surface has strong side lighting.

The sun rose and struck the shelter. As light began to reflect strongly from the floor and back wall, the mural on the ceiling had its greatest illumination of the day and my earlier anxiety was put to rest. Then and now, I see the paintings at El Batequi as a supreme example of primitive art. I went over it again and again. I suffered once more over its lost and damaged parts. And I rejoiced anew at its essential survival, its power, and its unity.

The overpainting, especially at the right end, attracted attention. In that strong light, shadowy figures could be seen underlying what I had perceived earlier. At least five different layers of paintings could be counted, and the thought crossed my mind that they must represent a rather large span of time. The freshest, the uppermost layer, must be several hundred years old, but its total weathering appeared far less than the difference between it and the oldest.

The works of that right end invite wonder and comment. They are unique in their style—which seems to me to be the most formal and sophisticated of all the Great Murals. The galloping deer and the arresting monos alike have a refinement and a classic simplicity that may be the highest expression of this culture.

The other parts of the grand cavalcade are curiously different. In the central section, two monos and a large deer are positively crude, and the left end seems to have been decorated by artists of widely varied talents. At first it seemed odd that these differences should be so marked in different parts of the mural rather than in different layers. However, a more thorough examination suggested a partial answer. The quality of the rock changes gradually across the mural. The smoothest and

A striking composite of the Painters' practices

This detail from the right end of the painted ceiling illustrates several of the Painters' conventions and techniques in four or five distinguishable layers of overpainting. White outlining is conspicuous, as are two examples of twisted perspective. Breasts on the woman at the upper left appear to issue from her armpits because they are depicted in double profile. The same distorted perspective causes dewclaws on the deer to appear unnaturally splayed, producing curious handlike hoofs.

El Batequi

hardest is on the right and it looks progressively softer toward the left. The condition of five tall, nearly identical brown and pale red monos tends to bear this out. Two on the right are in a good state of preservation, while the others are successively poorer as they are found farther to the left. It is possible that the entire ceiling was decorated during early periods of the painting epoch and that what we see on the right dates from those times. Corresponding works on the left must have been lost to erosion and then replaced by successions of later paintings. In any event, it is that beautiful right end of this great panel which will command the greatest attention and stir the strongest emotions.

At last it was time to go. I gathered up my things and, with many a backward glance, left my proudest discovery. I am amused now at my parting thoughts. What I confidently believed to be final farewells would be followed by four more pilgrimages.

As we rode down the arroyo, no more than a quarter of a mile west of the great painted site, Tacho remembered another, a place was called Mezquite Verde. Thirty years before he had to chase a wounded deer and, while returning, noticed some paintings. Presently, he pointed to the place: some poorly sheltered respaldos on the south side of the arroyo and perhaps 80 feet above the caja. I got out my binoculars and scanned its 100-yard length. The wall was in deep shade, and at first I could make out nothing but the speckling of numerous rocks cemented into the general matrix. Then I saw the head of a deer painted on one of the protruding rocks. With that we dismounted and climbed up a steep rock face to reach the level of the paintings.

The place once was a large center of primitive art. The entire length of the respaldo retains intermittent showings of painted groups, some on as grand a scale as those at El Batequi or La Natividad. All are in advanced stages of deterioration. I could not find a single profitable subject for a photograph, but finally I forced myself to select three or four representative groups to record the site.

One unique feature remains quite visible. At the western extremity, the rock face is eroded into a fantastic tracery of pockets and baseball-sized lumps. The smooth, rounded ends of the protuberances have been painted in different colors which have now faded but still gave the place the air of a bizarre parody of the pointillist school of French painters. It is the only example of such painting that I ever encountered. Caves at Cuesta de San Pablo over 15 miles north have similar knobs, but no paint.

The poor condition of the art at Mezquite Verde precluded any simple estimate of its worth, but it did offer some more evidence as to the causes of destruction. After analyzing El Batequi, La Natividad, and Mezquite Verde in the same arroyo, I believe I know why their art and that of most other sites has deteriorated.

The principal culprit is the rock itself. At some sites, the rock is hard and strongly resists all agents of weathering. At others, the rock seems to disintegrate at a fairly uniform rate due merely to exposure to air with its attendant changes in temperature and humidity. The site at Mezquite Verde offered dramatic proof of the differences caused by the character of the rock. The material of the painted walls is a conglomerate of volcanic debris: ash, pebbles, and some fairly large included rocks, occasionally softer but usually harder than the matrix. In some places a figure that can be made out only dimly on the wall as a whole is clearer and shows stronger colors where the design carries over onto the harder included material.

Paintings on western sierra slopes are, on the whole, in poorer shape than those on Gulf slopes. Since the rock formations of both slopes have common origins, it is probable that the deterioration of the paintings they bear is largely due to changes in humidity. The Pacific slopes are generally exposed to much moister air. When the somewhat porous agglomerate rock absorbs moisture in its outer layer, that layer expands slightly. Then, when dryer air sweeps those slopes as it occasionally does each year, the hydrated layer of rock loses its moisture and shrinks. In time, these expansions and contractions cause the layer to detach and slough off, a phenomenon noticeably more common on the western side of the peninsular sierras.

Exposure to sunlight alone seems to have been a minor factor in most cases of deterioration. On the dry eastern slopes, parts of paintings exposed to direct sun survive almost as well as those in year-round shade, other factors being about equal. On the west sides of the sierras however, paintings exposed to sun fare less well. The cycles of taking up and losing water are accelerated from seasonal to daily — absorption by night and drying by day. On either side of the mountains, direct exposure to rain or run-off from rain is disastrous and most paintings so exposed are virtually erased.

A few minutes' further ride brought us to Rancho El Batequi, which stood unoccupied just then despite its water, corrals, and sound buildings. Our animals needed water, so our objective was the batequi that gave the place its name.

Many Baja California arroyos have hard rock bottoms over which water flows underneath a bed of sand. A *batequi* is a shallow pit dug in the sands of the caja to reach that water. Spaniards probably learned the technique from Mexican natives; certainly the word *batequi* has an Indian origin. On the California peninsula, Indians, and later the *gente de razón,* or Hispanic settlers, found many of these sites and used them as water sources. The construction at El Batequi was classic. Three sides of the hole were fenced to prevent animals from breaking down the edges. The fourth side was dug back to form a long shallow ramp by which the stock could approach the water.

About two miles below Rancho El Batequi, the arroyo takes the form of a large dogleg by turning north and then abruptly back to the west. For the purposes of mapping and record keeping, my companions and I have dubbed this place *La Vuelta del Batequi,* The Bend of El Batequi. On the west wall, just before the second of these turns, is a series of small caves. In them we found a number of paintings in poor condition. The principal subject is deer, and one figure is noteworthy. The usual distribution of red and black in a bicolor deer is reversed; this one is

principally black with red on the belly and the inner legs.

Across the arroyo to the northeast is another shelter with unusual form and content. A low bluff protrudes into the sweep of the arroyo, its extremity pierced by a cave which passes through like a tunnel. The chamber is not large and its two entrances are no more than 50 feet apart, but within that small volume an amazing amount of ancient activity took place.

The inner space is divided into a broad passageway at ground level and, on the north or uphill side, a shelf two to three feet above that floor. The entire surface of this raised portion is engraved in a lavish and complex design of pits and grooves. Such work is not unknown in other places within the Great Mural region, but to date, nowhere has such an elaborate and extensive example been found. The carvings are also unusual in their depth; most are chipped or scratched at least two inches into the rock surface.

A carpet of rock engravings defies interpretation

Paleolithic cultures on every inhabited continent produced pit-and-groove rock engravings, but even very similar works may have been done for different reasons. A creative act which was part of a puberty rite in one group may have been a shaman's means of divination in another. So, perhaps, with rock art. No matter how similar, works of different times and places may have had different inspirations. The media available to artists are far more limited than the range of ideas they attempt to express.

La Vuelta del Batequi

All this work creates a puzzling spectacle for today's visitor. Such engravings may appear decorative to us, but they could be a purely incidental by-product created for specific ceremonial purposes. Similar works in other regions of the world have been associated ethnographically with tribal rites of several quite different kinds. Here we can only look and wonder at what is clearly a meaningful artifact.

The rich array of rock carving at la Vuelta del Batequi distracted us from other modest remains. On walls above the pits and grooves were vestiges of paintings and on the floor were several extremely worn metates. We also found some of the rarer *manos,* or hand stones, used in grinding on the metate surfaces. (Manos are less commonly encountered because they are smaller and hence more easily scattered, buried, or taken away for use.)

The art of El Batequi stands in the most marked contrast to that of El Parral. El Batequi has far fewer sites. No more than five or six truly separate locations can be counted, but four of these are major painting centers, each with over 100 figures.

The site that I have chosen to call El Batequi is distinguished by many masterfully executed figures. More important, it shows an unprecedented degree of cooperation among its major artists. Painters unknown numbers of years or generations apart not only respected but added to what they found; the product is a powerful composition. This attribute spotlights the place among the Painters' work because the norm is diametrically opposite—most assemblages of figures from different hands and times have resulted in disarray and chaos. In a land where overpainting was the rule, successive artists usually obliterated the works of their predecessors. The priceless mural at El Batequi shines down from its ceiling as a glorious exception.

Immediately to the north of Arroyo del Batequi is a small arroyo called San Esteban that does not penetrate to the heart of the sierra. North of that and generally parallel to both the others is La Ascensión, a major arroyo that originates on the south flanks of Cerro de La Laguna, a mountain with an elevation of 5,300 feet—the highest and most central expression of the sierra. La Ascensión was named for an old ranch located where the arroyo walls tower highest. As a curiosity, at least for people unfamiliar with local usage, the same arroyo below the ranch is called La Matancita, after another ranch. This practice is common; the name of an arroyo in a given locale typically reflects no more than the name of the ranch it contains. At the turn of the century, what we now know as Arroyo del Batequi was called La Natividad, as was the mountain now known as Cerro del Batequi. But Rancho La Natividad fell and Rancho El Batequi flourished.

Arroyo de la Ascensión

José Leree at Rancho La Ascensión was surprised at our interest in rock art—surprised that anyone would ride for weeks in the sierra seeking all the paintings strewn about by antiquity. But he did not laugh at us. He knew three painted places and, on reflection, he decided we would never find two of them without help. He offered to devote a day to our cause.

The arroyo divides at the ranch. The north fork is called Cañada de la Tinaja and the main trunk continues east to divide again. José instructed us to pass that second north fork, Cañada del Cerro, and follow the trail until we found a cave with some paintings—he called the place Los Monos. We could see it for ourselves and pass the night nearby. José would join us in the morning.

Los Monos must once have been an attractive place with a small but choice collection of art. A modest cave shelter on the north side of the arroyo still retains remnants of painted figures of deer, rabbits, birds and men. Unfortunately, these works are severely damaged by rock deterioration and further obscured by heavy deposits of soot from fires built within the shelter. Only a single attractive red and black bird survives both scourges.

The subject of fires and smoke in the caves of Baja California badly needs study by qualified scientists. In places like Los Monos de la Ascensión, it seems likely that ranchers of the historic period were responsible for the smoke stains.

Large painted cave(with major art)
Small painted cave(with major art)
Large painted cave(with minor art)
Small painted cave(with minor art)
Ⓡ Ranch

La Cuevona
Los Monos
Cueva Obscura
Ⓡ La Ascención
Las Calabasas
La Matancita

After all, this cave lies only a few feet from a trail connecting Rancho La Ascensión with Rancho Las Calabasas and then continuing to Santa Marta, long a portal to the sierra. But such smoked caves form a small fraction of the total. Most caves are far from modern trails and some are in places where people would have had no conceivable activity during historic times. In addition, while many painted caves are smoked, the majority are not. Moreover, smoke-blackened caves without signs of painting are frequently found near unsmoked caves that are heavily painted. Certainly the soot on the walls and the charcoal mixed with the earth, materials datable by the analysis of isotopes of carbon, have a story to tell. This subject is discussed further in Chapters V and VII.

Directly across from Los Monos, a soft rock stratum has eroded to produce a long, low recess about 15 feet above the wash of the arroyo. At one place in this shelter, a group of small paintings is visible on a large included rock weathering out of the greater mass. They depict young deer or perhaps rabbits and are a graceful and attractive lot. The intention of the painter seems obvious; most of the plump little figures were shown as pierced by arrows.

La Cuevona de la Ascensión   José Leree arrived at an early hour, and he had us climbing up a bedrock shute on the northern side of the arroyo before the sun got down to those depths. The ascent was slow and precarious with much loose material to avoid and many level changes involving dubious handholds and footholds. When we arrived at an impassable palisade, we turned west and rounded a point. For an hour and a half the climb continued until we reached the spine of the hill separating the arroyo from Cañada del Cerro. The whole hike was impeded by exceedingly steep, rough terrain, and by an unusually heavy growth of *garabatillo,* a long-limbed shrub with wicked hooklike thorns.

Finally Señor Leree brought us to the edge of a precipice that drops more than 300 feet to the floor of the cañada. We had arrived, he said, at a painted cave, and

it was directly beneath us. A quarter of an hour of confusion followed. Lerée had discovered the cave while seeking strayed goats. He had come upon it while working his way along what even he described as a difficult ledge, and he had left the place by climbing up a fluelike crack to a point near where we stood. Now he could not find the hidden stairway that would take us down, and we all looked along the perilous edge at what appeared to be an impossible descent.

At last the missing access was found and we let ourselves down in a cautious fashion and by that means entered La Cuevona, 3,500 feet above sea level and the largest true cave I have visited in the Painters' realm.

For once the setting stole the show from the promise of art or even the possibility of ancient treasures within. The place is vast and it is beautiful. Under the brow of the cliff, the elements have eroded an ovoid space about 200 feet long,

A *huge, windswept void houses Great Mural art*

This immense eye-socket cave in a steep wall of Cañada del Cerro is one of the least accessible of the Painters' sites. Although the few paintings of giant men and deer on its walls are not outstanding examples, this cathedral-like space, and the experience of reaching it, create beautiful memories of the land.

La Cuevona

60 feet high and 80 feet deep. The floor was windswept and clean of all traces of recent activity; there were no footprints and no animal droppings. The initial impression was that we were the first humans ever to disturb the place's isolated serenity. A brief tour dispelled that notion. Several metates sat about here and there and three giant monos and five successive deer seemed to stare down from the walls.

A thorough examination of the entire cave surface produced no further evidence from the Painters' hands. We were scarcely surprised; the wonder was that people had labored up to such a place to paint at all, not that they had failed to return in repeated cycles. Unfortunately, the painted figures are in a very diminished state. The same erosive forces that created the cave persist, and its art has not been spared. The relatively soft agglomerate rock the Painters chose as their canvas continues to loosen bit by bit, and falls to be scoured away by winds that whip those towering heights. While one mono at the center of the cave's back wall is only a shadow, two others still assert a degree of their half-red and half-black presence. Off to the right, the procession of deer is gradually weathering away.

We said our farewells to that eagle's lookout, profoundly moved by the grandeur of the great cave, by its enigmatic past association with humanity, and by the effort expended to reach it. Then we left and followed José Leree to take a devious path to the caja of the cañada below.

Directly across from La Cuevona but only fifty feet or so above the floor of the waterway we passed an open rock shelter, an unimpressive geologic event but a lively place from the standpoint of rock art. On a wall a little less than 100 feet long were painted several dozen figures, large and small, dominated by two fine large deer and three monos—two large and one small—which gave the impression of being a man, a woman, and a child. The large male mono is unique in being drawn with a heavy red outline filled in by horizontal bars that led us to dub him "ladder-man." The deer's distinction comes not in any unusual character but in the sure and simple way in which their grace was captured.

Cueva Obscura   The most northerly side canyon tributary to Arroyo de la Ascensión is called Cañada de la Tinaja. Its mouth is near Rancho La Ascensión and its origin lies about six miles north, high on the west face of Cerro de la Laguna, the central peak of the San Francisco range. The old trail leading from the ranch to San Francisco starts up the bottom of this watercourse and, after about a mile, makes a sharp turn to the west and leaves Cañada de la Tinaja by way of a steep cuesta. By looking north up the cañada from almost any point on the upper two-thirds of this cuesta, a black hole, an obvious cave on the opposite bank, can easily be seen. This is *Cueva Obscura* ("Dark Cave") and, upon inspection, it proves to be an exciting addition to the connoisseur's collection.

Cueva Obscura is about 80 feet deep, 50 feet wide, and 30 feet high at its apex, the largest true cave with significant Great Murals known to me. Few others sites are interior spaces with openings as small, or smaller than the cross section of the

Within the largest true cave decorated by the Painters

Three walls of a deep, small-mouthed cave display handsome, sophisticated groupings of animal and human figures.

Cueva Obscura

void within; most would better be called rock shelters, overhangs, or respaldos. As a result of its depth and true cave configuration, Cueva Obscura not only has a back wall but also two pronounced side walls, and all three have been painted with fine examples of the art typical of this region. Regrettably, unstable rock surfaces offset the advantage of superior protection from the elements, and the result is a mediocre state of preservation for the otherwise choice collection of about 30 figures.

On the long left wall as you enter, a succession of three red figures, two borregos and a deer, seems to press forward toward the mouth of the cave. The black deer following them is so deteriorated that only a head and some excellent antlers allow it to be identified. On the better rock of the rear wall a similar progression, moving from left to right, consists of four splendid black deer, and the two central ones are in unusually good condition. Of these two, the deer on the right is superimposed onto a distinctive mono done in red outline only, but with the torso lines strengthened, an emphatic device that also can be seen at La Palma and Cuesta del Palmarito.

The right wall slants uphill at the rear because the entire floor and ceiling of the cave are tilted so as to be higher on the right (south) side. As a result, figures in the paintings grouped near the rear seem to be moving uphill. The first group is overpainted more than others at this site: three red deer overlie three red and black monos and all of these appear to have been painted over a black deer, once part of a running frieze of similar figures that may have covered most of the wall. Moving closer to the mouth of the cave, the next group consists of four red deer

55

The Sierra de San Francisco

Cueva Obscura

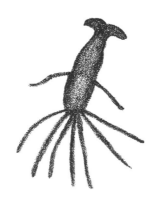

facing left and laid over three more of the original black deer, all of which face right. Yet another group of four red deer follow them, and finally, quite near the mouth of the cave, two large human figures, one red and the other bicolored, seem to stand like a pair of sentinels guarding the entrance to lonely Cueva Obscura.

As you leave Cueva Obscura, you can look across the cañada and see a conspicuous cuesta leading steeply up to Mesa de la Puerta, Rancho El Represo, and San Francisco. A small but well-preserved rock painting site called El Pilón de la Puerta is located near the top of the cuesta and a few steps off to the southwest along a low respaldo. Larger-than-life figures of three deer, a *borrega,* or female mountain sheep, and two birds occupy a single panel some 30 feet long. All were rendered in exactly the same light red-brown paint, all are in similar, generally good condition, and most look as if they were painted by the same hand. The exception is the highest and most westerly of the figures, a deer executed with greater skill and flair. Below the large figures and in the same red paint are scattered a few *pinturitas*—the local name for small paintings. One of the best preserved of these is a most unusual image which I believe represents either a squid or a spiny lobster; the only similar images I have seen are the equally difficult to identify pair painted above the shoulders of the mono at El Corralito, described earlier.

There is another painted site upstream in the main trunk of Arroyo de la Ascensión. East of Los Monos, the watercourse narrows to become a spectacularly deep and twisting gorge. Beyond that it emerges in the uplands as an open valley created by a pair of minor seasonal streams. Exactly at the place where the narrows end is Rancho Las Calabasas, inhabited at the time of my visit by Tacho's brothers Ignacio and Loreto and their families. High on the north side of the arroyo and looking directly down on the ranch is a small, undistinguished cave hollowed from the usual cemented volcanic materials. Loreto Arce pointed it out and then showed us the trail.

The granular walls of this shelter retain the clear but fading images of several monos and deer, plus a rabbit. Three of the monos have an unusual distinction. Although divided vertically in the common San Francisco fashion, they were painted in brown and black rather than the usual red and black. Elsewhere, Indian remains were scarce. We found a number of horseshoe-shaped engravings on a rock outcropping along the bed of the arroyo a mile below Rancho La Ascensión. At La Matancita, under an open respaldo, there appeared to be a *vivienda*, the local ranchers' name for a seasonally occupied prehistoric living place, this vivienda was replete with metates and so much charcoal in its dirt floor that the color was gray-black. In general, however, although La Ascensión is a major arroyo and penetrates to the heart of the sierra, surface evidence suggests it was not a major access route nor a place where aboriginal people spent a lot of time. Over the mountains to the north, another waterway provides a striking contrast.

Arroyo de San Pablo

From the drainage of the north slopes of Cerro de la Laguna arises Arroyo de San Pablo, a watercourse that cuts down to depths of over 1,000 feet and traverses two-thirds of the length of the sierra. Its extent and importance are suggested also in the number of names by which it is known. Beginning at its source and ending as it passes out into the Vizcaíno Desert, its successive parts are called Agua Verde, El Cartucho, Santa Teresa, San Nicolás, San Pablo, and finally, according to old-timers, El Salón. Along the way, there are numerous important tributary cañadas— El Dátil, La Banderita, San Jorge, El Bajío, La Soledad, El Cacariso, San Julio, Los Vainoros, and San Nicolás—which make this arroyo not only the longest but by all odds the most complex drainage system in the Sierra de San Francisco.

The ranch village of San Francisco, seasonally occupied in the early 1970s by as many as 16 families, sits at the head of Arroyo de San Pablo. In those days, the village had a school and a rudimentary airstrip. In the early 1960s, Erle Stanley Gardner landed here on his way to visit a group of caves in the San Pablo drainage. Leon Diguet came here in the 1890s. One of the sites he visited and specifically identified is a 20-minute walk from the village. It is called Cueva del Ratón, and it is located at the highest elevation of any painted cave of importance in the Sierra de San Francisco.[*]

*Diguet's numbered list of his Baja California rock art finds can be found in an appendix at the end of this work.

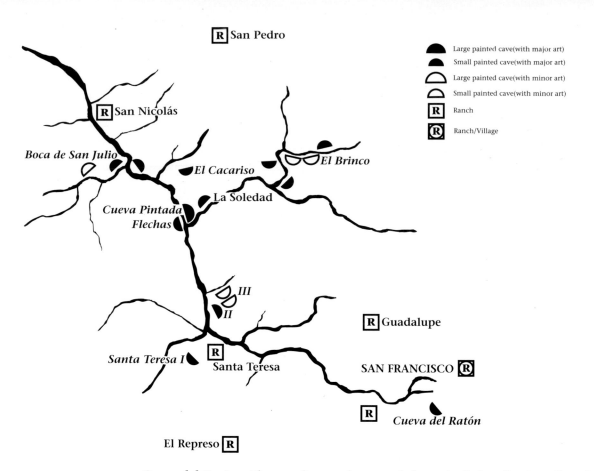

Cueva del Ratón   The cave lies southwest and above the little collection of ranch houses at San Francisco. It is on the eastern edge of a ridge dropping down from the high ground of Cerro de la Laguna, and it is more of an overhang or rock shelter than a true cave. The painted area is about 40 feet long and exhibits a small but choice collection of the Painters' art: colorful figures of deer, borregos, rabbits, humans, and a mountain lion. The rock seems to be above average in its resistance to weathering and, when we visited, the paintings were more complete than at most sites we had seen. In spite of this advantage, the works have been dulled and their contrast reduced by an unusually heavy layer of smoke residue on the cave's walls. A few little walls of piled rocks were evidence that the place had been used to shelter humans or domestic animals. That, and the proximity of San Francisco, once a ranch and visiting station of the San Ignacio mission, suggest that smoke damage occurred in historic times.

One large mono represents a rare type. The figure was divided into red and black areas along the vertical axis in the usual fashion, but a black oval was heavily painted over the area where we would imagine a face. In addition, both the red and black portions of the body were colored in fine vertical stripes rather than solid paint. This curious face patch has turned up at only four other sites: Cuesta del Palmarito about four miles to the southeast, and El Carrizo, Los Monos de San Juan, and El Cajón del Valle, 50 miles to the south and in a different sierra, that of Guadalupe. As a further curiosity, the coloring in vertical lines is much more common in the Sierra de Guadalupe than it is in the Sierra de San Francisco.

*E*vidence of itinerant Painters

Certain artists appear to have worked in several of the great painted centers. The mountain lion and the rare black-faced human shown here were virtually duplicated at Cuesta del Palmarito and elsewhere. Similar resemblances seem to link the histories of many painted caves. However, other artworks may be unique to their sites. For example, no counterparts are known for the elegant murals at El Batequi or the Serpent Cave.

Cueva del Ratón

59

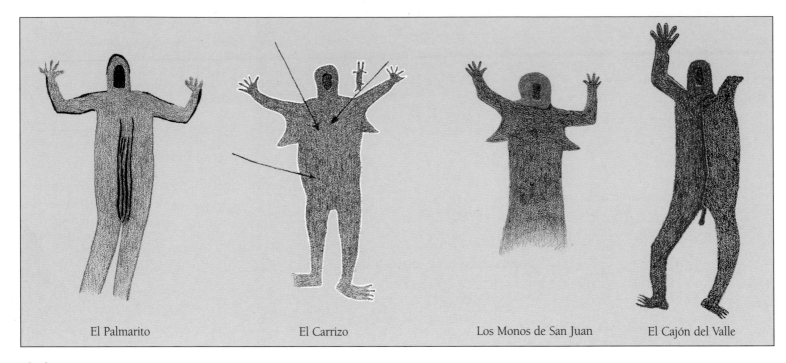

| El Palmarito | El Carrizo | Los Monos de San Juan | El Cajón del Valle |

**The known paintings
of human figures
with black face patches**

A black león also commands attention. Such painted representations of mountain lions occupy a special niche in the Painters' repertory. For some reason which I cannot possibly surmise, mountain lion figures vary less than any other, animal or mono. They all have long, stiff, extended tails and short legs cocked at similar angles. There is virtually no neck, and a round, short-muzzled head is set with small round ears. Most leones are black but several red examples have turned up, and even one in ochre — at El Ademado in Arroyo del Infierno. Oddly, the painted images of these animals are never bicolored. They are unique in this respect.

Below Cueva del Ratón, the great arroyo drops to the northwest. At San Francisco it is no more than a bunch of deep scratches on the backbone of the sierra, but within a mile these have consolidated into a sizable canyon called Agua Verde, a name taken from a large tinaja in its floor. Within two miles the arroyo has cut 1,000 feet below the mesa to form a spectacular winding corridor with almost vertical sides. That extends for two more miles in a run called El Cartucho. With its vistas of towering red rock walls, its course choked with boulders 20, 30, even 50 feet in size, and its groves of lofty palms, El Cartucho should eventually become a national park. As a better solution, the entire Sierra de San Francisco should achieve that status and El Cartucho would be one of its jewels.

Below, the arroyo opens up suddenly into an amphitheatrical space called Santa Teresa. This 1,200-foot-deep dish is the result of the confluence of the arroyo with four tributary cañadas. From the east descend El Dátil and El Bajío, and from the west, larger La Banderita and San Jorge. Around 1940, Fernando Arce Sandoval founded a ranch in this space and, at the time of our visits, it was one of the two or three most beautiful ranches in all the Baja California sierras. Don Fernando and his sons had built four substantial buildings of mortared masonry, plastered, painted, and beautifully thatched with fronds of the abundant native palms. They had also created two *huertas,* or garden-orchards, and built over a mile of flume to carry water to them from a spring.

When queried about rock art, these men deferred to Fernando's grandsons. The older men had been busy building and farming, they said, but the grandsons herded goats all over the arroyo, up into the cañadas, up the faldas, and onto the mesas far above. Thus, one or the other of two teenage brothers, Santo and Bernardino Arce, would take us to see the nearby sites, including those visited earlier by Erle Stanley Gardner and Clement Meighan.

Santa Teresa I   Directly above Rancho Santa Teresa and to the southwest, a typically steep and precarious trail leads to Rancho El Represo on the mesa above. Halfway up that cuesta, in a ravine to the right, we came to a very high respaldo with some minor caves at its foot. A curiosity of this place was the presence of a fan palm, grotesquely bent and distorted, which grew from the rock at the base of the respaldo. Since palms are usually restricted to watercourses, we sought its source of water and found a tiny spring weeping from the rock at the level of the caves.

This place was known to the Painters. Looking up, we could see three major groups of paintings on a smooth surface above the caves. At the left is a large ceremonial assemblage of monos. In the middle is a group of two deer and a borrego in an attractive design created by the partial superimposition of all three figures.

Such apparent compositions will remain a mystery; we will never know if they were the product of chance, or whether some artists in reusing a surface consciously or unconsciously took advantage of the existing art. At El Batequi, simple statistics told us the result was intentional. The odds on aligning 20 or more figures in the same direction by pure chance would be astronomical. But with small groups like the one here at Santa Teresa I, direction is not involved and evaluations are entirely subjective. Certainly, most of the hundreds of groups created by overpainting are not successful as compositions. In most cases, the result diminishes individual figures without creating artistic composites. The third or right-hand group at Santa Teresa I seems to illustrate the latter conclusion: it consists of a formless melange including monos, deer, and borregos.

Santa Teresa II   Entirely across the arroyo, on the east side just south of the opening of Cañada del Bajío, there is another site also located halfway to the mesa and at the foot of a high vertical rock face. This place, which we called Santa Teresa II, is a mixed bag in every sense. The basic shelter is unusual and, because of its exposure, conspicuous. A high, smooth layer of rock with a vertical face runs

The magical power of place

Certainly, some aspect of the Painters' religion dictated that art be located in specific places—a dictum that took precedence over convenience and maintaining the integrity of earlier works. Shamans apparently were stern taskmasters: Some art can be found at amazingly inaccessible sites, and other works, like this one, seem unnecessarily high on a wall that is otherwise unpainted.

Santa Teresa I

61

The Sierra de San Francisco

for hundreds of yards along the top of the falda. At one point an arch-shaped piece of this face has dropped away, leaving an alcove 60 feet high, 60 feet wide and 20 feet deep. This regular depression can be seen readily from any part of the valley.

Within this shelter, both on its back wall and the two wing walls, we found a score or more of monos and deer, all very faded. Some of the monos are quite large; one female figure is around 10 feet tall. Nearby, there is a painting of a doughnut-shaped figure about a foot in diameter, oddly abstract in a land where realistic art was the rule.

To the left of the great arched alcove, a low overhang contains some additional small works including more nonrepresentational figures. Most conspicuous is a set of parallel and partially broken waving lines, an unusual apparition among the Painters' display. Just beneath, the delightful, long-legged figure of a fawn was drawn in the expected realistic style. Elsewhere a rabbit in red is ringed by the black forms of several bat rays.

Our young guide took us another level up the mountain to a cave just below the trail to Rancho Guadalupe. There we saw three medium-sized red and black deer crudely painted. This site also includes a most curious cave, wide and deep with a low ceiling of such rough rock-hung conglomerate that not even the most ambitious Painter could have rendered a figure on it.

Cañada del Bajío is short and steep. According to the brothers who guided us, it had little to offer, perhaps a handful of faded figures. I was too curious to pass without a glance so I asked Bernardino to take me up for a look. About 200 to 300 yards from the mouth of the cañada on the south side, we came to a long, low overhung wall. A few painted figures were, as reported, small, faded, and uninteresting. Later, I heard that a cave farther up the cañada contains a handsomely worked group of fish.

Bernardino led us a mile and a half down the arroyo from Santa Teresa. After half a mile, the trail quitted the caja level and worked its way along an irregular shelf on the canyon's west wall. As we made our way along the bumpy and occasionally perilous path, it was easy to believe that the level caja 100 feet below would have been a better choice. This form of self-deception is common among the uninitiated on foot in rough country. Any other route tends to appear better than the one with which you are afflicted. Experience has shown conclusively that the local people know what they are about. On a later occasion I tried to return by that same caja and found out how tiring it is to walk on sand and over and around large boulders.

Our guide led us off the trail, down a bedrock chute, and across a small broken falda to a cave and painted respaldo. Our first glance showed the striking group of figures used by Dr. Meighan as a frontispiece in his book, *Indian Art and History*. We were standing on the floor of the site he called Flechas Cave.

Cueva de las Flechas   Visitors to this place find themselves distracted. The principal display of art is superb and the rest is above average in conception and exe-

Bernardino Arce

The enigma of arrows:
icons pierced, icons
overlaid, icons immaculate

The central effigy is impaled and overlaid with arrows, one of many puzzles in the Painters' symbolic vocabulary. Images of animals transfixed by arrows are common in the Sierra de San Francisco, but human figures so treated are rare. However, in the sierras of Guadalupe and San Borja, both are common. Some sites in all regions fairly bristle with figures wounded by spears and arrows, yet El Batequi, with its many figures, exhibits no weapons at all. What was the message? These powerful figures act out an elaborate charade for which we have not yet guessed the first word.

Cueva de las Flechas

cution; most is well exhibited and in excellent condition. But there is competition: The view out of the cave is a work of art in its own right, a handsomely framed living picture of a great canyon cut deeply through colorful layers of rock. In the lower part of that image, the feathered heads and tall poles of native palms form a line that serpentines out of sight with the curves of the arroyo. And, as another distraction, the overhung form of Cueva Pintada—another site made famous by Gardner and Meighan—beckons from across the arroyo, some of its copious art in plain sight.

Cueva de las Flechas* itself presents an opportunity to study the formation of a new respaldo surface. The massive layer of volcanic agglomerate from which its main walls are derived overlies a softer layer only three or four feet thick. The latter has been eroded selectively and to rather great depths. At the south end of the

*The Spanish form of the name "Flechas Cave," bestowed by Clement Meighan. See discussion on page 72 below.

63

Flechas site this layer is hollowed back into the mountain for over 30 feet forming a curious cavern 50 feet wide, 30 feet deep, and only three to four feet high. At some point in the not-too-distant future, when this cavity grows a bit deeper, the strain on the harder layer above — created by the ever-increasing weight of its over-hanging element — will cause a fracture. The unsupported mass will drop as a great scallop-shaped block onto the apron of the cave or into the chasm below. The freshly exposed material that remains in place will be a new respaldo, typical of those seen on all sides. Most of the art will be lost in the process — as it has been at several other sites on the peninsula where fragments of fallen walls still reveal scraps of painted surfaces.

Once the visitor's attention turns to the art of Las Flechas, its small but select gallery can be savored. The principal group, mentioned before, includes three of the most elegant monos to be found anywhere. Besides their noble proportions and great stature, they exhibit some unusual distinctions. The two at the left and center have tiny figures upside down over their shoulders like elaborate, detached epaulets. In the case of the red and black giant on the left, these small images appear to be a mono and an indeterminate animal, perhaps a sea turtle; in the case of the central figure in the trio, the inverted figures are a mono and a deer. That same central mono and the one to the right were painted as overlaid, or impaled, by half a dozen black arrows each. A pair of the arrows overlying the central mono have carefully painted points representing arrowheads similar to the obsidian projectile points found quite commonly in the greater area. These primitive Saint Sebastian figures suggested the name *Flechas,* or Arrows, to Dr. Meighan because they were the only human figures so mutilated in the four caves he visited. He was singularly fortunate in his choice of a name. In the sierras of San Borja to the north and Guadalupe to the south, such arrow-impaled representations are common and make up a large percentage of all human figures. But in the Sierra de San Francisco, images of humans are associated with arrows, to my knowledge, at only three sites.

Some forty miles to the southwest, in the Sierra de Guadalupe, there is a site called El Carrizo where I noticed a combination of features that make it, in some ways, a counterpart to this group at Cueva de las Flechas — and suggest that it might be the work of the same artist. El Carrizo displays a pair of sizable monos. The larger and higher one has no arrows, is red and black, and has a headdress similar to the one on the red and black upper figure at Las Flechas. The second mono at El Carrizo is female and painted in solid red except for a black face patch. Three black arrows with carefully drawn points are painted over its body. In the manner of the mono at Las Flechas, this image features a tiny "epaulet" animal figure inverted over one shoulder. Another instance of this oddity is found at El Corralito, as described earlier.

A further peculiarity in the Flechas group is the black cap on the otherwise red central figure — it is worth noting that all three monos have particularly fine, if not rare, types of headdresses. Regrettably, the central mono was painted over the head part of a highly stylized image that probably represents the relatively rarely depicted *gato montés,* or bobcat.

Elsewhere the site is distinguished by a fine bicolored borrego with two rare attributes. First, one horn is red and the other black. In the vast majority of such bicolored borrego paintings, both horns are the same color. Another of these rare exceptions is located just across the arroyo at Cueva Pintada. The second oddity of the Flechas borrego is found in the treatment of its forelegs which appear to have been painted twice, once straight down and a second time extended forward. This is not the result of overpainting another figure; I believe that it was an artistic device intended to simulate action. As photographs and drawings elsewhere in the book show, the Painters devised several techniques to give a sense of animation to their images.

A second probable method of implying movement is common at Cueva de las Flechas and throughout the Great Mural area. In this technique, two or more figures—usually similar images of deer or rabbits—were painted in succession, often cocked in slightly different positions to create a sense of animated progression. At least four such pairs can be seen at Las Flechas and one is especially interesting. Two rabbits were outlined in sure, fine lines of red paint that included an arrow in each. But the fields within these outlines were never painted. Such incomplete figures are found here and there among the Great Murals, creations interrupted by exigencies of the moment, pauses that became eternal.

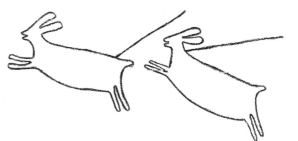

The remaining figures and groups at Cueva de las Flechas include a large black deer, a red deer painted over a large black bird, and numerous small figures representative of all the usual subjects. These miniatures, ranging in size from about eight inches to a foot and a half, are common at most sites and should not be confused with the truly tiny figures, drawn in outline only, noted at La Natividad. Dr. Meighan drew attention to the fact that a number of the small monos at Cueva de las Flechas retain only half of their usual form, the half painted in red. In each case, the black half that an observer would expect to see is missing, and Meighan assumed it had never been painted. After inspecting hundreds of figures and sites, I am inclined to another opinion: I think it likely that the figures were completed and that the black side has entirely weathered away. Some of the black paint prepared by the Painters apparently weathered more quickly than the red; perhaps some artists were so ill advised that they used charcoal as their black pigment. Whatever the reason, figures with strong red parts and weak black parts are common, but in no case have I found the reverse to be true.

Cueva Pintada   Across the arroyo and down a scant quarter of a mile is Cueva Pintada. Stating the distance, however, conveys little sense of the experience of traversing that stretch. First, one has to pick his way carefully down about 150 feet to the caja over a crumbling, slippery bedrock inclined at an exceptionally steep

65

The location of Baja California's foremost center of primitive art

The largest collection of Great Murals, and those in the best condition, are found in this shallow recess eroded from the nearly vertical east wall in the central part of Arroyo de San Pablo. Note the situation of the cave and the proximity of native palms that could have been used to make ladders or scaffolding to reach high up on the backwall of the shelter. Although the cave appears small here, it measures 500 feet across the base of the opening.

Cueva Pintada

angle. Then he must traverse a caja filled with small obstacles such as deep pools, boulders, and thickets of a woody plant called *guatamote* and, finally, climb to Cueva Pintada up a slope almost as steep, if not as high, as the descent from Las Flechas. However, with the contemplation of the new surroundings, all is forgiven and forgotten.

This grand cave is the most painted place in the most painted part of the entire range of the Great Murals. It may rightly be considered the focus of the phenomenon. The larger physical setting, as with nearby Cueva de las Flechas, is very beautiful. This slightly lower cave has an even more intimate view of the deep canyon, palms, and pools of water. The cave itself, while close to 500 feet in length, is not as impressive as that figure implies. At no point is it very deep, perhaps 40 feet at most, and for half its length it is low ceilinged and shallow as well.

Both La Cuevona de la Ascensión and La Natividad are caves of much greater volume—but no other site has so much appreciable art.

The quantity of well-preserved painting at Cueva Pintada is a function of two factors that extend beyond the will of the Painters: the size of the cave and the durability of its rock surfaces. In the latter respect, this place is remarkable. Many other sites were as heavily painted per square foot of wall space, but in very few is the ratio of survival so high. This is due in part to a relatively recent event in the history of the cave's formation.

At the south end of the shelter, a section of the back wall some 100 feet long is covered with over 40 grand images, principally monos, deer, and borregos. Although these were overpainted to a depth of at least three layers, the group is in the best condition of any with a comparable number of large figures to be found in the entire range of Great Murals. A line of large rock fragments lies just below this heavily painted respaldo. Inspection shows that they fell relatively recently from the wall above, leaving it a clean, little-eroded surface. It appears that the excellent condition of these paintings is due in large measure to the fresh character of the rock on

The most renowned and most visited of all Great Mural panels

Erle Stanley Gardner publicized this magnificent location in 1962. Most of its 500 feet of walls and ceilings exhibit paintings of men, women, beasts, birds—even sea mammals. The great south panel, pictured here with the author and Tacho Arce to provide scale, is remarkable for its fine condition and the homogeneity of its painted figures.

Cueva Pintada

67

which they were painted. Most other respaldos apparently were already weathered and beginning to disintegrate before any paint was applied. Afterward, the process continued and the paintings suffered.

The rock in a part of this special area appears particularly fresh and it is interesting that the style of painting on what seems to be the freshest surface is homogeneous and the range of color is amazingly limited: only black and a single hue of red are evident. I believe that this particular section collapsed sometime during the painting epoch, and that the Painters decorated the new surface in a fairly short period of time. Someday this hypothesis could be tested by tunneling under or turning over one of the fallen fragments to see if its lower side is painted. Should this prove to be the case, the problem of dating might be simplified. Organic materials found lying on the floor that was covered by the fallen rock would almost certainly date from the Painters' time.

Elsewhere the art of the cave contrasts strongly with that just described. The subject matter is more varied, more styles are observable, and more colors were used. Just to the left of the abnormally fresh-looking works, there rises a gigantic figure depicted in sketchy red strokes with a chalklike substance or a dry brush. This monster, the largest figure in the cave, appeared to me to represent a whale.

Paintings on the low ceiling of a slit cave

Cueva Pintada is so wide and irregular that it provided the Painters with two very different sorts of rock shelter. The previous photograph showed a recessed wall painted to a height of 30 feet. Here in the central part of the cave, the back wall is too soft to sustain paintings, but a ceiling of excellent rock supports an amazing gallery. This view looks south toward Cueva de las Flechas on the opposite wall of the arroyo.

Cueva Pintada

Chapter 3

The forepart, head and fins, are admirable but the tail region is drawn more like a pair of elephantine legs than the fluke of a whale. In the time since I made my observations, others with greater knowledge of sea mammals have offered the opinion, based on those rear appendages, that this figure and the similar one at San Gregorio represent one of the larger pinnipeds: sea lions or elephant seals. Farther to the left, beyond a rather large area with little or no painting, is a group of additional monos and deer in a pale, chalked-line or dry-brush style similar to that used to produce the aforementioned "whale" and the well-preserved group of deer at La Natividad. My observations all over the sierra lead me to believe this was a technique used late in the epoch of the Great Murals.

The entire northern half of the cave has an unusually low ceiling, the greater part of which is heavily painted. The colors are exceptionally rich, the figures range from large to small, but the latter predominate. Overpainting is the rule; in places it is as heavily applied and as wildly confused as any to be encountered among the Great Murals.

The smaller figures include an unusual variety of subjects and styles, forming a subgallery of special interest. Birds are represented more frequently than usual; over a dozen can be discerned. Fish figures, on the other hand, are few and the three or four that appear are undistinguished in concept or execution. Five times the number of fish can be seen on the walls of a single small cave at Cuesta de San Pablo, a few miles down the arroyo. Rabbit figures abound at Cueva Pintada. From 15 to 20 depictions can be counted—the disparity allows for differences of opinion about representations of rabbits and fawns. (Indians preyed heavily on fawns, easy to run down as compared to older deer or, for that matter, rabbits. A rather large percentage of the paintings that outsiders instantly assume to represent rabbits or hares probably depict fawns. Many visitors to Baja California are not familiar with mule deer, the only species the Painters knew. The ears of mule deer are very large, and in the young their proportion relative to the head size is comparable to that of a rabbit. The length of legs is a better way to distinguish the paintings of these animals.)

Cueva Pintada by no means contains all the different sorts of images created by the Painters. It does not necessarily include the most artistic representations of the subjects that do appear. However, it exhibits about three times as many clear, well-preserved figures as any other location, and it is the Great Mural site most visitors would choose to experience the phenomenon in a single visit. Even the indifferent people of the sierra—before they were aware of outside interest—were moved to call it La Cueva Pintada; to them it was The Painted Cave, despite the many other shelters known to preserve Indian art.

Obviously, this large, long slit of a cave on the wall of a remote arroyo was an important center in prehistoric times, but it has a short history in written and oral tradition. The missionaries missed it because their roads ran either east of the sierra or over its mesas far above the caja of the arroyo. Some of the Cochimí neophytes at the mission rancho of San Francisco at the head of this arroyo or the

Each wall an altar, each painting an offering?

We do not understand the reasoning that led to the placement of the Painters' art. Most of the time, they superimposed new images on old, showing little concern for the visibility of existing works or of those being added. They obviously valued the act of painting in particular places more than they valued the show that resulted.

Cueva Pintada

visiting station at San Pablo nearer its mouth, must have known of the paintings. But apparently they either did not mention them or their reports failed to interest the missionaries—who had already seen or knew about the phenomenon from places closer to their beaten paths.

When Buenaventura Arce acquired legal title to Rancho Santa Marta around 1840, its vaguely stated boundaries included the mission ranch at San Francisco. No one today knows whether the great painted caves of the arroyo were known to Arce, his family, or his tenants. Everyone assumes that Cueva del Ratón was known all along because of its proximity to the ranch, but the deep parts of the arroyo had no inhabitants and few visitors in those days.

In pursuing this history, I queried all the sierra's old-timers and got a fairly consistent report. By about 1890 at least two men knew of a large cave with many paintings in Arroyo de Salsipuedes, as the stretch between San Francisco and San Pablo was then known. They knew it as Cueva Pintada. Tacho's father, Severiano Arce, at age ninety, recalled that when he was a child, his father, Cesario Arce, discovered such a cave. It was talked about for a while and occasionally visited by other sierra men. Cesario was a grandson of Buenaventura Arce and, during the older man's life, moved up to the mountain ranch as the first family member in full-time residence. According to family legend, Cesario was an *andariego,* a restless traveling type, and knew every trail between San Borja and La Purísima.

Pedro Altamirano, living at San Pablo in 1972, was sure that his father, Francisco, apparently the first post-mission rancher in the lower arroyo, also knew of Cueva Pintada. Pedro was born in 1890 and believed that his father knew the cave and traversed the entire arroyo several years earlier.

Subsequent neglect is easy to understand. The Arroyo de Salsipuedes was passable only on foot and then with great difficulty. No one had a reason to abandon the far faster mesa routes that connected the sierra ranches of the time. When Diguet visited San Francisco in 1893–94, he missed Cueva Pintada. This does not tell us that no one knew of it then. We do not know who guided him during this trip as a whole, nor who, if anyone, advised him in San Francisco. Only two or three families lived at the ranch in those days and then, as now, they had to move seasonally to pasture their animals. We do know that Diguet's list of painted places included few, if any, that were not on or near main trails. A study of Sierra de San Francisco place names derived from the various Diguet publications reveals his probable route. He entered the north end of the sierra at Cuesta Blanca and came up Arroyo de San Pablo as far as Rancho San Pablo. Then he ascended the cuesta to the southwest which put him on Mesa de San Julio. He took and published a photograph of Rancho San Jorge on that mesa, which shows that he passed to the west and 1,000 feet above Cueva Pintada. From there he stayed on mesas all the way to San Francisco, passing through Rancho Santa Ana on the way. Since this route was a main road from Calmallí to the San Ignacio area, many people who had little knowledge of the country on either side could have guided Diguet competently over that trail.

When Fernando Arce Sandoval founded Rancho Santa Teresa in the heart of Arroyo de Salsipuedes around 1940, he significantly changed the travel patterns in the area. His wife was an Altamirano from San Nicolás, four or five miles down the arroyo. A regular trail was established between the two ranches and every passerby could literally have seen into the great cave from that trail. Thus, by 1962, when Erle Stanley Gardner got wind of the place, a lot of people were aware of La Cueva Pintada.

Sam Hicks, of Temecula, California, was a member of the Gardner party that flew into the sierra and was told about cave paintings. He, J. W. Black, John Straubel, and helicopter pilot Bob Boughton went to San Francisco the day after Gardner's visit and were taken to Cueva del Ratón, as Gardner had been. Then they were told about giant Cueva Pintada far down Arroyo de San Pablo. As they flew back to share this revelation with the others in their party, they took the route described to them by the people of San Francisco. By good fortune, Hicks spotted the cave, so they landed and took a few pictures.

Fernando Arce Sandoval

That incident opened the door. The photos convinced Gardner that he was on to something big and he organized the return expedition with Dr. Meighan. Nat Farbman from *Life Magazine* went along and national coverage resulted. For a brief time the affair commanded international interest. I and millions of others read about this discovery on our neighbor's land and settled back, assuming that studies were under way.

My historical inquiries raised a thorny subject. Dr. Meighan had named three painted sites—Flechas Cave, Gardner Cave, and another nearby which he called Pájaro Negro. But the question of nomenclature reaches beyond the cases of these three caves. How are places in remote regions to be known, mapped, and reported? It seems simple enough when only three sites are involved, but when there are hundreds, the situation cries out for a philosophy, a system that respects history, local usage, and the needs of everyone involved.

Local usage should take precedence. If a name is employed regularly by local people, even if they are few in number, then that is the place's legitimate name. I believe this should apply even when a more general place name is applied to a cave. The mountain people bestowed few names as directly as they did in the case of Cueva Pintada. Usually, they chose the practical recourse of association by locality: "The Cave in Cañada de la Natividad" communicates perfectly to someone who knows the sierra well. Since that cañada has but one cave of consequence, Cueva de la Natividad makes an ideal name. This can be legitimately shortened to La Natividad in any context where it is clear that caves are the subject.

When a named geographic area like an arroyo embraces several caves, the problem becomes complex and more arbitrary decisions have to be made. Additional designations are called for and Arabic or Roman numerals seem to be indicated. I prefer the latter, hence the use of such designations as Santa Teresa I, Santa Teresa II, etc., in this book. The simplest way to apply any style of numerals is by the order in which discoveries are made. That leaves the door open to the indefinite extension of the system.

This digression on nomenclature properly ends as a review of three cave names that Dr. Meighan chose. His "Gardner Cave" already had a recognized legitimate name, Cueva Pintada. The translation, Painted Cave, is certainly not a marvel of originality or distinctiveness, but that is not the question.

Meighan's "Flechas Cave" apparently had no name of its own even among the people who lived a few miles above or below it. It was known to them only as "The Cave Across from Cueva Pintada," which is scarcely a satisfactory designation for such an important place. Since Dr. Meighan's name is descriptive and distinguishes the place from others, it seems appropriate to vote for its continued use. This vote has additional support in new local usage. My guides and many other local people picked up the name "Flechas," not so much from Meighan, whom they never met, nor from his book, which they never saw, but from outsiders who came to see the caves. The mountain folk heard "Flechas" over and over in connection with this cave. Since they had no local name for it, and this Spanish word applies to a salient feature of the cave, they began to call it Cueva de las Flechas — a satisfactory solution that places it entirely in the language of the land.

Meighan's "Pájaro Negro,"or Black Bird, is the only painted cave in the main trunk of Cañada de la Soledad. When I arrived on the scene seven years after Meighan's visit, local people called it Cueva de la Soledad, or simply La Soledad, when caves were being listed or discussed. Even if this name were not in use, it is debatable that Pájaro Negro would be appropriate because several other caves in the same sierra offer prominent paintings of black birds. Furthermore, Cueva de la Soledad displays a red bird of similar proportions and prominence four feet from the black one.

Cueva de la Soledad   Cañada de la Soledad enters Arroyo de San Pablo at a right angle from the northeast where it has made an abrupt drop between unusually high walls. The intersection takes place a few dozen yards upstream and across from Cueva de las Flechas. A quarter of a mile up this cañada and on its north side, a large rock shelter can be seen at the top of a falda so steep it could almost qualify as a cliff. This shelter is Cueva de la Soledad.

The basic space is simple. A series of thick agglomerate layers were cut through by the cañada and then cross-cut by a smaller watercourse at right angles to the main drainage. This second cut produced a freestanding corner of rock out of which large pieces have fallen away to create an alcove about 30 feet high by 80 feet wide. The back wall is in two quite different sections. The southerly end consists of a simple curved surface that reaches to the full height of the shelter. That wall displays about a dozen clear monos, half as many deer and, most notably, the previously discussed pair of nearly identical large birds, one red and one black. The latter figure was responsible for Clement Meighan's choice of names for this cave.

The northern end of the back wall is much rougher and has a complex form. Its lower half is undercut and eroded to form a tiny cave within a cave. On the roof of this recess is the most complex example that I know of an abstract, geometric painting among the typically naturalistic Great Murals: a checkerboard made up of ochre yellow lines with the boxes filled in neatly in red and black. The whole is about four feet long and one and a half feet wide. One row of squares was partially drawn in yellow but never completed or colored in.

On the same surface as the checkerboard are a pair of ornate red and black birds, a red rabbit, and a rich confusion of overpainted works that cannot be identified. In a higher alcove almost outside the north side of the shelter are three figures: a red and black mono, a black borrego, and a black deer. The latter two are notable for the vigor of their representations.

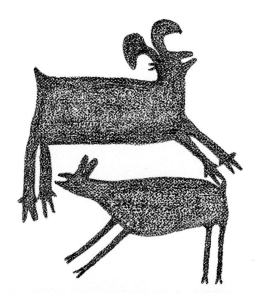

On the principal wall the greatest artistic interest centers on the great pair of birds and three black deer, all apparently from the same hand. Spaced well across

the 40-foot span and moving from left to right are a buck, an immature deer, and a doe. The representations are executed in a simple, confident style suggesting a thoroughly practiced artist. Careful depictions of details such as antlers and dewclaws are particularly noteworthy.

Above Cueva de la Soledad the cañada has formed a region of twisting, steepsided gorges. About a mile from the cave the watercourse divides into two and before long the northern branch divides again. All of this branching and twisting and cutting deeply into the many-layered rock produces the most labyrinthine passages in the entire sierra—indeed, on the entire peninsula. For large parts of the length of Cañada de la Soledad, a person literally cannot climb out of the caja, and even where it is possible, the exits are precipitous. In precisely those places where no exit is possible, some excellent paintings are found in galleries high above the restricted waterways.

The middle branch of the cañada is called El Brinco because, at its head, a trail once scaled a precarious palisade layer of rock. The *brinco,* or jump was a short and particularly steep ascent. By the time of our visit, recent trail work with large iron bars had made this into a respectable stairway which no longer challenged a sierra mule, but the name persisted.

The mountain people have little reason to enter Cañada de la Soledad, much less El Brinco. They apparently never enter from below. The Arces of Santa Teresa knew nothing about it and I might have missed it altogether but for Leandro Arce Sandoval at San Pedro, a rancho high on the mesa and north of this whole drainage complex. The subject came up on my second visit to San Pedro when, for a second time, Tacho and I were attempting to obtain useful details to bolster Don Leandro's vague references to local rock art. We had disposed of the mesa as totally barren and our host professed to know of no Indian remains whatsoever in Arroyo de San Pedro, the location of a tinaja which provided water for his ranch. In truth, Leandro was not interested in paintings; only his politeness and our persistence kept him on the subject. Finally there was a flicker, a recollection. Years before, many years before, he had lost a number of goats, a dozen or so. He had searched for days and finally ventured down from the top to look into the abysmally deep Cañada del Brinco. After a long scramble he found them on an "island" created by the deep-cutting vagaries of the cañada. Now he recalled that during the chase he had noticed a large cave with some paintings, but he remembered nothing about them. I wanted to go immediately, but Leandro, at 60-some years, obviously did not relish acting as a guide. Although Tacho knew the trail over the brinco, he knew nothing of the cañada. A grandson of Leandro was said to know the terrain, but he was far away. I would have to wait.

The wait lasted two years and through two more visits. Finally the young man was available and the trip began. We set out on the trail connecting Rancho San Pedro with the village of San Francisco, a trail that follows the absolute spine of the

74

Chapter 3

sierra and permits wonderful views of the Gulf coast and the sierras of San Juan and San Borja.

Shortly before coming to the actual brinco, our guide led us west on foot down a slope that became steeper and steeper and finally had to be descended with the utmost care, one halting step at a time. After twisting downward for 40 minutes, we were nearing the notchlike bottom of the gully when we suddenly found our trail leading to the floor of a large cave shelter.

El Brinco I   The shelter has an unusually regular form: a high respaldo arched over a wide, level floor area. On the tall curved plane of the wall are a large number of figures, primarily red and black monos and deer. Most are in very poor condition and require some effort to interpret. Among the highest images on the wall is a large mono with a distinctive headpiece, the whole delineated in the rather common dry-brush technique seen at Cueva Pintada and elsewhere. This figure represents perhaps the commonest type among monos in this sketchily painted genre. The headdress hangs rakishly to one side and resembles an old-fashioned nightcap. For convenience in taking notes, I adopted the title "sackhat man" for this configuration and took to greeting each as an old friend. The version here at El Brinco I also exhibits the infill pattern most typical of his type: his red upper body changes to black exactly at the waist, giving people of our mind set the impression that he is wearing trousers. Elsewhere, a red león is quite visible and a large manta ray, a rare form indeed, appears toward the extreme east end of the shelter. The diamond-shaped form of this great fish was bisected vertically by a straight line from the center of the head through the center of the tail. One half was then painted red and the other black. Finally, the entire figure was outlined in a rich orange pink. The image can still be made out readily and it is obvious that it was elegantly painted, but all the paint is dimmed by mineral deposits, some parts are damaged by erosion, and the tail is missing. The rareness of such representations makes the loss especially galling.

After much study of the poorly preserved works, I realized why a few of the deer looked so familiar: their style is reminiscent of La Natividad. I had not made the connection because of their radically different condition. At La Natividad they had looked like yesterday's work, but at El Brinco I they look like ancient artifacts.

El Brinco IV   A hundred yards down the caja we were shown the second and third painted places at El Brinco, but only small, worn paintings remain. We climbed out of the wash and worked our way along a shelf on the north side. The cañada turned south and we followed around the turn. Our guide stopped and pointed up to a steep cliff. Under its brow is a small shelter, his own discovery. Like his grandfather, he had come down to look for lost goats. A group was trapped on that ridge and when he went up to investigate, he noticing the paintings as he passed.

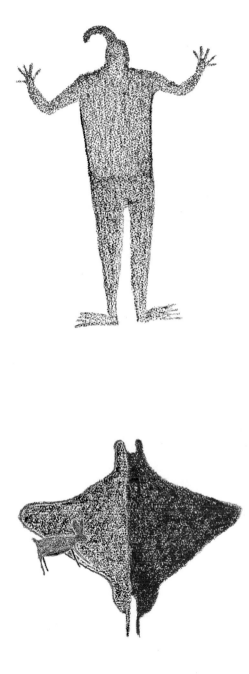

75

The Sierra de San Francisco

A small, open gallery with a fine offering

The approximately 300 different painted caves and shelters thus far discovered in the Great Mural area vary widely in size, exposure, rock condition, and other factors that affect the survival of painted art. Many combinations are possible. Large, well overhung shelters often were formed from soft rock and lost their paintings quickly. Here, a small, little-protected site includes a durable rock surface that preserves an attractive group of paintings.

El Brinco IV

After the sad losses at El Brinco I and the poverty of II and III, El Brinco IV proved to be an absolute joy. The small, open cave fairly glows with color and, for a blessed change, most of the figures are quite clear. The weathered edge of one rock layer forms a single panel six feet high on which there is a continuous frieze of painted figures some 30 feet in extent. The subject matter offers few surprises—monos, deer and perhaps rabbits—but the palette is most unusual: instead of reds, there are rich browns and a burnt sienna, while a deep umber substitutes for the more usual black.

The parade of forms is easily dominated by the largest and darkest, a strikingly composed deer that displays a curiosity other than its color. Fitted exactly within its body is a square whose sides are made up of two or three parallel black lines. This is the only example of this, or any similar device, that I have seen.

While we photographed El Brinco IV, Tacho's son, Ramón Arce, was out scouting farther along the ledge. He returned to report that he found nothing on our side of the cañada, but he had spotted a huge cave on the other side and some 500 hundred yards downstream. Our next exertions help to give a picture of the terrain. There was no question of a direct descent—a sheer drop of 80 feet intervened. So we returned as we had come, hiking a quarter of a mile upstream to reach the bed of the cañada. Then we had to ascend that wash another 200 yards before it was possible to climb the opposite bank. The walk to the new cave was a fairly easy half mile march over a sloping shelf high above the caja.

El Brinco V   The cave is the most impressive of its kind that I have ever seen. Two successive layers of fairly soft rock underlie a thick layer of harder material. The soft strata have eroded until the hard layer above overhangs them by 20 feet

or more. Since the two layers that are now recessed have a thickness, in sum, of over 20 feet and since the whole outcropping is about 400 feet long, the void is immense. The whole is formed of a very pale gray-beige agglomerate, almost a white. The floor is level and smooth and, as I walked along, I felt I was traversing a great open gallery. I had a marvelous view on one side and an art collection on the other.

Actually, the painted works are concentrated in a run of only fifty feet or so while the rest of the gallery wall is spotless. But what paintings they are, and in what condition! The inventory is short: six monos, four deer, three rabbits, and one fish. In addition to these, a mono and two rabbits were neatly painted in white outline only and abandoned in that incomplete condition. These "ghost" rabbits, like those at Cueva de las Flechas, included arrows as an integral part of their initial drawing.

The joy of this place is created by the quality and condition of its few works as well as by their beautiful surroundings. As a group the paintings are better preserved than those of any other site. They are almost as colorful and complete as those of the great southern wall panel at Cueva Pintada. Overpainting is limited to a slight confusion of the feet of two monos with the figures of the two large deer—no problem for anyone who has puzzled over some of the Painters' really complex overlaid mazes.

Each of three monos is divided vertically into a red area and a black area, one of several patterns traditional with the Painters. One of the monos has a truly droll little headdress resembling a miniature palm.

The other three monos represent women and are painted in a red ground color overlaid by vertical black stripes. One of these also has an unusual black line

77

The Sierra de San Francisco

emerging from the top of the head that could represent either an arrow or a very simple headdress. A pair of deer or fawns are beautifully realized. The use of black accents around ears and tail is especially noteworthy The fish is bicolored but the division of red and black is highly individual. A rabbit carefully painted on an included rock is an unusual drawing with an equally unusual color combination. The dark upper part is painted in a rich red brown and the pale belly in a soft beige.

Our guide from San Pedro had never heard of this cave although he had a name, Banco del Carrizo, for the slope and hill on which it was found. We learned later that the people of Rancho Guadalupe on the mesa to the south did know of this place and had taken visitors to it a year or two before. They, in turn, knew nothing of our El Brinco IV site, all of which illustrates the rugged and isolated state of the upper reaches of Cañada de la Soledad.

El Cacariso   Back in the principal flow of Arroyo de San Pablo and about a mile below the mouth of Cañada de la Soledad, a trail climbs out of the depths of the arroyo and commences the long and notably indirect ascent to the north which eventually leads to Mesa de los Gajos. The greater part of this cuesta lies in a short, steep cañada called *El Cacariso*—the pockmarked—after an oddly eroded bluff at its mouth. The trail ascends the north wall of the cañada and, as it does so, affords a good view of some respaldos on its south side and perhaps a third of the way up. On the basis of a tip from young Bernardino Arce at Santa Teresa, we went over and checked these potential sites.

We worked our way along the lower of two respaldo levels without success and climbed with difficulty to the second. There, in a large overhung shelter, were metates and numerous rock chips but no paintings. However, perhaps 100 yards farther to the east, we found what we sought, a small but heavily painted respaldo. On the principal face are 15 deer and five monos including a clear red representation of the ubiquitous "sackhat man" in his usual position high among the other works.

The rock is soft and the paintings are badly eroded, particularly a lower row. The general level of artistry appears to have been rather low and the figures entirely routine except for one four-foot-long oddity in red and black. Here, I feel certain, we found one of the few Great Mural paintings of rattlesnakes. This one, however, could scarcely compete as art with the superb rattler we found later at Cueva del Rosarito in the Sierra de Guadalupe.

The trail that leaves Arroyo de San Pablo and goes up Cuesta del Cacariso divides before it starts up the cuesta. The right branch ascends the cuesta and continues north to Rancho San Pedro. The left branch does not actually leave the arroyo but proceeds along a shelf some 100 feet or more above the caja, As you ride along it, you can see that, on the opposite side and half a mile below the opening of El Cacariso, another cañada enters from the southwest through a narrow channel. This is Cañada de San Julio which takes its name from that of a prominent volcanic cone on the mesa to the west.

As we rode along on my first visit to the area, we were inspecting every suspicious rock surface with care, inspired as we were by viewing the great sites around Cueva Pintada during the previous days. Looking up San Julio from the aforementioned trail, I thought I saw several possible shelters, one high and distant and others near the caja and closer. I wanted to investigate but was frustrated by the terrain; there was no descent at that point. Finally, after riding another quarter of a mile north, I was able to climb down to the caja and hike back to the opening of the cañada.

This part of Arroyo de San Pablo is impressive for its depth and for its wild character. There are pools of water hundreds of feet long and up to 20 feet deep; there are huge boulders scattered about, numerous stands of palms and thickets of dense undergrowth. Working my way back was neither quick nor easy. Finally, however, I was able to start up the actual cañada and soon found, on its floor, a stand of *palo blanco,* a beautiful white-barked tree. After scrambling up the cañada about a hundred and fifty yards I looked to my right up the steep wall and saw a beautiful cave shelter carved from a soft cream-colored rock. I climbed the bank and entered a place I call *La Boca de San Julio,* the mouth of the cañada of San Julio.

A *minor cave with major art*

The author makes notes while sitting below the east end of the single, 50-foot-long painted panel at one of the Sierra de San Francisco's most beautiful and readily accessible small sites. In addition to elegant images of deer, the cave is notable for paintings of several shorebirds with elaborate plumage.

Boca de San Julio

79

The Sierra de San Francisco

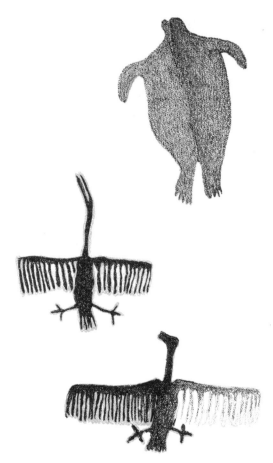

Boca de San Julio   There is no more beautiful painted place in all the mountains. The cave is about 70 feet long and 8 to 12 feet high. The floor is a level, spotless expanse of pale sandy stone raised above the shelf outside. The whole is sufficiently inaccessible to keep cattle and goats from using it for shelter. The ceiling curves gently downward, its slope accelerating as it approaches the floor. The little cave faces south, and its interior is brilliantly lighted all day by sunlight reflected from the floor.

This cheerful place was once liberally painted and a considerable showing survives. Unfortunately the stone of Boca de San Julio is quite soft—it sheds its substance in a constant sloughing of grains, and all the paintings have been damaged in the process.

At the west end is the greatest concentration of works, several large and small deer much overpainted. Two stand out for their fine condition: a heavy-bodied doe in red that could well have been drawn as pregnant, and a red and black buck arched as if in flight. Around and under them are a large number of smaller figures including rabbits, birds, monos (actually half-monos as at Cueva de las Flechas), and an odd half-red, half-black image in a damaged state. This last figure taught me a lesson. As I looked at it, and later in looking at pictures, I took it to be a rare image created as a hybrid of human and animal forms, in this case man and turtle. Later, while carefully sketching the surviving paint, I found that it appears to be a depiction of a chubby seal or sea lion.

At the right end is an exceptional show. Four birds rendered in dark red, pink, and white decorate one small rock panel. All are badly damaged, but mercifully the two larger ones are in good enough condition that facsimiles can be made. These depictions of birds with wing spreads of about 30 inches appear to represent some sort of shorebird or water fowl; perhaps one is a cormorant and the other a duck or goose. In each case the painting is beautiful; the basic form has been drawn in dark red and the whole image is outlined in pink and white. The technique makes the display of flight feathers appear alternately red and pink.

A long climb to the farther, higher cave revealed only vestiges of paint on its ceiling, but a very exposed shelter facing the trail on the way up produced two striking sentinels: a large red and black mono, his black half almost eroded away, and a larger female mono. With their upraised arms, this weather-beaten pair seem to be blocking the passage to some secret place beyond.

Later, a real curiosity turned up just a few yards above the trail facing the opening of Cañada de San Julio. On the ceiling of a small cave clogged with a huge fallen block of rock, an absolutely unique group of tiny red and black monos are scattered in a tight but apparently random pattern. Drawn across them in dazzling white are two groups of lines resembling musical staffs. The effect is peculiar in the extreme—the monos look like dancing notes on two bars of music.

A mile below the mouth of San Julio is Rancho San Nicolás, and four miles below that is Rancho San Pablo, the home of Pedro Altamirano. This man, past

80 years of age when I first met him, was a living legend in the greater region. As a young man, he associated himself with the revolutionaries of 1910 and served them with distinction. In two well-remembered incidents, he risked his life to save men of the region from government reprisals. When the revolutionaries prevailed, Pedro was decorated and, in his old age, received a pension from his grateful nation.

We found the old man sitting in the sun on a chill morning wearing a much-favored knitted cap. He was hard of hearing but soon understood who we were and made us welcome. After a stiff-gaited excursion into the house for his glasses, he commenced an intelligent, lively account of his family's experiences with local Indian remains in general. First he remembered a string of caves in a respaldo just off a cuesta ascending the south wall of the arroyo — "the old Cuesta de San Pablo," he called it. Then he and his first cousin, Tránsito Quintero, a man almost Pedro's age, fell to discussing a site in a place called El Salón. They had not seen it for 60 years and their recollections proved vague. Finally he gave us some pointers on finding numerous small painted sites farther down the arroyo and off to one side of Cuesta Blanca that leads northward over a low pass to the arroyo of the same name. Obviously the old man had never taken much interest in paintings, but he had been very observant and now was kind enough to review his formidable store of memories. I am very grateful. Cuesta de San Pablo alone proved to be a tremendous gift.

A mile and a half below Rancho San Pablo, a historic site can be observed from the trail down the west side of the broad wash. Across the way to the east a towering bluff, a high sheer outcropping of intensely red volcanic rock strikes the eye. Its substance is so colorful that it may once have been ground to produce some of the Indian paint. Opposite and downstream a couple of hundred yards are the remains of a large adobe chapel.

This is the site usually indicated by those who interpret history to include a mission called Los Dolores del Norte. Actually, no such mission was ever founded although the name was suggested around 1750 by Padre Fernando Consag, missionary at San Ignacio and ardent explorer. His explorations and his proposals led to the establishment of Misión de Santa Gertrudis, and this site at San Pablo was developed as a visiting station of that mission. Ample remains of a large, beautifully made road constructed in typical Jesuit fashion lead from San Pablo to Santa Gertrudis.

The ruins of the chapel structure are about 130 feet long by 21 feet wide and show that it consisted of three rooms of approximately equal size. The adobe walls were erected on stone foundations and still stand to three or four feet along the sides and almost to full height at the four gable walls. Just south of this church is a massive stone corral. On the ancón of the opposite or east side are the remains of a huerta buttressed by rock against the ravages of flood, and an irrigation system, much damaged but quite visible.

Pedro Altamirano

Altars were discovered, not built

Occasionally, as here, a cave or rock shelter provided naturally framed panels or alcoves that attracted the Painters. In such cases, they were particularly apt to paint image on top of image rather than spreading them out—as they were more likely to do when they had access to large, undifferentiated rock surfaces.

Cuesta de San Pablo I

Chapter 3

Another great artifact scars the hillside to the west. A conspicuous trail diverges at the chapel and leads up the slope. After an extremely steep series of switchbacks—steep even for the Sierra de San Francisco—the trail heads up onto a mesa and then south by way of San Jorge. This was once the main road in use between San Ignacio and such northern places as Calmallí, El Arco, Rosarito, and Punta Prieta. During small mining booms it was heavily traveled and it continued to be used until the need for an auto road resulted in a new construction entirely west of the sierra.

The part of this road leading up the falda to the southwest is called Cuesta de San Pablo. About two-thirds of the way up the cuesta, the trail is forced to make a radical turn to the north in order to get over a vertical impasse breached only at one point. Following Altamirano's instructions, Tacho, who had never seen the caves but knew the trail, led us to the right along the base of the cliff which so blocked the access to the summit. In less than 100 yards, we arrived at a small cave with its floor raised above the head of the falda.

Cuevas de la Cuesta de San Pablo   The walls of this cave eroded from a gray conglomerate made up of fine particles. The form of the eroded surface is unusual in that it mimics the character of draped material. This curtained pattern parts to leave two fairly smooth clear areas about twelve feet high. That on the left was decorated with a rather stylish if unintentional grouping of three distinguishable figures: a deer; a *gato montés,* or bobcat; and a mono. The bobcat closely resembles the Painters' depiction of a mountain lion except that it bears a well-defined, stubby tail. The right grouping is larger and more confused. It appears to consist of at least three deer and a mono with smaller figures frolicking at their feet. Despite the disarray of overpainting, both groups are attractive, in part because their color contrasts effectively with the pale gray of the walls.

Another 50 yards of scrambling took us past a huge fallen rock mass and into a second cave. This one, too, has curiously formed walls. Here, the entire surface is textured by a pattern of protruding knobs four or five inches in diameter. The paintings, however, were so compelling that they quickly put the subject of the textured wall quite out of mind. Although we saw a large black deer and several attractive smaller bicolored deer and rabbits, our immediate attention was drawn to four similar and much rarer depictions. There, grouped together in the central part of the cave are four superb paintings of mobula or manta rays done in elegantly simple detail. The cephalic fins on either side of the mouth cavities and the extended whiplike tails had been precisely indicated. One image clearly shows the trailing claspers of the male fish. All were outlined in white with a single sure line; two were painted completely in red, while only one half of each of the others was colored with the same hue. Below them are perhaps two dozen smaller fish of more conventional types as well as a few nicely drawn birds and small monos. The beautiful images of the rays, however, absolutely dominate the small cave.

Uncommon images in a world of repetitive art

A few subjects made up the majority of the Painters' artistic images; humans and deer abound. However, if one is patient and looks into every corner, he will find diversity. Here, in a small cave, seldom-portrayed manta rays provide the principal show. The Painters visited their two shores and knew many forms of sea life in detail—as they proved with skillfully created images of fish, turtles, sea mammals, and shorebirds placed on cave walls more than 25 miles from the nearest arm of the sea.

Cuesta de San Pablo II

By pushing farther along the top of the falda, we came to a cave so smoked that its interior is still a solid black. Through that heavy patina, a few vestiges of painting are visible. A number of engraved images stand out boldly because they were added by cutting through the smoked surface to the pale rock.

After a hiatus of 100 yards in which no art remains appeared, we encountered a final cave, the largest and most dispiriting. On its back wall, we found a long group of painted figures, all deer, mostly bicolored and heavily overpainted. The figures were elegantly conceived and executed with a real sense of style, but the artists' finesse is nearly obscured by the confusion of superimposed lines and colors and by heavy losses to erosion.

From the chapel, the aforementioned Jesuit road makes a five-mile run down the broad ancón on the east side of the arroyo. Then it heads north, obliquely up the falda, and over a striking white way that gave the ascent its name, Cuesta Blanca. Near the pass on the north side is a long line of small caves in a soft light-colored rock layer. Because of their proximity to the trail, it is most probable that these are the rock shelters to which Leon Diguet referred when he specified a site at Cuesta Blanca. Most of these small cave-shelters once were painted, but the deterioration of the art was far advanced at the time of our visit. Scattered in various shelters are deer and monos; one black figure is probably either a borrego or a rare depiction of *berrendo,* the pronghorn antelope.

One group of these deteriorated paintings may be of special interest to archaeologists. In a small, open shelter are a couple of monos: one red and black, the other black. The soft, fine, sand-textured surface on which they were painted has since weathered away to a depth of a few millimeters. Almost all the paint was lost with it, but a strange "ghost" of the black image penetrated deeper and remains as a perceptible stain. This stain could provide a clue to the liquid medium used to make the paint.

83

No summary is required for the art in Arroyo de San Pablo, the epicenter of the Great Mural phenomenon. The works retained on the walls of this long, deep watercourse are so numerous, so relatively well preserved, and so often elegant that they establish the standard against which others are compared.

Arroyo de la Cuesta Blanca

The north end of the main mass of the Sierra de San Francisco takes the form of a grand outpouring toward the northwest. In its original state, it must have been a rather featureless fan of volcanic rock, gradually descending to the level of the surrounding plains. Today that early simplicity is scarred by a series of nearly parallel watercourses which cut deeply through the successive layers that made up the thickness of the fan. San Pablo is the largest of these watercourses. Just to the east and over Cuesta Blanca, the next arroyo, with a certain paucity of imagination, is named Arroyo de la Cuesta Blanca. At just about the point where the old Jesuit road descends from that cuesta, the arroyo is joined from the east by the next major watercourse, Arroyo de San Pedro. The latter runs far into the sierra and roughly parallels Arroyo de San Pablo. Arroyo de la Cuesta Blanca, sandwiched between these larger neighbors, extends about five miles to the southeast where it originates as a group of rivulets collecting off the surface of the great flow.

As one proceeds to the north and crosses the high point of Cuesta Blanca, a series of cliffs can be seen to the right; they run southeast and proceed almost unbroken up the west wall of Arroyo de la Cuesta Blanca. That part of the cliff nearest the cuesta has various caves and the larger ones show abundant traces of past human activity. Metates and manos are more common than at most other cave sites, which is to say they are plentiful indeed.

Cuevas del Arroyo de Cuesta Blanca   A mile and a half from the prominent white scar of the cuesta, the line of cliffs on the right or more southerly side of the arroyo lies close to the caja and turns a rather sharp corner to head more south than east. Exactly at that point, the rocks of the cliff begin to show a multitude of petroglyphs—perhaps the largest and most interesting collection within the boundaries of the sierra proper.

On my first visit, we poked along the base of the cliff for an hour or more inspecting and photographing these engravings, most of which are on the *in situ* rock of the bluff rather than on the numerous large fragments scattered about. This is atypical; at most petroglyph sites, the larger free boulders were chosen at least as frequently as the living rock. Many of the engraved images resemble petroglyphs found all over the greater Southwest: lines, grids, circles, and other abstract symbols. Some are engravings of figures otherwise employed by the Painters: rabbits, deer, grotesque human dolls, and so forth. However, several are unique or rarely seen symbols that appear to depict such unusual subjects as the sun, flowers, and plants. One grouping of a plantlet and a vulva symbol would surely be identified as a vernal celebration in any part of the world.

A hundred yards south of the greatest concentration of these engravings the cliff becomes honeycombed with small caves. We were surprised when our search revealed only one with paintings. That cave contains a superb red and black deer in the high San Francisco style, fully eight feet long and in excellent condition. Several monos in a more exposed location are terribly deteriorated, as is an interesting red deer whose head and forelegs are entirely missing. Only the body survives, and it shows a pattern of red and black running down its side like a racing stripe.

Another cave in the complex yields additional realistic petroglyphs: a procession of tiny deer. Two other caves exhibit networks of pits and grooves dug into their rock floors. However, taken altogether, they contain only a fraction of the expanse of the engraved floor found at La Vuelta del Batequi.

About a quarter of a mile farther on, we came to a large respaldo covered with a veritable tapestry of painting in terrible condition. Soft rock and exposure had long since ruined any chance for long-term survival. We stood in frustration looking at what once had been an amazing display. Photographs disclose its extent but not much else. Our on-the-spot analysis linked the artists here to those of Cuesta de San Pablo I and IV and, interestingly enough, to Santa Gertrudis Norte, a site 20 miles to the north. The similarities extend to pigment colors, groupings, and individual stylistic features in the drawings.

Two miles to the south the arroyo divides and a short but steep grade, Cuesta del Marcial, zigzags up to the mesa. That trail took us on to Rancho San Pedro, the goat ranch midway between the arroyos of San Pablo and San Gregorio. Just before starting up the cuesta, we found a final respaldo site similar to that we had just visited — and possibly in poorer condition. Its place in my notes only serves to emphasize the amazing degree to which the Painters decorated this sierra in the practice of their now-obscure customs.

Paintings in Arroyo de la Cuesta Blanca are generally in very poor condition. Their chief contribution may be to assist in showing a close linkage between the painters of this region and those of Santa Gertrudis. The petroglyphs are handsome as well as unusual and should be carefully considered when a major study is made of this other field of aboriginal art.

In that connection, and before leaving this geographic area, I make note of a final and very different petroglyph site nearby: Departing Arroyo de la Cuesta Blanca via the aforementioned Cuesta de Marcial, the trail leads some three miles to San Pedro, a goat ranch on a mesa at about a 2000-foot elevation. Water for the ranch is obtained from a large tinaja in a cañada half a mile to the northwest of the ranch. From that tinaja, looking to the west and up the extremely steep wall of the watercourse, the wide, low opening of a cave can be seen just below the crest of the slope. That cave is much larger than it appears from the tinaja — and farther; the

A *petroglyph in place of a painting*

The soft, gray agglomerate rock of this cave ceiling attracted artists who engraved a series of large symbols and animal images — to date, a unique display in the Great Mural area.

Tinaja de San Pedro

85

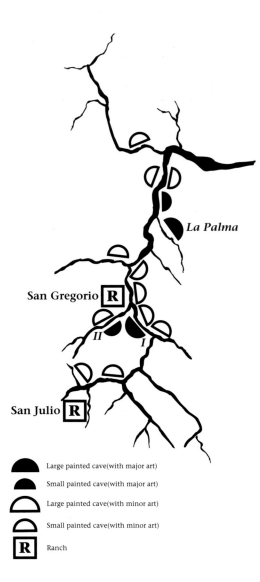

La Palma

San Gregorio **R**

II *I*

San Julio **R**

◖ Large painted cave(with major art)

◣ Small painted cave(with major art)

◖ Large painted cave(with minor art)

◗ Small painted cave(with minor art)

R Ranch

climb to reach it required an hour. No paintings survive within; perhaps none were ever attempted. The material of the cave, walls and ceiling, is a relatively soft, granular, metallic-grey agglomerate, different from any I have encountered elsewhere. Earlier visitors or occupants, the Painters or others, carved elaborate images into the rather low, flat ceiling. Some are geometric and abstract, like a large, elegant sunburst motif. Others are realistic, like a deeply engraved four-foot lizard figure, the largest single petroglyph image I have seen in the Sierra de San Francisco.

I have not had the opportunity to explore the northeast corner of the Sierra de San Francisco beyond Cuesta Blanca. In that area, from west to east, the arroyos of San Pedro, El Tabardillo, another whose name I do not know, and Buenos Aires flow to the northwest into the general Pacific drainage. Over the peninsular divide, an arroyo with the invitingly provocative name of Los Monos flows into the Llano de San Gregorio. None of these to my knowledge has been surveyed for paintings, but the probability is high that some exist. As evidence, we have seen that each of the arroyos to the west offers several painted sites, and the next arroyo which will be considered, San Gregorio, is adjacent to Los Monos and is extremely heavily endowed with painted art. In addition, the Sierra de San Juan, which will be covered later, lies just to the north and has numerous painted sites, some of which are no more than four to eight miles from the various parts of the unexplored area. To temper the enthusiasm these suggestions might engender, there is a sobering reality: Even the natives of this arid land consider this region dangerously lacking in water.

Arroyo de San Gregorio

The eastern slope of the sierra has almost the character of a wall. Its arroyos start just as high as those on the west side, but they drop to an elevation of 1,000 feet in an average of about one-third the distance required by their western counterparts; in brief, they are steep. These are places where occasional storms produce thunderous floods and where the terrain is so broken that all travel is difficult and the choice of routes is severely restricted. Arroyo de San Gregorio results from a confluence of four relatively short cañadas. One of these, San Gregorito, the most southerly, is considered as a separate arroyo in this work.

The array of painted art in this drainage basin is simply bewildering. Arroyo de San Gregorio has as many sites as Arroyo de San Pablo although it is only a fraction of the size. Along some stretches of its watercourses, caves and shelters run with chainlike continuity and most of them have at least a few paintings still in evidence.

San Gregorio I   Rancho San Gregorio, which figures prominently in the introductory chapter of this work, lies at about the geographic center of the area's rock art locations. Less than a quarter of a mile up the arroyo to the south of the ranch is

Who makes it a mural — artist or observer?

This 60-foot-wide "mural" is, in fact, a progression of many dozens of interlaced human and animal forms painted at different times and partially overlapped. As this parade developed, each artist may have been concerned only with adding his new figure, but a modern viewer finds it easy to synthesize the separate images into a meaningful work of art.

San Gregorio I

the great site that so amazed me during my first visit. This place, which I call San Gregorio I, consists of a low cave about 100 feet long located at the base of a formidable respaldo. The ceiling of the shallow cave is heavily painted with large and small figures of nearly every sort found in the Great Mural area. Most of these are in reasonably good condition and this assemblage alone would constitute a major example of the Painters' range and skills. However, on the respaldo outside and above this ceiling exhibit there is a procession of men and beasts surpassed only by El Batequi in artistry and composition — and by no other in power and thrust. As at El Batequi, the effect was fostered by a tacit cooperation among the artists who painted different areas or repainted those already used. It is noteworthy that the flow of running, pressing animals here is from right to left, the reverse of El Batequi. In further comparison, San Gregorio has a harder, rougher rock and its colors are the more vivid as a result. The drawings at El Batequi seem finer and surer. In balance, both these grand canvases are profoundly impressive: San Gregorio the more immediately striking, El Batequi the more sophisticated expression.

Unfortunately, a large area to the right of the existing mural at San Gregorio has fallen away and lies in huge fragments on the apron of the cave. Several painted figures are broken at the line of this fallen area indicating that the work once proceeded from a point farther to the right; it could well have been double its present size.

The ceiling menagerie within the cave proper is difficult to appreciate and requires careful study. The difficulty is the same as at some areas at Cueva de las Flechas: a ceiling so low that a good view is difficult to obtain. This becomes a critical problem for photography. Several really beautiful figures are painted so far back that the camera must be less than two feet from them. It is impossible to photograph some groupings even with wide angle lenses.

The Phoenix of San Gregorio

87

The Sierra de San Francisco

A *rich tapestry on a low ceiling*

Whereas the grand exterior panel displays a parade of large figures, the roof of the inner space is painted and overpainted with a complex assortment of smaller images—small mammals, birds, snakes, and fish—rich in colors and forms, but difficult to isolate and appreciate.

San Gregorio I

Apparently the painters of San Gregorio were not as bound by convention as most of their fellow artists. Of course, it is also possible that something about the magical or ritual character of this cave permitted or encouraged depictions of unusual creatures. Several animals were carefully delineated but fall into no obvious category.

A thorough inventory of all the overlapping figures reveals other curiosities. One which can be classified still has no known precedent in this sierra: a white serpent, very sinuous, and neatly and heavily outlined in red. Unfortunately, while some parts are clear, others are heavily overpainted including its head and tail. A noticeable bulge in the serpent's midsection may have been designed to indicate that the snake had fed. Finally, an unusually large number of birds are represented; at least half a dozen are prominently displayed and others are at least partially visible.

About 100 yards north is another long, overhung shelter that I call San Gregorio II. This contains at least 30 distinguishable figures but all are dominated by one great group: a giant fish or dolphin, a large red borrego, and a huge whale or sea lion, perhaps the second largest single image—after the similar figure at Cueva Pintada—to be seen among all the Great Murals. And, like the painting at Cueva Pintada, this one has strange rear appendages; they scarcely recall the fluke of a whale and lend credence to the opinion of some that these two figures represent sea lions or elephant seals.

La Palma   A little over a mile below Rancho San Gregorio is an inconspicuous cañada called La Palma that enters the arroyo from a southerly direction. Two hundred yards up that unprepossessing watercourse is one of the richer galleries left by the Painters. The site consists of a 200-foot respaldo located 50 or 60 feet above the caja on the east side. Near the north end of this wall, the lower part is undercut to form a deeper shelter. At the north end of the greater respaldo, a small cave has formed which penetrates the base of the respaldo to a depth of 20 feet. Each of these areas is painted in its own significant and distinctive fashion.

At the right end of the large outer face of the respaldo, an array of monos exhibits a degree of order unmatched at any other site. Two rows of larger-than-life figures are ranged one above the other. These monos are spaced at about arm's length. The style, paint, and proportions are similar in all figures and the rows are the result of plan, not accident. The one break in this regular scheme is an image of a large borrego over which the grid was apparently superimposed. These monos are typical of those created late in the epoch of the painting phenomenon: All are lightly colored, the paint applied sparingly and in streaks that suggest chalk or dry-brush strokes. In a very rare combination, the single female figure in this group, clearly identified by breasts jutting from the armpits, is wearing a headdress of three small featherlike projections, one of few instances in which a female mono was outfitted with any sort of headgear. Several male figures have headdresses of the sackhat variety, and in one case the lower half of the body and legs are painted black, a decorative scheme that gives the figure the appearance of

Monsters of the deep impressed the Painters

A stranded whale or great ray would have attracted much attention since it could supply a whole band with an unprecedented cache of protein. This painting seems to show a whale broaching, an event the artist could have seen at Scammon's Lagoon; but the strange rear appendages lead some viewers to identify this figure as a pinniped — either a sea lion or an elephant seal.

San Gregorio II

89

The Sierra de San Francisco

wearing trousers. The body and legs of another sackhat figure are infilled with a regular pattern of alternating red and black stripes. Two counterparts of this curiosity are found side by side at Cuesta del Palmarito and another has been described at El Corralito. These four figures are so similar that they constitute one of the few cases where we can be quite sure we are seeing the work of a single painter at more than one site.

This group displays at least one other peculiarity. Two of its figures are clearly represented as impaled by, or overlaid with, arrows. Although this also occurs at Cueva de las Flechas, such representations are uncommon in works found in the Sierra de San Francisco.

Farther to the left, the outer wall is profusely decorated with other less regularly placed monos and several large borregos. These representations of bighorn sheep are as fine as those at any other place, and they occur here in impressive combinations. One pair overlaps, creating the effect that they are leaping in tandem. Both appear to have launched themselves simultaneously as if startled by the same stimulus. Nearby is another group of three borregos that barely overlap, and all were painted with heads raised to best exhibit noble representations of their distinctive horns. Another noteworthy feature of the middle wall area is the presence of four rather crudely drawn fish. One of these almost certainly represents a shark and is delineated as a profile — a rare occurrence.

The lower, better-sheltered part of the respaldo is decorated with a remarkably integrated group of monos. Unlike the rows of their regularly spaced fellows already described, this group of eight is arranged shoulder to shoulder in a partially superimposed fashion which suggests an actual event. Other factors contribute to the perception by modern viewers that these were real people: The group is painted near the level of the shelter's floor so that one confronts the figures more at eye level than is customary. The figures are unusually naturalistic; their heads are rounded and set on perceptible necks. The decorative pattern used on two of the figures suggests clothing, and finally, a small black mono is placed in such a way that it creates the illusion of being a child. The total effect of this assemblage is very compelling; it is perhaps the most human of all the Painters' efforts. My companions and I have come to call it The Family of Man.

Just above and to the left of this most appealing work is one of the rare representations of a pronghorn antelope, the *berrendo,* now almost extinct on the peninsula. Fortunately, this skillful and lively representation is in excellent condition.

The small cave at the north end of the La Palma site has a ceiling formed into a low vault perhaps 20 by 15 feet in extent. This surface has one of those incredibly painted and overpainted histories that result in a profusion of color but little distinguishable art. Even if this were the whole story, the rich interplay of orange-red, velvety black, and white outlined fragments would create a beautiful artifact. But there is more and the place is transformed by it. Late in the painting cycle two large and beautiful black borregos were added. Nothing covers or obscures

Chapter 3

them and they stand out like two ebony appliques on a background of rich brocade. This juxtaposition creates one of the most opulent effects I have seen among the Great Murals or in rock art anywhere. La Palma, already abounding in fine paintings of mountain sheep, with these becomes the Painters' apotheosis of all that is borrego.

A small cave near Rancho San Gregorio has been heavily smoked, and only a single figure — a damaged but soaring bird — survives quite near its less blackened mouth,. That one painting could brighten a far greater place. With its triumph over the forces of time and fire, this bird rises as the phoenix of the Painters' spirit.

The walls of the Arroyo de San Gregorio are lined with more art than those of any other natural avenue in and out of the Sierra de San Francisco, including the Arroyo del Parral which led down to the major oasis of San Ignacio. A look at the map suggests an explanation: In ancient times, San Gregorio must have been not

The Family of Man

An artist with an individual and compelling style created this oddly affecting scene. The sure, bold representations have an unusually human air about them; their arrangement and the presence of the childlike figure suggest a family group.

La Palma

91

The Sierra de San Francisco

only the major access route for the northeast third of the sierra, but also part of the
most direct route from any part of its highlands to the Gulf coast. The logical course
of a trail would have run down Arroyo de San Gregorio and across the Llano de
San Gregorio to the Gulf shore near Punta de la Trinidad. Shell mounds abound
in the latter region and the entire sierra is littered with evidence of ancient marine
harvests. Shells are found scattered profusely along every trail and here and there
in observable quantities on ancones, faldas, and mesas. The placement and fre-
quency of ceremonial art probably reflected, in part at least, the patterns of traffic
vital to a paleolithic society.

Arroyo de San Gregorito

This watercourse is actually a large southern tributary to Arroyo de San Gregorio
which it joins at a point about four miles downstream from Rancho San Gregorio.
Like Arroyo de San Gregorio, it originates in a series of extremely steep runoff gul-
lies at the very crest of the sierra.

During my early explorations of the sierra, I picked up no specific information about paintings in San Gregorito. But in the fall of 1973, during the survey of another area, Tacho and I encountered Angel Ojeda, a resident of the village of San Francisco, and fell to discussing cave painting. Angel surprised us with the statement that he had seen a painted cave near his seasonal ranch at La Candelaria in the headwaters of Arroyo de San Gregorito. We got directions and in the spring of 1974 arranged to go up the arroyo to investigate. On this occasion I brought my wife, Joanne, and our older daughter, Ristin Crosby Decker, who were preparing to create illustrations for this work. We all looked forward to a grand tour of this most painted sierra. I had high hopes for Angel Ojeda's cave in any case, but I was particularly eager to share the excitement of a new discovery with family members.

Near the mouth of San Gregorito, a trail from the southeast drops into the main arroyo. This is the direct link to El Camino Real. Three miles upstream in Arroyo San Gregorito, the ranch of the same name is located on a shelf above the west side of the caja. This prosperous goat ranch was founded around the turn of the century by Patricio Arce, the father of Loreto. At the ranch, we made the acquaintance of Jesús Arce, a nephew of both Loreto Arce Aguilar and Pedro Altamirano, and his cousin, Salvador Arce. Both were also kin to Tacho and eager to help as soon as they understood the nature of our mission. We sat around and discussed what we had seen elsewhere and they were put on their mettle to produce results in their area. Despite early protestations that the place had little more than *pinturitas,* small works of no great interest, it soon developed that they knew several sites.

First they took us to a place a quarter of a mile below the ranch. There the arroyo branches and a minor cañada runs to the west. In the immediate environs of this fork we saw six small shelters, each with a handful of paintings. None was difficult to reach and we passed a couple of pleasant hours finding and enjoying an outstanding group of smaller works. Many proved to be in unusually good condition. A beast painted in rich red-brown and black defied our efforts at identification. The prize of the collection is a precisely drawn group of black figures: a four-foot deer, and a borrego and a stylized mono, each about one foot in length.

The following morning we saddled up for a ride to La Candelaria and some other places up the arroyo that the cousins knew. An hour's ride brought us to a spot called the *Enjambre de Hipólito,* or "Hipólito's Hive," meaning the place where Hipólito collects wild honey. Jesús Arce pointed to a place high on the north wall of the arroyo and said that paintings had been found above a ledge out of our sight. He proposed that we see it on our return. Soon we passed through a wildly beautiful angostura, a place where the high rock walls virtually lean together. In that shady canyon, great *zalates,* wild fig trees, grow to 50-foot spreads with their white-barked roots running madly over and through broken rock to the sources of water below.

Large painted cave(with major art)

Small painted cave(with major art)

Large painted cave(with minor art)

Small painted cave(with minor art)

Ranch

San Gregorito

Enjambre de Hipólito

La Candelaria I

La Candelaria

93

The Sierra de San Francisco

Beyond the angostura, the arroyo broadened and we soon came to La Candelaria, the ranch of Angel Ojeda, then standing empty. A few hundred yards beyond it we arrived at a stand of fan palms and a spring of clear water. The cousins had us dismount and tether our animals to some of the tough arroyo shrubs.

For a quarter of a mile we labored up a steep, rocky falda, climbing toward the northwest. Joanne and Ristin had worked hard to condition themselves for the trip and here for the first of many times they were rewarded as they managed a stiff climb in the hot sun without delays or undue exhaustion.

When we arrived at the head of the falda we were up against a wall, and our guides led us to the west along its base. We turned a corner and found ourselves in a small cave with a few paintings in mediocre condition. At first we imagined we were seeing Angel Ojeda's painted cave and began to prepare ourselves for disappointment, but in moments Jesús and Salvador led us a few yards around a corner and into the marvelous cave of La Candelaria.

La Candelaria   At its mouth, the cave is about 100 feet wide and 40 feet high and its interior is complex in form. The opening faces west and the northern part of the cave is quite shallow with a nearly vertical back wall. The southern portion is much deeper, running back 50 feet or so from the entry. Between these dissimilar areas is a structure unique to La Candelaria: A sort of natural staircase leads from the central part of the cave up to a point quite close to the ceiling and near the center of the back wall. This ready-made scaffolding was not wasted by the Painters. Exactly at its top, we found the supremely beautiful deer of La Candelaria, its antler-crowned head thrown back as if in the agony of the chase. This image, in spite of its damaged condition, asserts itself in any company as an expressive work of art.

Elsewhere, as well, the cave proved to be a treasure house. Much, much art has been irrevocably lost to erosion, but the surviving works include a high percentage of rare and beautiful images.

The last major figure at the north end depicts a berrendo in the Painters' best bicolored tradition. This and the all-red berrendo at La Palma are among the few representations of this animal found in peninsular art, and this is the finest of the lot. The drawing and execution are exemplary and the image apparently includes a rare example of the Painters' techniques for suggesting animation; in this case the animal was given two pairs of forelegs, one thrust down and the other forward (another example at Cueva de las Flechas has been described). Laid over the antelope's body is the painting of a slim arrow with a well-defined point.

Abstract, semi-geometric figures occupy wall spaces adjacent to the antelope image. Above the antelope is a shield-shaped white outline filled in with a carefully painted checkerboard in alternating hues of black and ochre-yellow. Below the antelope is another prominent checkerboard done all in ochre. On the south side of the "staircase" are two more checkerboards in red and black, larger than those described above. More figures with this abstract pattern — seven in all — appear at La Cande-

The bond between hunter and hunted

Whatever their motives for decorating caves, the Painters displayed an affinity for the creatures they pictured. Deer are shown impaled by arrows or spears; with legs broken by throwing sticks; or gasping, open-mouthed, perhaps run down in a chase. Nevertheless, the grace and symmetry of the animals shine through. They were not merely pieces of meat on the hoof; they were given spirits. There was a bond between artist and animal.

La Candelaria I

laria than at any other site in the Sierra de San Francisco. As unusual as checkerboards are among the typically realistic Great Murals, there is another figure on this panel that is unique in the Painters' world: A three-foot mono which looks like nothing so much as a piece of Meso-American funerary pottery. Such breaks with convention are inexplicable, but they do add spice to the quest and the questions.

Directly behind the beautiful deer is a neatly executed red fish about five feet tall, and directly in front of the deer, superimposed on its front legs, is a bicolored fish or dolphin about half as large. The former is a rare type but the latter closely resembles fish figures in El Parral, San Julio, El Infierno, and San Pablo. In fact, these widespread fish and the many "sackhat man" representations argue more than any other artworks for the idea that some of the Great Mural figures were products of itinerant painters. Obviously, the painting tradition, with all its conventions, influenced many people over a rather large area. These figures suggest that, in addition, some individual painters may have practiced their art over much of that area.

The south wall, the closed end of the deep half of the cave, is the sad chapter in the Candelaria story. The fragments or faded remains of two to three dozen large figures can be made out, and the indications are that they were a fine lot. But, as was so often the case, the rock proved false and a painted wall with excellent protection from the elements was nevertheless reduced to a hint of its original state.

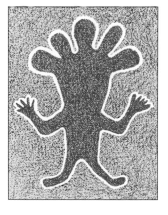

95

The Sierra de San Francisco

A *rare depiction of a pronghorn antelope*

I have found only three painted images that can confidently be identified as antelope. This example shows the long neck and short body common to all three. Visible also are two examples of the rare ochre yellow "checkerboards" in the abstract style that may postdate the majority of the Great Murals.

La Candelaria I

A large, soft rock lies at the foot of the grand column that divides the cave into two chambers. A variety of petroglyphs have been cut deeply into this inviting medium. One figure appears to be a virtual replica of the "supernova" painting in El Parral, but at about two-thirds the scale.

When we returned to our animals, our guide remarked that a small cave a few steps away also displayed some painted figures. Since we were down in a brushy caja, we had a bit of a scramble to arrive in a low overhung shelter with just two painted figures, both deer. The wall on which they were painted had, at its center, an alcove reminiscent of a huge fireplace. A life-sized red doe occupied the panel to the left of this depression, and a rather more elegant black doe was placed in a similar position on the right. The red figure had been painted, obviously with intent, at the center of a patch of whitish mineral deposit on the rather smooth face of the cave wall. Since the local people had no specific name for the site, we resorted to the obvious *Dos Venadas*, two does.

On our return trip we spotted some paintings on an exposed wall just upstream from the beautiful angostura. Close inspection showed that once there had been a group of 15 or 20 large red and black monos ranged in a tight group. Now there are only faded remnants.

The hour was late and the sun was nearly down by the time we returned to the Enjambre de Hipólito. We attacked a steep, treacherous slope and arrived at the upper level, exhausted and breathless, with just enough light to allow us to glance about and snap a few pictures.

El Enjambre de Hipólito   The site consists of a respaldo painted for about 60 feet of its length. At the right end of the painted area is a deeper alcove about 10 feet tall and 20 feet broad. This recess was heavily painted with large handsome figures primarily in red and outlined strikingly in white. The massing of the figures and the form of the shelter suggest a primitive shrine, and a close inspection showed, within this niche, a high percentage of figures notable for artistic merit and good preservation. Although there are fine deer, borregos, monos, and striking depictions of birds, this site is dominated by the unusual prominence of large stout-bodied fish. It is a rare experience to see fish portrayed almost as large as human figures and given equal footing in the presentation.

springs in Los Cerritos, San Gregorio, and San Gregorito. During the 19th century various strangers lost their lives in this region and others had harrowing experiences trying to get from San Ignacio to Santa Gertrudis. Unguided, they followed the larger, better marked version of El Camino Real instead of taking the trail that jumped from Santa Marta over Cuesta del Palmarito.

The Painters knew all about water sources; we find their characteristic work near every one of these springs. Of these, only the watering place in El Palmarito offered no inviting caves or respaldos but the Indians spotted an eminently suitable substitute at the top of the cuesta to the south. Standing at that pass, they saw a mammoth respaldo running south in an unbroken arc about half a mile long. In this prominent rock layer are numerous small caves and one that is very large, Cueva de la Cuesta del Palmarito, a great shelter about 150 feet long, 40 feet high, and perhaps 50 feet deep at the extreme of its inward curve. Its opening and prominent overhead respaldo are very visible from the *portezuelo,* or pass at the highest point on the trail.

No important painted place was so exposed to the missionaries' view. Jesuit Padre Fernando Consag probably knew this place or at least noticed it. It is almost certain that Padre Joseph Mariano Rothea, Consag's successor at San Ignacio, knew it well. His description of Great Murals quoted earlier fits this site better than any other despite the fact that his estimated measurements are all at about half scale. Allowing for error created by the passage of 10 years and the occurrence of events that shattered the man's career and transported him and other Jesuits 8,000 miles away, Rothea's description is admirable.

During his 1893–94 trip of exploration, Leon Diguet visited Cueva de la Cuesta del Palmarito. From his published work it is clear he understood the relationship between the cave and the cuesta. He wrote: "But on the eastern slope of this sierra one can discover, from a steep hillside known under the name of cuesta del Palmarito, a number of pictographic representations forming the ornamentation of a rock shelter located on the upper part of the cliff."

What Diguet apparently did not know was that the place itself was not Palmarito but only a point on the cuesta leading in and out of Arroyo del Palmarito. As a result, he referred elsewhere to the site simply as Palmarito and others have followed suit. None of the sierra people use this name, and it should be discouraged. In Diguet's time, it was simply inaccurate; now that painted places have been found in Arroyo del Palmarito proper, such a usage is actively confusing.

Erle Stanley Gardner and those who flew in with him somehow confused Cueva de la Cuesta del Palmarito with Cueva del Ratón. Since both were visited by Diguet and correctly identified, this is difficult to understand. A possible explanation lies in the fact that both these otherwise dissimilar sites are in the general vicinity of the village of San Francisco and both have conspicuous black mountain lion figures. Diguet did show the león of Cuesta del Palmarito in an illustration, and Gardner's group may have seen the one at Cueva del Ratón and jumped to a

A *site known for centuries to missionaries and travelers*

During both prehistoric and mission periods, major trails passed within easy view of this cave's great arched entrance—which probably made it the most visited of all Great Mural locations. In its highest row of paintings, a collection of human figures displays unusually varied headdresses and decorations. Some appear clothed, a possibility so welcome to the decorous Jesuits that it contributed to their belief that the region had once been populated by a more civilized people.

Cuesta del Palmarito

The Sierra de San Francisco

conclusion. As noted previously, the painted likenesses of leones vary less from place to place than do those of any other creature.

From the portezuelo of Cuesta del Palmarito, there are two feasible paths to the great cave: One strategy is to approach by trail to a point directly below the cave and then climb up the falda. The other is to start at the pass and skirt along the base of the respaldo until the cave is reached. I have tried both and the latter, though longer, is preferable by far.

When the latter approach is used, a small painted cave is passed at about the halfway point. It contains several sizable paintings including crudely delineated monos, some small deer, and a large fish. None is artistically important or memorable, but at the feet of the large figures runs a chain of tiny deer exquisitely conceived and executed. Ten of them in black outlined in white follow each other in a thoroughly intentional procession. No two are exactly alike and they are subtly cocked, up and down successively, which suggests motion in the whole line. The painter of the tiny deer almost certainly understood what he was doing; this artist was an independent creator of animation.

Cueva de la Cuesta del Palmarito   The principal cave was once a great showplace of painted art. The entire concavity was heavily painted to a height of 20 feet and a large number of later works go from there to a height of 35 feet. The lower paintings are so mutilated by rock erosion that few can be appreciated, but most of those above are still quite clear and many are in exceptional condition. The age and style of the upper figures appear similar to those of the carefully spaced monos at La Palma. These are not arranged in rows, but here, too, the artists largely avoided overpainting.

Few animals appear among the higher figures, but two exceptions—a pair of large red deer which stand face to face as if contesting—offer a handsome example of the Painters' skill and inspiration. Other deer and the black lion mentioned before are pedestrian entries in this catalog. The real show at Cuesta del Palmarito is the collection of monos. About 15 stand out clearly, and they are as diverse a group as can be found at any site. Headdresses abound; there are half a dozen "sackhat men" and, uniquely, a "sackhat woman." Several bicolored monos were painted with the colors divided horizontally, creating the illusion of men wearing red shirts and black pants. Two others are painted in vertical stripes and appear very similar in style and technique to the striped figure described earlier at La Palma. Nearby is a red mono with a black facial area, a counterpart of those described at Cueva del Ratón and La Candelaria and a design which we encountered again at two sites in the northwest part of the Sierra de Guadalupe. This black-faced figure has an additional feature not seen elsewhere: a vertical central panel outlined in black and filled in with vertical black and white stripes that suggest a decorative stripe on a garment.

Some viewers have imagined that these strongly vertical patterns on monos represented capes or robes. These figures are almost certainly the paintings described by missionaries as depicting a decently clad folk who walked the land in times before those of the naked and shameless natives that the padres knew. However, anyone who argues that these paintings were truly intended to represent clothed people has two difficult questions to answer: Why are the outlines of all the supposedly clothed monos identical to those whose forms are filled in simply with red or black? Why are animals frequently decorated with all the same devices that are interpreted as clothing on people?

Four of the upper group of monos at Cuesta del Palmarito exhibit a fascinating ornament or accessory. A black sphere about the size of the mono's head is suspended over the biceps of the upraised arm on the viewer's right. This device appears in single instances at several other sites.

Of all the Painters' sites, none compels more awe than this one for the Painters' ingenuity and technology as they solved the extremely difficult problem of gaining access to a forward-sloping surface higher than a three-story building. As a further complication, the floor of Cueva de la Cuesta del Palmarito is composed of slippery, crumbling material that is irregular and sharply slanting. Overcoming such obstacles was no simple task but it certainly was not superhuman. Obviously, a construction was developed, probably something that could be dismantled and reused. El Palmarito in those days was full of 50-foot palms and then, as now, 30-foot wands could be extracted from the skeletons of the ubiquitous *cardón*, the giant cactus of the peninsula.

After our final visit to the great cave, we discovered one more small site in its vicinity by climbing in a westerly direction from the oft-mentioned portezuelo. At the top of a steep falda, a layer of hard basalt palisades crowns the slope. From there, we proceeded to the right, or northwest, and worked our way along the top of the falda, finally coming to a place where we could view the entire upper end of Arroyo del Palmarito, below and off to the west of us. At about that point we found a small respaldo of light colored, rough rock decorated with several handsome, well-preserved paintings of deer and borregos — red and black in the best San Francisco tradition.

Arroyo de Santa Marta

From Cueva de la Cuesta del Palmarito there is a view that covers the lower part of the mountain-ringed amphitheater of Santa Marta. Cerro de las Cabras, a dark bulky mountain, rises in the midst of the scene. Beyond, Arroyo de Santa Marta flows east and then swings south on its way to join Arroyo de San Ignacio, 25-five miles away.

As far as paintings are concerned, Arroyo de Santa Marta is a large puzzle. It drains an area containing numerous signs of an extensive human past. Its walls are liberally sprinkled with caves and shelters and many of these, especially a few miles east of Santa Marta proper, abound in metates, charcoal, and other evidence of previous human occupancy. But, thus far at least, very few paintings have been found. The only sites worth mentioning are a painted wall on Cuesta de San Antonio and a small painted cave near the mouth of Cañada de los Platos, six or seven miles downstream from Santa Marta. The former site is in a very faded state although monos, a deer, a borrego, and perhaps a sea turtle can be made out. The Los Platos site is in plain view of the trail and situated about 100 yards to the west where it can be seen as a depression in a respaldo that is 100 feet higher than the bed of the arroyo. The principal chamber has been heavily painted and over-painted and much of its color survives. Even from the trail the interior has a fiery look, but on close inspection the figures are badly degraded and confused. Just to the north, a more exposed shelter shows the much eroded remains of several smaller paintings.

For the present that is the Santa Marta story—a major access arroyo almost without aboriginal art. Possibly people will explore its many tributary cañadas and discover more. There are rumors of other paintings; logic and probability argue in their favor.

Arroyo del Infierno

After El Camino Real crosses Santa Marta heading south, it climbs a short cuesta and enters the headwaters of an arroyo called El Infierno. The old road, and almost certainly an Indian trail before it, follows the arroyo out of the sierra, then turns south and proceeds over fairly level ground to San Ignacio. That part of the road traversing the uppermost part of El Infierno is a troublesome stretch, steep, tortuous, and rocky. The name Infierno probably was bestowed by the Jesuits more for trials imposed by these hazards than for the heat of the place, which is no worse than that of other boxed-in canyons on the Gulf slope of the sierra.

With El Infierno, my study completes a clockwise circuit of the Sierra de San Francisco's arroyos. Our entrance was by El Parral, which was the southern drainage of Cerro de Santa Marta. Now we arrive at El Infierno, which drains part of the east slope of the same eminence. The Jesuits tried both of these arroyos as

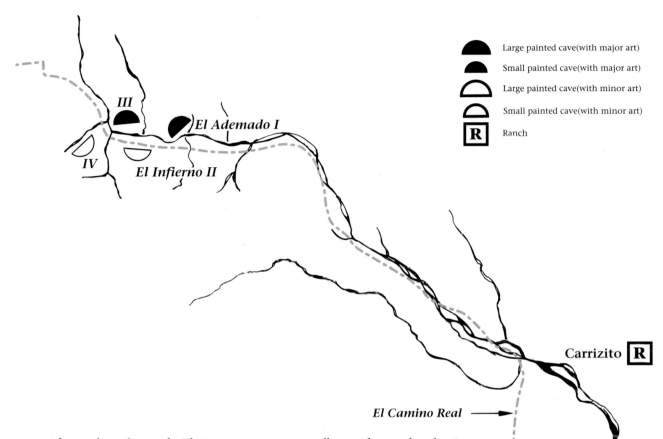

Large painted cave(with major art)

Small painted cave(with major art)

Large painted cave(with minor art)

Small painted cave(with minor art)

Ranch

III

IV

El Ademado I

El Infierno II

Carrizito R

El Camino Real →

routes for roads to the north. Their constructions are still in evidence when leaving San Ignacio and bearing for the respective mouths of these natural avenues into the sierra. After both routes were constructed and used, the Infierno route apparently was chosen as better; it is the Camino Real of history. The Indians, or at least the Painters, appear to have made the reverse decision. El Parral, as we have seen, was heavily painted; El Infierno has only a few very modest sites.

Possibly because of its fascinating written history and visual charms, I rode through Arroyo del Infierno three times before I ever looked for a painting. Tacho and I had asked about such things both at Santa Marta and at Rancho El Carrizito* in the mouth of El Infierno. No one had suggestions and, at the time, we bowed to what we believed was local expertise. Subsequent experiences in other places finally made us suspicious. Our informants did not run livestock in the arroyo; their real business in the place, like our own, had been to use it as a road.

In the spring of 1974, we made an all-day project of the short stretch from Carrizito to the head of the arroyo. We examined every suspicious rock formation with 10-power field glasses and climbed to investigate those showing evidence of

Carricito is the proper Spanish spelling of the diminutive form of *carrizo,* a giant, canelike grass. However, the spelling used above and hereinafter reflects common usage among Baja California ranchers.

paint. The result was the discovery of three sites, two of which had been in plain view to us—and every other daytime traveler—since the paint was fresh.

In the upper three miles of the arroyo, the trail—which is to say El Camino Real—stays on the south falda. At one point a considerable stretch was built up, or reinforced, by a retaining wall made of carefully laid large fragments of basalt. This sort of construction is called an *ademe* and it has given that place its name, *El Ademado,* the supported or retained place. On the opposite bank, across from El Ademado, is an unimpressive cave and to its left a respaldo angles back toward the hillside. A magnified view of the cave revealed little, but an obvious red painting appeared on the respaldo so an investigation was made.

The paint proved to be part of a good red and black borrego—not a memorable figure but a nice trophy from previously barren El Infierno. The west wall of the cave, however, yielded an unexpected treasure: the unique and beautifully crafted figure of an ochre-yellow león about five feet from tip to tip. The pose is conventional but the drawing is as unusual as the color. This cat is not the heavy, clubfooted creature we were accustomed to seeing; it is lean, almost gaunt, and all its parts were drawn with unusual attention to detail. A careful examination showed that its paws were armed with claws.

A few hundred yards to the west Ramón Arce spotted a small, steep cleft in the arroyo wall and went up to investigate. Around a corner and after a steep climb, he found a large cave with a few paintings including some rather original but crudely made monos.

Near the head of the arroyo there is a sharp turn from west to north. The obstacle around which this turn is made is a high, steep-sided bluff. As we rode up the arroyo we could see a cave near its top. When we were as close to the cave as possible on the trail, we inspected it with our glasses. Paintings fairly leaped out. We tethered our animals at the turn and made a laborious climb.

The contents of the cave, or cave complex as it proved to be, were enough to remind us once again that we have no simple explanation for the Painters' choice of places to paint. This one is high and difficult to access. In the course of our study we investigated dozens of others that contain no art despite offering better facilities in locations easier to reach. Of course, we also had found dozens that are easier to reach and yet heavily painted. It is baffling; perhaps ours is the wrong logic altogether. Perhaps such choices were controlled in part by magic or divine guidance. We will never know.

The paintings in this high and out-of-the-way place are, with a single exception, routine. We found several large red and black monos, deer, and the stereotypical red and black fish noted at La Candelaria. Definitely not routine is a huge red form outlined in white and lying in a horizontal position along one wall of the cave. Several figures had been painted over it and the rear portion is badly eroded, but it appears to represent a whale. Sea creatures at other sites typically were painted in a vertical posture with head up and tail down. Here, the size of the wall permitted no such orientation. If the figure is that of a whale, it would be a rare case in which the Painters' conventions were modified to conform to a practical necessity.

Later, in the fall of 1974, we finally followed Padre Fernando Consag's road up El Parral and made its great jump over the mountains to Santa Marta. Prior to this, Roberto Ojeda from Santa Marta had told Ramón about a painted cave he discovered while herding goats on the mesa over which the old road passes. During our crossing, Ramón found the cave high on the cliff overlooking El Infierno from the west. There, in a modest cave shelter, we found figures of a pair of large and very faded deer and four apparent coyotes, two in the rare ochre yellow paint.

The principal value of our visit to this minor site was its reminder that the Great Murals probably cannot be explained simply or in purely practical terms. This place, like La Cuevona, certainly never had large numbers of casual passersby. Anyone who came here did so in order to express the impulse that lay behind the paintings, or to commune with the works themselves or the spirits they mediated. Because so many of the painted places openly display their artworks to trails or natural avenues, we might regard such exposure as fundamental—if it were not for numbers of immensely secluded painting sites that prove that other factors were involved.

La Llavecita   Oddly enough, my next encounter with the art of El Infierno's drainage turned up another site that is even more secluded, perhaps because it is not near a major route or, indeed, any route at all. In November of 1975, we went back to Rancho El Carrizito where Juan López, one of the brothers who owned the ranch, told us about a painted cave recently discovered at the head of one of the forks of the cañada which supplied water to the ranch by means of a four-inch pipe. A spring in that cañada inspired El Boleo, a French copper mining company in Santa Rosalía, to install the pipe and build the ranch in the first years of the 20th century. The cañada is carved out of a most unusual setting, a detached mini-sierra, called El Aguaje, divided from the main mass on the west by Arroyo del Infierno and defined on the north by the much wider Arroyo de Santa Marta. The spring within this *sierrita* accounts not only for the ranch, but also for the names of the hills and the watercourse; *El Aguaje* means the watering place; *La Toma* means the outlet of a spring or reservoir; and *La Llavecita,* the little valve, refers to the control device used on the pipe carrying water down from the spring.

We rode some two and a half miles to the northwest up Cañada de la Toma to the point where the watercourse divides. La Toma continues to the west-northwest; a side branch, Cañada de la Llavecita, climbs steeply to the north. We walked up the latter gulch, which became narrower and steeper as we approached its end on an abrupt, palisade-like barrier of rock. After a nearly half-hour climb, we stood in a handsome true cave—called, naturally enough, La Llavecita. As we stood in its 50-foot-wide mouth, we commanded a bird's eye view of the steep and narrow cañada below. High on the north wall of the cave and just inside the opening, a large red mono seemed to look down upon us as well as upon the rocky world outside. The figure was painted on a fragmented block in a stratum of hard, basalt-like rock. To the right of the mono, a confusion of overpainted figures occupy the surface of the next great rock fragment. Below both, a pair of *pinturitas,* small monos, also in red, were painted on a softer agglomerate that has sloughed away and degraded the images. Elsewhere in the cave, large and small figures can be made out but barely identified; their rock surfaces have proved even less durable than that supporting the small monos. Despite the small size of the gallery, the visit was worthwhile: a few paintings in good condition, a dazzling setting, and another example of Great Mural art far from any thoroughfare, habitation site, or food supply. Perhaps the dependable spring a little over a mile away helps to explain the presence of the Painters and, hence, the paintings.

Clues provided by the distribution of art in the Sierra de San Francisco   This account of art discoveries has been structured around the separate drainage systems in the Sierra de San Francisco. That plan fits the terrain and the distribution of paintings very well, up to a point. The arroyos certainly are logical as geographic subdivisions, and several of them clearly served as avenues for prehistoric humans. However, this clockwise circuit of the sierra's arroyos has not revealed the whole story or even all that is observable at present. At least four arroyos on the west side of the sierra were not entered in the course of my study, and the same neglect applies to the large piece of ground on the northeast corner of the sierra, a region whose potential was discussed earlier.

Apart from areas not investigated, the pattern of this presentation also neglects several interarroyo relationships that may someday help us to understand the Painters' activities in the sierra and their relationship to the occupation of nearby lower ground and the coasts. On the basis of their heavily painted state, it was surmised earlier that El Parral and San Gregorio were major routes in and out of the San Francisco highlands. El Batequi and Cuesta Blanca seem to have been lesser arteries. All of this could be deduced to some degree from evidence found within the individual arroyos. But a great deal of art (and, hence, proof of human activity) has been found along Cañada de la Soledad and in Arroyo de San Pablo within a mile of the cañada's mouth. The region thus defined is in the heart of the sierra and, up until now, was assumed to have been very isolated. In fact, this may not have been the case. A look at the map of the whole sierra shows that Arroyo de San Gregorio, heavily painted, drains the northeast portion of the high ground. Its upper reaches, the arms called San Gregorito and San Julio, both touch the very divide of the mountains, and they do so within 100 yards of the corresponding fingers of La Soledad that drain the western side. Thus, the most heavily painted avenue on the east communicated directly with the drainage in which we find the great complex of painted places including El Brinco I, La Soledad, Cueva de las Flechas, and

Cueva Pintada. This connection seems more than a coincidence. Even without the painted record, the route could be identified as the most direct trail with permanent water to cross the central high ground. Further exploration west of Arroyo de San Pablo may indicate an equivalent route or routes in the direction of the Pacific.

The ancient paintings in the Sierra de San Francisco are just beginning to be studied for their obvious value as elements in reconstructions of regional prehistory. However, unlike many humbler artifacts, the more inspired of these paintings embody a timeless genius that speaks to us in any context — art for art's sake.

CHAPTER *4*

The
*Sierra de
Guadalupe*

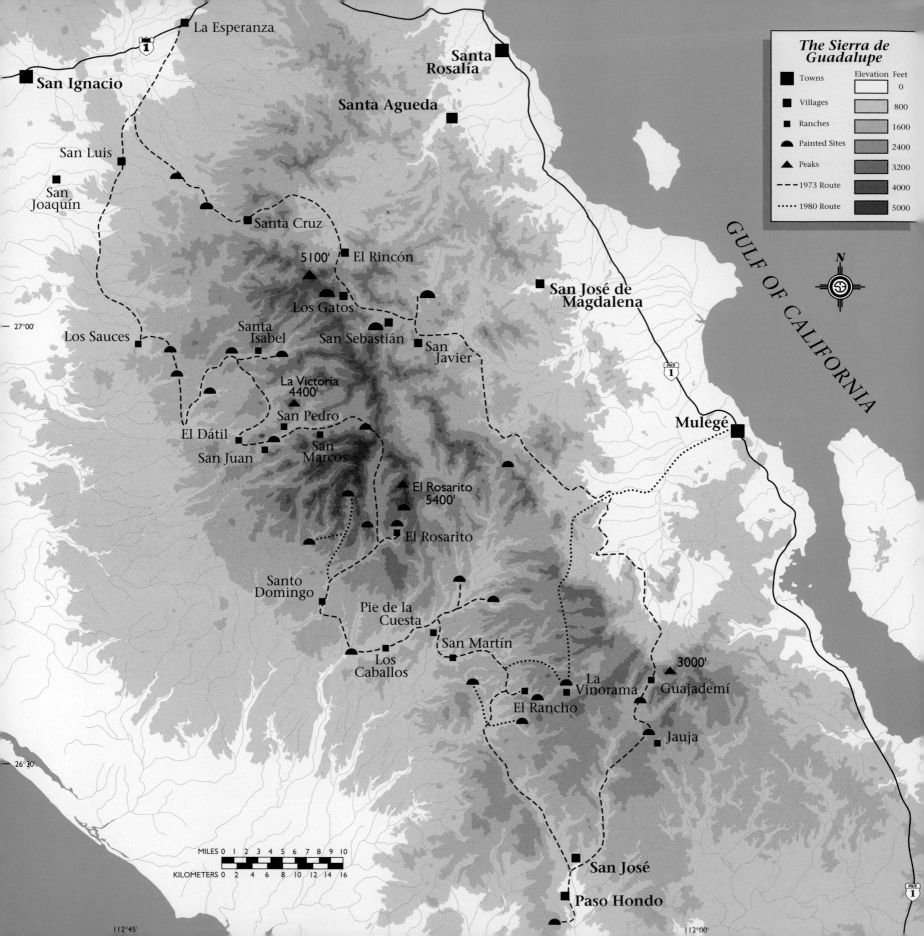

S tretching southeast from San Ignacio to a point beyond Bahía de la Concepción looms a jumbled mass: over 2,000 square miles of mountains with peaks rising 4,000 and 5,000 feet all along its central axis. This is the most complex terrain in the Great Mural area. Missionaries found many people here as well as the resources to feed them. A mission and its satellite ranches prospered materially, but the human flock could not cope with the combination of an introduced culture and introduced diseases. The religious establishment closed and its Hispanic soldiers and servants took over the lonely sierra where their descendants still live, tucked into its isolated pockets of watered land. No one knows the whole of this intricate maze, but its people know it bit by bit. Under patient questioning, they produce the lines that add up to the sierra's tale; the Painters were here and, range by arroyo, they left their telltale art.

San Borjitas   Before the many striking discoveries of the mid-20th century, the best-known rock art of Baja California was located in a cave at a place near Mulegé called San Borjitas. The description of a cave provided in 1772 by Padre Francisco Escalante,* the Jesuit missionary at Mulegé until the expulsion of his order in 1768, most probably referred to San Borjitas despite underestimating its dimensions. Leon Diguet visited the site in the 1890s, photographed it, and later described its artwork as the most impressive he saw on the peninsula. In 1951, San Borjitas was the subject of a study by Barbro Dahlgren and Javier Romero for the Instituto Nacional de Antropología e Historia (INAH). Erle Stanley Gardner visited San Borjitas and described it as a wondrous sight.

A single factor explains the early and repeated attention paid to this rock art site in a land with many others: San Borjitas is close to a village continuously populated from early mission times to the present. The people of the Mulegé area knew the cave and its contents before the missionaries came, and that knowledge was never lost. Furthermore, the trip between the two places is not difficult; no high mountains need to be crossed, and there has been a functioning ranch in the vicinity since mission times.

San Borjitas today is an abandoned ranch within a greater cattle-raising area known as San Baltazar. Since the late 19th century, the whole spread has been the property of the Gorosave family of Mulegé, the purchase of Vicente Gorosave, an educated immigrant born in 1844 in the Basque region of Spain. According to family tradition, Vicente was well acquainted with the French colony at Santa Rosalía, so it was probably he who informed Diguet of the cave and its art.

After earlier experiences with the aboriginal paintings of the Sierra de San Francisco, I became curious about famous San Borjitas. I wanted to compare its art with what I had seen to the north. During earlier visits to Mulegé, I was privileged to meet and become friendly with Doña Refugio Gorosave, a granddaughter of Vicente Gorosave. By December 1971, I was ready to visit San Borjitas. A commu-

*See Chapter II for the text of Escalante's report.

113

nication with Doña Cuca, as she is familiarly called, put me in touch with a man who had worked at the ranch and could act as a guide. We drove 14 miles north on the main road toward Santa Rosalía and then 19 additional miles west into the sierra to a ranch called Las Tinajas. From there, an hour-and-a-half mule ride to the south took us to the site of the abandoned ranch, and a 20 minute walk up a brush-filled cañada put us at the base of a slope leading up to the cave.

As usual, such sites are unimpressive when viewed from below. As I made my way up, it looked like no more than a modest respaldo at the foot of a high bluff. But from its own level, the form and scale of the place underwent a dramatic change. A broad opening appeared at the base of the respaldo, and, as we approached, it could be seen as an overhung cave of impressive depth. Furthermore, some of its paintings were immediately apparent. That part of the ceiling visible from without is heavily decorated with a network of large monos in random orientation (see photograph on page 12).

At first glance, the cave seems small, probably because of its low ceiling and the great mass of towering rock above. Therefore, I was surprised when I paced it off. At 100 feet wide by about 80 feet deep and an average of 12 feet high, it is no match for La Cuevona or even Cuesta del Palmarito in the Sierra de San Francisco, but it is impressive nonetheless. Even more important, its broad, unusually smooth and accessible ceiling made an extremely satisfactory canvas to which a large amount of art was entrusted. The narrow focus of this art is most unusual; the eighty identifiable figures are all monos larger than life size.

The monos of San Borjitas are varied, but strikingly related. Their pigments were drawn from an unusually broad palette: red, black, ochre, gray, white and combinations of these colors. The artists treated the fields within the outlines of monos in more ways than I was accustomed to seeing at a single site: solid fields of one paint; fields divided vertically into areas of two colors; and fields of stripes, checkerboards, or more complex geometric lattices. Despite all this variety, most of these human figures share some characteristics. Their bodies are long compared with their legs and appear to bulge as if they were inflated. Arms are thrust more out than up, and heads are short, often rectangular in outline, and rest directly on shoulders without the suggestion of a neck. In all, compared with monos in the Sierra de San Francisco, these figures are stiff and ill-proportioned. An emphasis on arrows embedded in the bodies of the monos, or laid over them, provides an additional contrast. This theme certainly appears here and there in the sierras of San Francisco and San Borja (discussed in Chapter VII), but not with the emphasis seen at San Borjitas. More than a dozen figures are transfixed or overlaid, some with as many as six arrows.

The monos of San Borjitas en masse present another unusual characteristic: They appear to form an open network of bodies woven together at consistent 90-degree angles. This is because the figures are oriented rather randomly toward three different points of the compass. The heads point predominantly toward the west, but many are left to point north or south. This odd practice was probably a response to the relatively horizontal plane of the ceiling that allowed the artists to choose their own versions of "up." East was avoided by all because a figure whose head pointed in that direction would be seen as upside down by observers approaching from any direction. The spectacle of adjacent and overlapping figures at right angles to each other is most unusual among the Great Murals and, at present, can be considered characteristic only of San Borjitas.

Prototypes for a regional school of grotesque human images

Stiff, slightly bulbous human figures, many with out-thrust arms and vertical stripes, define a parochial Guadalupe style. A number of the more than 50 figures in this painting mimic San Francisco conventions: characteristic headdresses and bodies divided vertically into red and black sides. But spread legs and heads divided between the two colors identify these as works of Guadalupe artists. Perhaps this ceiling mural symbolized warfare between the folk of the two sierras.

San Borjitas

115

The Sierra de Guadalupe

Ramón Arce and Tacho Arce

The side and back walls of the cave consist of a soft tuff. Originally the entire void was filled with this material and the ceiling was the contact face of a harder agglomerate layer above. The tuff layer bears water—a spring drips from it year-round—and this contributed to the erosion that formed the cave. The soft side walls, particularly on the north, provided an attractive material for engravings. Literally dozens of symbols, predominantly vulvas, decorate its surface. On the back wall, a fire-blackened area has been scratched through to produce handsome figures of a deer and fish.

The visit to San Borjitas produced immediate food for thought. The paintings are not those of San Francisco. Indeed, this style—one could even call it a school—of painting would look quite out of place at any of the sites with which I had become familiar. Nevertheless, they are simply different, not alien. Apart from style, the painters in the two sierras shared a common impulse, employed the same techniques, and depicted the same subjects. Suddenly it seemed important to me to link San Borjitas to San Francisco. I began to have a vision of finding a sequence of splendidly painted caves leading me from the northern foothills of Guadalupe all the way to San Borjitas and linking the artistic styles of the two sierras into a continuous chain.

The plan that leaped into being so simply took a long time to put into practice. I had to work on other things to support these adventures and I was not able to return to the Sierra de Guadalupe until the latter part of 1973. During the intervening time, I met Enrique Hambleton, a young Mexican then living in La Paz, who had been educated in Mexico City and at Saint Mary's College in the San Francisco Bay area. Enrique was beginning to develop a career in photography and when he saw my pictures of rock art, he was interested. I liked the idea of having another active, intelligent companion to share in the search and I had no trouble enlisting Enrique for the Guadalupe adventure. I retained the services of the excellent Tacho Arce and his son Ramón, and asked them to rent animals. We also asked them to obtain the guide or guides we would need, since we would be leaving the region with which they were familiar. When the time came, Tacho had a commitment to guide an old hunting client and was unable to go with us. Fortunately, he was able to arrange for a guide, Arnulfo Villavicencio, his distant cousin. This man, nicknamed Coco, was a wiry, 40-year-old cowboy who had grown up near Guadalupe and seemed well acquainted with the northern part of the mountains.

We planned to start our exploration on the northwest corner of the sierra and proceed down its Pacific slopes to the region of La Purísima. There we would turn north and follow an ancient Indian and mission route toward Mulegé. Once on the Mulegé plain, we would return to the north by way of the Gulf slopes and finish where we started at La Esperanza. The exact itinerary, of course, would be determined by clues to painted sites that we might glean along the way. For a beginning, I had Diguet's list, but it was not much help in laying out a route because we would not be able to identify most of his named places until we reached their immediate vicinities.

The sierra to be surveyed loomed on the horizon to the south, a line of jagged peaks at the east end giving way to a long slope down toward the Pacific. Maps showed a mountain mass extending 80 miles to the southeast with a width varying from 20 to 30 miles. Thus the area involved is greater than 2,000 square miles, and I was acutely aware that I would be more dependent than ever on local information. If that broken pile of mountains and mesas were deserted, a man could spend years finding all the nooks and crannies. Fortunately the area is sprinkled with ranches, many of which date back to mission times. In addition, the north end of the Sierra de Guadalupe—the part we planned to visit first—was the scene of much activity during the heyday of El Boleo, the French copper-mining concern at Santa Rosalía.

Between 1900 and 1925, El Boleo bought, confiscated, or founded more than 50 ranches in the hinterland around Santa Rosalía. These were used primarily to raise beef, but goats and goat cheese were also important. In addition, several ranches had enough water to serve as fruit and vegetable gardens. El Boleo lavished a great deal of money on this ranch system. The French hired a large percentage of the local people and put them to work building huge corrals of stone, digging wells by hand, and building *pilas,* or stone-and-mortar reservoirs, at each ranch. The company also constructed an elaborate road system for driving stock. In 1973, that system was conspicuous in aerial photographs of this arid, rocky region, and parts of it still served to connect ranches.

For two days we rode south over these Boleo roads and visited ranches formerly possessed by the company. No one seemed to have information about rock art, but we were neither surprised nor disappointed. The terrain promised little, consisting as it does of large mesas and broad arroyos; there are few rock formations that would appear to invite painting.

A small change of fortune occurred at Los Sauces, the first ranch that could be said to occupy a corner of the sierra proper. After days of riding over very open, very dry country it was a surprise to come to the edge of a deep cañada carved from colorful rock. The trail wound down a very steep road, built by the rancher, leading to the ranch house and the welcome shade of its open porch. The *dueño,* or owner, Venancio Zúñiga, heard our questions and in answer led us below his orchard and across the cañada. There, on a low *cantil,* the broken-off edge of a flow of basalt, we saw paintings, but they could scarcely be considered Great Murals. Painted in rose red on a smoothly fractured surface of columnar basalt are five fish and an unidentifiable zoomorphic form suggestive of a pelican. The figures range from a few inches to a couple of feet in height. Vertical stains on the painted panels indicate that they have been washed by running water during and after rains; as a result, a deposit of salts leached from the cliff above has streaked the paintings. We marveled that the primitive paintmakers' product had persisted so well despite

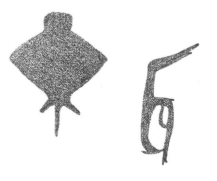

117

The Sierra de Guadalupe

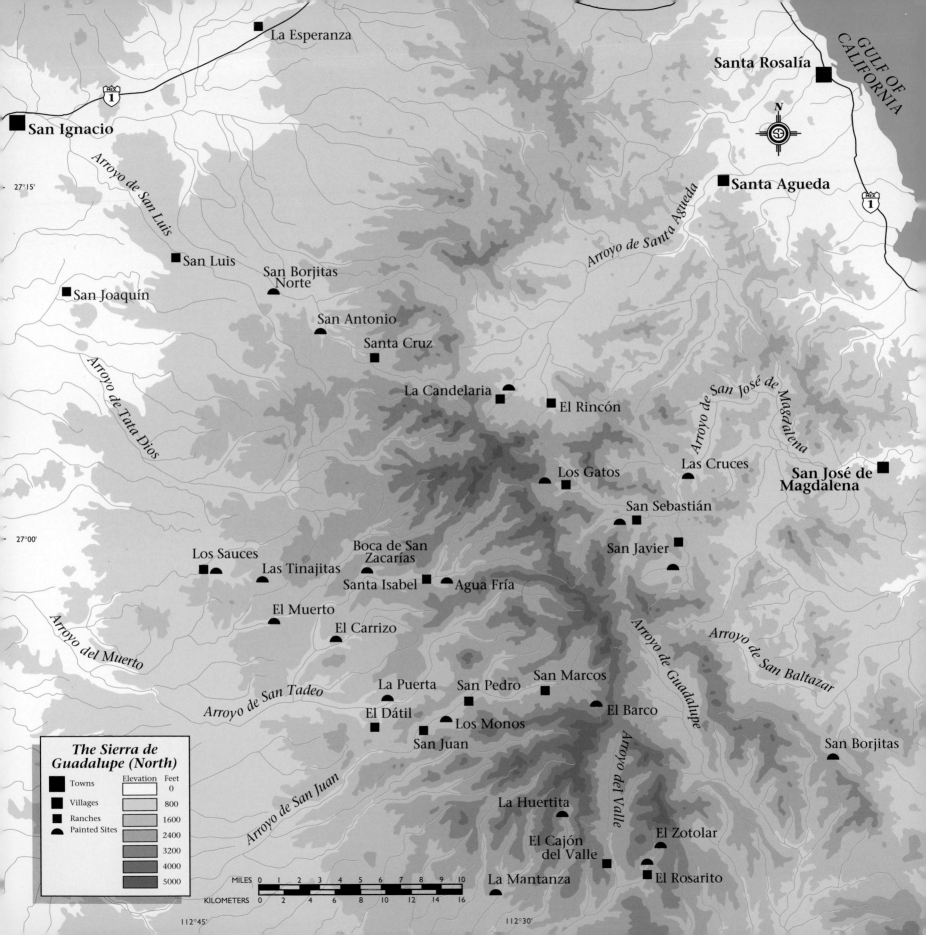

GULF OF CALIFORNIA

La Esperanza

Santa Rosalía

San Ignacio

Santa Agueda

27°15'

Arroyo de San Luis

San Luis

San Joaquín

San Borjitas Norte

San Antonio

Santa Cruz

Arroyo de Santa Agueda

Arroyo de Tata Dios

La Candelaria

El Rincón

Arroyo de San José de Magdalena

Las Cruces

San José de Magdalena

Los Gatos

27°00'

San Sebastián

San Javier

Los Sauces

Boca de San Zacarías

Las Tinajitas

Santa Isabel

Agua Fría

Arroyo del Muerto

El Muerto

El Carrizo

Arroyo de San Tadeo

Arroyo de Guadalupe

Arroyo de San Baltazar

La Puerta

San Pedro

San Marcos

El Dátil

Los Monos

El Barco

San Juan

San Borjitas

Arroyo de San Juan

Arroyo del Valle

La Huertita

El Cajón del Valle

El Zotolar

La Mantanza

El Rosarito

The Sierra de Guadalupe (North)

◼	Towns
▪	Villages
▪	Ranches
◗	Painted Sites

Elevation	Feet
	0
	800
	1600
	2400
	3200
	4000
	5000

MILES 0 1 2 3 4 5 6 7 8 9 10

KILOMETERS 0 2 4 6 8 10 12 14 16

112°45'

112°30'

centuries of annual washings. Four of the painted fish were so crudely drawn that they could be called shorthand symbols for fish, but the fifth is a skillfully executed bat ray. Unfortunately, all the works have suffered the fate of antiquities near ranches. Someone had scratched fresh outlines around the paintings, and numerous initials had been worked lightly into the hard basalt.

The trail left Los Sauces by going up its cañada and heading east. We were now coming into the real foothills of the sierra, where each successive arroyo is wider and deeper. Coco was in his element now, and for the next two weeks our routes and objectives would be in his hands or subject to the suggestions of residents in the region.

Two hours' ride took us to a place called Las Tinajitas, a succession of water catchments in a basalt flow. Countless blocks of basalt are scattered all around, and a profusion of petroglyphs has been hammered into the surfaces of those located close to pools. Most of the themes are natural if not actually realistic. Many of the human figures are rather grotesque, but the animals—deer and rabbits, for the most part—were depicted much as they appear in the Great Mural assemblages. It was surprising to see a pelican-like figure very similar to the puzzling painting at Los Sauces. Such a correspondence in so complicated a figure invited the thought that they came from the same hand.

Arroyo del Muerto   Another hour took us to the south edge of a mesa and down into an arroyo by way of a steep trail that works around and through a tremendous slide of tumbled blocks of basalt. In a few moments, we became aware of thousands of artworks engraved on the undisturbed bluffs of basalt above and on the jumble of boulders lying on either side of the trail as it descends. We had arrived at Leon Diguet's eighth site, "Cañada del Muerto, about 27 degrees, petroglyphs and cliff with paintings."

From the crest of the mesa to a point over halfway down the cuesta, most boulders in that great slide are covered with pictures pecked into their patinated surfaces. Human, deer, bird, fish, and what appear to be insect forms abound. We saw dozens of depictions of spears and arrows as well as many symbolic devices—or perhaps zoomorphic forms—too stylized to recognize. The prospect of photographing it all was discouraging; a proper recording of Cañada del Muerto's petroglyphs would have used up my entire stock of film.

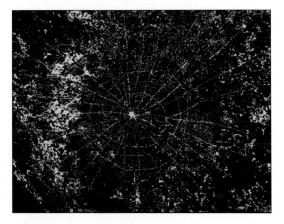

We hiked back and forth across the slope looking for prime examples. Many arrangements or groups of figures call for attention, but one of the most striking compositions is also the simplest: a pair of nicely drawn deer, one superimposed on the other. I was struck by the degree to which they resemble the deer in many Great Murals.

The most unusual and fascinating find is also the least conspicuous: Spread over two or three square feet of a flat surface is a delicate tracery representing a spider web. Working such fine lines into the hard basalt must have required the utmost in patience and skill.

We moved down to the caja of Arroyo del Muerto. Diguet had seen "a cliff with paintings" somewhere nearby, and I was too impatient to wait for morning so, despite approaching sunset, I climbed the cuesta exiting to the south. I found the paintings in the place Coco had indicated—an open, poorly protected respaldo near the top of the cuesta and facing east. On it is painted a singularly appropriate group. From left to right, the first image is a red and black mono with vertical stripes, a figure that in all ways is reminiscent of San Borjitas (which lies 28 miles east-southeast). Next is an even larger solid black woman, then a red deer and, superimposed on that, a perfect "black warrior" like the two near the right end of the ceiling mural at El Batequi in the Sierra de San Francisco. The whole thing seemed a perfect introduction to "Great Murals in the Sierra de Guadalupe," a sort of interface between the art of the two sierras. My joy was moderated, as was so often the case, by the terribly weathered condition of these exposed works. At best, they are clear but faint.

In the morning Enrique and I found more painted places, all in very bad condition. On the north side of the arroyo directly opposite the tinaja is a small cave weathered out of a gray-brown pudding stone. The lower and deeper parts are heavily smoke blackened, but the ceiling shows the remains of extensive paintings. At the left, a group of three life-sized monos survives well enough to be discerned if not to be enjoyed as art. Each was divided vertically into red and black areas, with the head on the red side, as usual. Noteworthy are the apparent headdresses on two of the figures, one with a single tall featherlike plume, the other possibly with a pair. A few smaller human figures are distinguishable at the right end of the opening and all the monos are unusually heavily outlined in white paint of the plaster type. A large metate lay broken on the floor, apparently the victim of heat during its use as a fire stone.

About 500 yards up the arroyo to the east is a slit cave on the south wall. Here we found a small painting of a bird delineated in the skillful fashion of those at Boca de San Julio, although in much poorer condition than its San Francisco counterparts. The basic drawing is in a brownish-red, outlined with a rich pink. Below, a dozen or more vulva symbols were carved into a soft tuff layer of the cave formation.

We left the Tinaja del Muerto by way of the cañada to the south, passed the painted respaldo, and were shortly on Mesa del Muerto at an elevation of 2,100 feet. To the east, we were presented with a sweeping panorama of mountains dominated by the sharp spike of the relatively nearby Pilón de San Matías and the great flat-topped block of Cerro de la Victoria. Due north, the sentinel tip of La Vírgen was still visible over the top of the intervening range.

We arrived at the south edge of the Mesa del Muerto and saw below us a vast and complicated system of waterways carved by the chubascos of countless summers. Here we received a lesson in a complex geography that allowed us to anticipate the directions our travels would take during the next several days. Coco, our instructor, pointed out the landmarks. An arroyo that runs east into the sierra, he called El Dátil. Arroyo de Santa Isabel branches from it just below the point on which we stood, and runs to the north. Other smaller watercourses branch from both of these to cut the country into a crazy-quilt pattern. Coco told us that both arroyos contain paintings and that based on our general plan, we should ride up Santa Isabel and see its offerings first. We descended a long, carefully made cuesta and turned north at the bottom.

El Carrizo Near sunset, after a break for lunch and a rest for our animals, and after over two hours of riding up the boulder-strewn arroyo, we arrived at a place called El Carrizo. Here we found the water we needed to camp as well as some real caves on both sides of the watercourse. The first one, a few feet above the bed of the arroyo and on its north side, yielded prompt but frustrating rewards. The cave had been heavily painted at one time, but its rough and crumbling surface retains only a few patches of paint with here and there a decipherable figure. The one real survivor, the white outline of a deer painted with a tenacious plasterlike paint, shone in the gloom of the cave interior, dimly lit by the sky at dusk. It was at once promising and disappointing. We had encountered paintings during each of the past three days, but not one was in good enough condition to really enjoy or photograph. When questioned, Coco said other paintings in his sierra were *mas o menos,* meaning, colloquially, "about the same."

At dawn our search began. We quickly found that the other caves are painted, but in equally poor condition. As I came out of one, something located well up on the south or opposite side of the arroyo caught my eye: a suspicious looking patch of red on a respaldo. Binoculars confirmed the suspicion; their 10-power magnification showed a pair of large monos with arms raised in the familiar salute. I scrambled down one bank, crossed the arroyo, and worked my way up the loose, sliding rock of the other. A few minutes after the discovery, I stood puffing in front of my prize. And a prize it was. The right-hand mono is about seven feet tall, bicolored red and black, divided vertically, and outlined in pink. It is crowned with a three-lobed headdress: a short central protuberance flanked by two longer lobes curving downward toward the shoulders. The other mono represents a woman and was painted in a plain red, outlined with pink, and overlaid with three black arrows, their heads carefully drawn over the body paint. Over one shoulder is a tiny inverted figure similar to the "epaulet" figures I'd seen painted over the shoulders of two monos at Cueva de las Flechas and one at Cueva del Corralito in the Sierra de San Francisco.

Above the two monos at El Carrizo fly three black *auras,* or vultures, wing to wing. Their heads were painted red, making this one of the rare instances in which more than the outline of a figure was painted realistically.

By this time my companions had joined me, and we walked around the site and found more paintings. Very high and to the left of the mono-aura group is a huge black deer with handsome antlers; the legs, however, had been painted on a

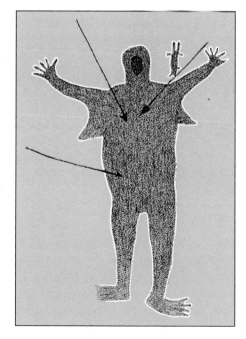

121

The Sierra de Guadalupe

softer layer of rock and are now completely gone. Several tiny monos are scattered about on included rocks. Other larger paintings near the bottom of the respaldo are now in the last stages of deterioration. On returning to the main group, I noticed a fourth *aura* in good condition partially overpainting the calf area of the bicolored mono. On the ground were numerous artifacts: choppers, scrapers, manos and, best of all, a metate and other stones unmistakably stained with red or black paint.

El Carrizo left me a warm sense of having arrived once again among the Painters; another half-hour's ride brought a further reminder: At a narrow corner of the arroyo, we waved to a faded mono visible high above us on a sheer rock wall.

Boca de San Zacarías   Two hours later we came to the place where Arroyo de San Zacarías flows down from the north and joins Arroyo de Santa Isabel. As we rode past the mouth of San Zacarías, Coco pointed up at the high, opposite bank. There in plain sight was a mammoth respaldo covered with monos so large and numerous that they make an impressive showing even from far below.

Remnants of a once grand prehistoric rock painting center

Once, 1,000 or more years ago, the Sierra de Guadalupe was dotted with a dozen or more sites where huge rock panels had been liberally painted with larger-than-life images, primarily of men and women. Today, only the paintings at San Borjitas and San Juan survive sufficiently to suggest what they were like in their prime. At a few other sites, like Boca de las Piedras and Boca de San Zacarías, enough painting can be detected to show that these sites, too, were important ceremonial centers.

Boca de San Zacarías

Thus we came to our first major Great Mural site in the Sierra de Guadalupe. The respaldo is long, at least 200 feet, and it is high. Several of the many dozens of figures are 25 feet off the floor, and they are still dwarfed by the height of the wall above them. Rows of giant red and black monos stand abreast, staunchly braving erosion, but theirs is a losing battle. The fine outlines are gone, the colors are washing away. Here and there flakes of rock had fallen and taken pieces of painted figures as they went. Seeing this site as a whole was a profoundly moving experience. With its huge dimensions, its sweeping visibility from two arroyos, and the remains of so much human endeavor, Boca de San Zacarías retains the atmosphere of a great ceremonial center.

A few items of artistic interest survive all the destruction. The most important is embodied in a style of mono distinctly different from any I had seen before. Near the center of the painted area is a pair of human figures; only their heads, shoulders, and arms survive. One was painted in a solid maroon outlined heavily in white, and the other was painted in maroon and black with a lighter white boundary. Their different appearance is characterized by a very short head so deeply sunk into the shoulders that it gives no sense of a neck at all, and by a strange, floppy "dog ears" sort of headdress on each figure. Below these and the rows of tall monos are animal figures, but they are terribly eroded.

Time did not allow an inventory of Arroyo de San Zacarías itself but, before we moved on, I took a few steps into it and found a tiny cave on the west wall with well-preserved paintings of two small black deer.

Brutal forms, unique paint: a painter with his own stamp

The massive black shapes of a mountain lion and a deer, each 10 feet long, exemplify the stylistic diversity of the Great Murals. Although many conventions were observed by nearly all the artists, their works are surprisingly individual. No other site known at this time displays figures that seem akin to these or that are colored with the same strange pitchlike, brown-black paint used here.

Agua Fría I

123

Art bridges the gulf between two sierras

Rock paintings like these in the northern region of the Sierra de Guadalupe show stylistic similarities to those of the Sierra de San Francisco, just to the north across the San Ignacio plain. But subtle differences are already apparent, and, as an observer moves south, additional sites reveal a progression of changes.

Agua Fría II

Agua Fría   Two hours' ride took us to Rancho Santa Isabel. The dueño, Tomás Murillo, gave us instructions for reaching the best-known paintings in his region. About a mile and a half away, precisely at sunset, we came to a place called Agua Fría. Ramón spotted paintings as we rode in. He directed our gaze across the arroyo to the east, to a conspicuous cave at the top of the usual steep, rocky falda. On its ceiling, well exposed to view, we saw huge paintings of a deer and a mountain lion brilliantly lighted by the last rays of the sun. I jumped down, grabbed my camera, and charged the slope. Minutes later and utterly winded, I arrived at the cave just in time to see the light die on the paintings. No matter. Being there was reward enough. I poked around in the pink light of the afterglow. The two large black figures survive marvelously well and, even in the rapidly graying dusk, I could make out the forms of several older figures partially covered by the lion and the deer.

Far above the painted cave, perhaps 1,000 feet higher, we noticed a gigantic cave illuminated in the setting sun. Coco called it Cueva Blanca and told a strange story about it. According to local lore the cave was struck by an *aerolito*, a meteorite, some 70 or 80 years before. The people at Santa Isabel heard a great roar and felt a smashing impact. When they examined the place they found a huge slide of broken rock tumbled down the mountain side and individual fragments scattered as much as a mile to the west. Coco had never been up to the site and had no notion if the remains of the cave were painted or not.

In the morning our climb to Cueva Blanca proved to be slow, difficult, and tiring. The entire slope is covered with fragments of relatively freshly broken rock set at about the steepest angle they could occupy and without sliding. In many places, large chunks are precariously balanced and we had to move with caution.

The cave turned out to be an exciting place but it is entirely barren of art. The covered space is huge, perhaps 300 feet long and overhung by a respaldo more than 100 feet high. Of the original deepest part of the cave only a pocket remains, but that is 80 feet wide, more than 60 feet deep, and 30 feet high. A tiny spring dripped from the roof and formed a pool of delicious water which was surrounded by a wreath of tiny plants with golden flowers.

The entire area, except the inner cave, is buried in clean-faced fragments of broken rock. The source of the tremendous cubage of fallen stone appears to have been an overhang that must once have formed a gigantic cave. No test we could apply told us whether the meteorite tale should be believed or not. All the stone we saw could simply have fallen and rolled or slid down the steep slope. But whatever the cause, the event left an impressive scar.

We were thoroughly tired by the time we got down again, but we launched right into the job of recording Agua Fría. The two large black figures offered a surprise. They were painted with a unique substance, a sort of bituminous material, perhaps natural tar or asphalt. Many of the painted caves, including Agua Fría, contain blotchlike exudations of a similar-looking material. However, when we have examined these stains they have invariably proven to be hard and dry.*

Lower than the two figures which so dominated the cave, we now observed a small, nicely painted rabbit and the eroded remains of a deer with elegant antlers, both rendered in the same curious paint. The older works that I had seen the night before turned out to be two deer, one a little larger than life and the other huge, even bigger than the black giant. Both of these are well preserved but painted in a soft pink that does not give a lot of contrast with the warm beige patina on the cave wall.

Early in the morning before our climb, I had used binoculars to look at Cueva Blanca and the hillsides in general. Just a couple of hundred yards south of the Agua Fría Cave and at the same level, I had noticed a respaldo with a suspicious stain on it. When we finished our photography at the first site, we scrambled along the rough falda and through the thorny plants until we reached the other.

This second site did indeed prove to be painted, and it also contained a mild surprise: conventional San Francisco-style red and black monos, divided vertically and showing off unusually elaborate headdresses. Here also are deer painted in the usual Great Mural fashion. It seemed odd to us that all of the figures at Agua Fría I should prove so unusual, and that those at Agua Fría II should be so familiar. A small pink deer seemed to form the only bond between the two sites.

The artwork at Agua Fría II, like that at Agua Fría I, survives unusually well; the colors are strong and the outlines distinct. We tore ourselves away reluctantly; nothing we had seen thus far on our trip had proved nearly so fine.

Now we needed to backtrack to a spot beyond Boca de San Zacarías before we could continue south. We mounted and started back to Santa Isabel. After we traveled half of a mile, Ramón pointed across the arroyo to a respaldo behind some trees. Just over a canopy of leaves, he had seen a telltale *mancha,* a spot or stain. Binoculars verified the presence of paintings. Enrique and I dismounted and sent Coco and Ramón on to Santa Isabel where they could ask the ranch folk to prepare us a meal. We crossed the arroyo and, somewhat wearily, began to clamber up the falda.

Mindful of the striking differences between the Agua Fría sites, we speculated about this one as we climbed. When we arrived we found additional art that was new to us—and quite unlike that on exhibit at either of its neighboring galleries up the arroyo. Ramón's attention had been attracted by the figures of two women painted high on the respaldo in solid red, outlined strongly in white. Each image is overlaid with a painting of a white arrow with a classically drawn head. Various

*These black encrustations exude from crevices in many respaldos and could be remains of bat excrement that accumulated long ago and has been acted upon by water percolating through fractures in the bedded rock. As far as I know, no one has tested a sample of this substance to determine its origin

other paintings are scattered about on the respaldo: deer, a red mountain lion outlined in white, and a group of large monos in the same colors.

We found other, smaller-scaled collections of paintings below, strung out in a series of little caves and shelters. One hollow contains a doll-like mono in red outlined in black. In a dark nook of another, I found a memento of Agua Fría I, a small black deer that is a virtual replica of the large one which so dominates the other site. A third recess offers a group of five red rabbits outlined in white plaster paint. The last cave to the west displays numerous small bird paintings and a fine, large bat ray, orange-red, and outlined in black.

We walked the mile or less to the ranch and, after dinner, packed up and continued backtracking. At sunset we passed La Boca de San Zacarías, the great wall of monos clearly visible in the shadows of the south slope. We camped, almost in their presence, a short distance west at the foot of a grade that would take us out of Arroyo de Santa Isabel.

Our ride in the morning was long and scenic, first up the cuesta, then across a mesa and through broken tableland. We took our midday break exactly on the pass crossing the north shoulder of the Pilón de San Matías, the most conspicuous and recognizable mountain in the greater area. We rested there awhile and then I climbed a short distance toward the bullet-shaped peak to get a look around. Ahead I could see the cuesta that would take us down into Arroyo de San Matías; I could also see a cañada Coco called San Matiitas, or little San Matías. The name sounded familiar. Checking back, I found that Diguet had visited a site he called San Matillita. I had never been able to find anyone who recognized that name and, indeed, an obvious error had been made in transcribing it. "San" is masculine and "Matillita" feminine. The sierra people are notorious mumblers, and swallowing the final "s" is almost universal among them. The more I thought about it, the more certain I became that this was the answer; Diguet evidently wrote down what he heard without questioning the logic of gender. The rest of his description—"La Cañada de San Matillita, situated near the 27th parallel on the Pacific watershed of the sierra, flows into the great Arroyo de San Adeo."— is simple to verify. Here, we were no more than five minutes south of 27 degrees north latitude on the Pacific slope, and Coco informed me that the cañada joined Arroyo de San Tadeo a short distance away. Since there is no saint on the calendar named San Adeo, it seems Diguet once again missed the mark in his transcription.

We descended the cuesta and arrived in a broad sandy watercourse. Enrique and I climbed to a small cave about 300 yards downstream, hoping to find the paintings seen by Diguet. The cave turned out to be in very bad condition, eroded and smoke-blackened, but it contains the remains of many paintings. None, however, is unusual in any way. Diguet had described a group of small and nearly abstract works, but we were looking at Great Murals, however, worn, stained, and pitted. It was late and we decided to go on. As tempting as it was to try to dog

Diguet's footsteps, our resolve failed when faced with the immensity of the area we would have to search.

At sunset, as we rode south in the bed of the waterway, we came to a curious sight: a basaltic dike had formed across this area in some distant eon, and now it stands like a wall, partially weathered out of the softer surrounding material. The exposed portion stretches across the valley, in places standing to heights of 30 feet or more, and looking like some ancient construction wildly out of place in those remote and deserted surroundings.

The next morning found us making our way down the same waterway and past the point where it is joined by Arroyo de San Tadeo. Despite the Diguet site, I decided not to ride up to Rancho San Tadeo itself. Coco said it would cost us a day or more and he knew of no paintings. We would have no local assistance because, just then, the ranch was *solo,* or "alone," the colorful mountain term for "unoccupied." To cap it off, Diguet himself had merely listed a rock shelter, presumably painted but never described.

About a mile and a half below the junction of the two arroyos, we came to a beautiful angostura, a place where the vertical walls of the watercourse approach each other to within 100 feet. We rode down this corridor admiring the play of light and shadow on the vertical surfaces of rich red-brown rock.

The southern mouth of this angostura is called *La Puerta,* The Door, and Coco had heard talk of paintings nearby. We were not kept waiting; Ramón spotted them through some trees virtually as we arrived. The eastern rock wall, which narrows to form that side of La Puerta, has a large flat face just above the high-water marks of the canyon. This panel is very slightly overhung by another layer of volcanic agglomerate. There, adjacent to The Door itself, is a grand array of painted figures, about 60 feet long. There are many deer. Two in black were cocked so that they appear to be seated on their haunches. Ten or twelve monos stand in a row like those at Boca de San Zacarías. Most interesting of all, an immense, heavy-bodied serpent undulates across the top of the entire group.

Joy at this discovery was heavily tempered by its condition. The entire panel, every figure, is in a very eroded, almost washed-off condition. The cause was unusual. Here the actual paint seems to have been worn away by exposure to wind and water. For a change, the rock does not seem to have been the culprit; its surface is hard and smooth. The site illustrates a basic observation: A really good survival depends on many factors. In order to descend to us in anything like the condition in which the Painters left them, the art must have begun with that rare combination of good rock and good protection—from wind, rain, and flowing water. La Puerta lacks protection and survives only as another sad and tantalizing reminder of all that has been lost.

A few minutes' ride below La Puerta took us to a large cave just above the caja. Enrique and I hastily dismounted to inspect it. Our efforts were rewarded with a painful lesson about the other half of the survival equation: The place has perfect protection against the elements, but its rock is so soft and crumbling that nothing on its surface could have survived.

By noon we were at Rancho El Dátil, the home of Juan Zúñiga, brother of Venancio. El Dátil was once the principal Boleo ranch in this region. Here, the foremen of all the other ranches gathered monthly to be paid, and here, in the first quarter of this century, was the liveliest scene in all the sierras of Baja California.

Rancho El Dátil occupies a rise just east of the confluence of the arroyo and a cañada dropping down from the south. Just below, the washes of the combined watercourses form a broad flat. Two sturdy corrals built in Boleo days still stood and were in use; a few cultivated patches scattered among thickets of brush and carrizo grew in what once must have been wide fields. That flat area, according to old-timers, was the site of the colorful monthly encampments that accompanied paydays. Falluqueros, the mounted dry goods salesmen of the pre-automotive age, arrived with anything that might appeal to the temporarily monied mountain people. Some of these men brought young women with them, exotic faces for the provincial ranchers. "Beautiful señoritas all the way from Guaymas," one old man told me, "and never the same from month to month." In addition to their obvious roles, the women added a lot to the public revels among the tents and clearings of that flat. According to the old-timers, few wives attended the post-payday parties, yet there was a fiesta every night. "Those young things never sat down; they danced every dance and sang every song."

Late in the afternoon we headed for the cuesta over the pass separating El Dátil from San Juan. We started up the cañada south of the house and passed the crumbling remains of a stone and mortar aqueduct that once brought water from a spring above directly to the fields below. Soon we started up a grade and, in a few minutes, found ourselves climbing steeply across a bleak and picturesque slide of tumbled basalt block. This is higher and steeper than the slide at El Muerto but, unfortunately, offers no petroglyphs. Two-thirds of the way to the top we heard singing above us and soon spotted a young man on a mule that was stepping spryly down the rock pile. In a few moments we met Jesús Valenzuela, the rancher at San Juan. He stopped to chat and, when he heard about our mission, he gave us the best possible news. He could show us a large painted site called Los Monos de San Juan located near his ranch. Further, he was sure the name was old. I, in my turn, was sure that it must be one of Diguet's sites — not merely a listing like San Tadeo, but a large and important center that Diguet had compared with San Borjitas. Señor Valenzuela was on his way to buy supplies and socialize at El Dátil, but he said he would return and show us the paintings.

We camped on the mesa and during the night were surprised when a traveler passed on the trail. The undaunted Jesús Valenzuela had completed his visit and was riding home over that awesome mountain trail in the pitch black of a moonless night.

On the morning of the 10th day of the trip, we rose early and headed east. In minutes we came to a lookout over Arroyo de San Juan and had a noble view of the country in which we would be riding for several days. Perhaps 800 feet below we saw a right-angle turn in the arroyo and the tract of level land usually found at such places. All of it had been cleared and plowed, and a tidy rock wall divided it from the bed of the watercourse. A man could be seen stacking brush in piles, several of which were blazing and smoking. An animal trail led up the waterway to a cluster of houses and then disappeared as it followed the arroyo around a corner of the hills. In the distance to the east we saw the highest peaks of our trip thus far, a really formidable wall running north and south.

Los Monos de San Juan   A leisurely descent brought us to the farm scene below. We completed the brief ceremonial visit expected at Rancho San Juan and were soon on the trail again with Jesús Valenzuela as our guide. The way was simplicity itself. We followed the bed of the arroyo and, in a little over half an hour, dismounted with Los Monos de San Juan in plain view up a slope on the southwest side of the arroyo. The actual site is somewhat reminiscent of Boca de San Zacarías: a long, high respaldo with monos quite visible from the trail below. The principal differences are the lower elevation of this site, only 50 feet or so above the bed of the arroyo, and the better condition of its paintings.

We shouldered all our gear, crossed the riverbed, scrambled up a slope, and I placed myself where Leon Diguet had stood almost eighty years before. To savor the moment as fully as possible, I rummaged in my papers and found a photocopy of Diguet's original report which included a photograph of this site. In a moment we located the place where it was taken, and I solemnly stood for a picture on the spot where a guide once posed for Diguet.

Los Monos did not disappoint us. The respaldo is about 80 feet high and hangs well over the art painted on its lower 25 feet. This rich tapestry of the Painters' art features an assemblage of human figures almost as numerous as those at San Borjitas and, to my eye, more varied and interesting. As usual, the stratum bearing the painting is of a different rock than the mass protruding above. As this bottom layer became recessed, erosion also broke its surface into the four areas that were used by the Painters.

From the left, the first painted area is a large platelike depression covered with about 25 monos, largely of the red and black, vertically divided ilk. That group is dominated by the figure of a gigantic red león seemingly suspended over the monos. Next and slightly higher, another concave panel, double the width of the first, displays a multitude of human figures — men and women. Beneath the right end of this panel, a shelflike protuberance overhangs a tiny cave, also heavily painted. Diguet's photo shows this area, including part of the large panel above. To the right of the small cave, and quite separated by a rock formation, is another little painted cave. The artwork in these two recesses is rich in numbers, styles, and

The first Great Mural site to be photographed (1894)

Leon Diguet, a French naturalist, published a picture, re-created here, in a French scientific journal. For 50 years, Diguet's article and its few illustrations were the world's only view of Baja California's great primitive art centers. In 1973, the Diguet photographs were compared to the locations at which they were taken. There was no observable change in the condition of the paintings.

Los Monos de San Juan

subject matter. However, it is all in relatively poor condition because it was placed low on the respaldo, here — as at other sites — the part with the least durable rock. Only a painstaking analysis and reconstruction would allow us to appreciate the remains that meet the eye.

Paintings on the two major panels above are in much better condition, with many complete figures that show little of the pitting or flaking that destroys line and color. However, these upper paintings have suffered a different sort of degradation. Water has seeped through the rock above, dissolved salts during its passage, and deposited them as a milky-looking film that covers the paintings. This coating dulls the drawing and mutes the colors. At first I thought it might be merely dirt or dust that had settled on the inclined surface, but a water-soaked rag removed none of the deposit. When wet, the colors became more vivid, but they shortly dried to their original appearance.

Our examination of the condition of the work at Los Monos soon prompted a comparison with the Diguet photo. This was a rare opportunity. To my knowledge, Diguet's are by far the earliest photographs of Great Murals, and the one taken at San Juan is the best of them all. The quality of the reproduction I carried was poor, but, according to what I could see, there had been no change in the painted area covered by the photograph. Subsequently, I saw a better print of Diguet's picture and compared it with mine. The results were the same: The art on that panel at San Juan had not deteriorated appreciably in eighty years.

Other parts of the paintings have fared differently. Outside the area covered by the 1894 photo, two large, irregular patches of the painted surface have flaked away, leaving several square feet of clean rock. Just below, the ground was littered

This grand panel exemplifies the style of rock painting found in the northwest third of the Sierra de Guadalupe. Note the sense of mutual participation—as if in some ritual event—imparted by the grouping and the attitudes of these larger-than-life human figures. Note also the variety of headdresses, unmatched by any other single display in the sierra.

Los Monos de San Juan

with painted bits. In answer to our obvious puzzlement, Jesús Valenzuela told us a heartbreaking story. Twenty years before, Luis Suiqui, a man from the Gulf coast, was working in San Juan. He fell out with his employer, was discharged, and left in a drunken condition. The people soon heard shots, "a real fusillade," Jesús told us, and feared someone had met the inebriate and come to harm. Riding out, they found to their relief that Suiqui had only discharged his .30-30 carbine at Los Monos de San Juan. Shots struck the right upper panel and partially destroyed a particularly beautiful and unusual deer painted in a strong red and outlined in black.

Enrique and I looked in frustration at the piles of colored tesserae, the residue of lost art. We recalled the terrible odds against the survival of the Great Murals; these had survived well with the gift of good rock and adequate shelter. We now agreed that another enemy of the paintings had to be added to our list: the most implacable of all the potentially destructive forces, the one with the ability to search and destroy.

Los Monos is a true gallery of the Painters, a place that requires time and concentration to appreciate. En masse, its human figures are particularly effective; all appear to be closely related. The paints are alike, the drawings oddly similar: figures with shortened legs and elongated bodies. They are arranged like a multitude attending a momentous event. Neighboring monos seem to create an atmosphere for each other; a certain suggestive flexibility in their lines creates static tension. They seem to express emotion, they bend as if recoiling from unseen dangers. One behind another, many abreast, they wait out the ages as witnesses to forgotten rites.

San Juan presents us with one of the most subtly varied of the great mono groupings. Close inspection reveals a variety of treatments in headdresses, several of which are unique, at least in my experience. The most characteristic San Juan headdress, and the most striking, takes the form of a double sackhat, creating a perception, for people of Western culture, of the sausage-shaped appendages depicted on the heads of medieval court jesters. A black male mono has a beautiful moundlike headdress that was created by engraving the rock into the pattern of a dandelion gone to seed. A black female mono has a red head with a large black spot suggesting a mask or a Cyclopean eye. This figure markedly resembles similarly painted monos at Cueva del Ratón and Cuesta del Palmarito in the Sierra de San Francisco, and, as will be seen shortly, a striking image in an isolated cave at El Valle, quite near San Juan.

The emotional and story-telling content I perceived at Los Monos de San Juan contrasted sharply with my perception of San Borjitas. At that site, an equally large number of less varied monos are arrayed neither with nor against each other; they are disposed in an unnatural but geometric order and cooperate only as an effective abstract design. Individually, San Borjitas's stiff, sausagelike figures impart less of beauty, of horror, of human involvement than those at San Juan. The contrast was especially interesting because the two sites are in the same sierra and only 20 miles apart. A visitor cannot observe these two sets of paintings without the immediate perception that he or she is looking at the work of quite different cultures, at least as far as artistic representations are concerned. As always, there is the fact, and the mystery, that such different groups nevertheless adhered to all the basic conventions that characterize Great Mural art.

We left Los Monos with the strangely mixed feelings that overcame us at most of the great rock art sites. We were awed and exhilarated by the marvelous display of art; we were saddened by its condition and the prospects for its future. We rode up the arroyo, each of us quiet with his own thoughts.

Along the way, we saw the impressive remains of a system of water pipes installed half a century before by El Boleo. Chubascos had since wrecked the whole enterprise, and most of the works were fallen or smashed into litter along that sometimes-tumultuous waterway. It was odd to see twenty-foot lengths of six-inch pipe lying about in a place so far from any vestiges of the culture that produced them.

A half-mile ride brought us to another of the sierra's beautiful angosturas. Once again, high rock walls rose on either side and we fell to looking for additional rock art that Jesús Valenzuela had mentioned before he returned to his home. As usual, Ramón first recognized the faint showings and we were soon toiling up a falda unusually steep in a land of steep slopes. The paintings at La Angostura de San Juan are minor after those of Los Monos, but still full of interest for us. The first thing to meet my eye, for example, was another of the floppy-eared monos that we first saw at Boca de San Zacarías. This one is overlaid by several arrows with carefully drawn feathers. Male and female monos had been outlined with white plaster but never filled in with color. A straight-backed black deer image still shows off a splendid set of antlers, but has lost his legs to rock erosion.

While Enrique and I admired and photographed that collection, Ramón was off to the east scouting along the base of the same continuing respaldo. He returned saying he had found a curiosity he had not seen before, a human handprint. That was exciting. Handprints are among the oldest and most common rock-painting devices known. They have been found on every inhabited continent and in just about every place frequented by ancient artists, yet I had not seen or heard of one among the Great Murals. We followed Ramón to the spot and he pointed to a broken rock face about seven feet off the ground. There, in plain sight, we saw a negative handprint—in other words, an image made by placing a hand on the rock and blowing paint at it. Curious, we placed our hands over the image and found that the painter was smaller than any of us. The original hand must have been about a tenth smaller than that of Ramón, a sturdily built man five feet and nine inches tall.

We resumed our ride, but shortly we reined up to a stop. The narrowest place in the angostura was filled with water from wall to wall. However, we soon determined that the depth was not alarming and splashed our way through.* In a few more minutes, we rode past the ruins of a dam and up out of the narrows altogether. That put us in a broad open arroyo and, as the sun set, we halted briefly at two small caves with insignificant and badly preserved paintings. In the gathering dusk, we rode into Rancho San Marcos where Coco had thought we might spend the night. As we pulled up, we were met by a most friendly man, Ramón Avila, master of San Marcos. He made us welcome, and we passed a pleasant evening catching up on sierra gossip.

In the morning, we headed east toward Rancho San Pedro. Señor Avila accompanied us for a quarter of a mile and showed us a painted rock face on the north side of the arroyo. There we saw a large woman's figure outlined in an orange-pink and various other smaller figures too deteriorated to justify a close inspection.

For the next two hours or more we rode up the ancón of a very broad arroyo on which grew large mezquite and bebelama trees. Ahead, the imposing wall of

*See photograph, page x.

133

mountains loomed closer and taller. A map check showed the reason. Some of those peaks have elevations close to 6,000 feet, we were at 2,000 feet, and they were only four or five miles away.

Just before noon we came to Rancho San Pedro, almost a village, with several houses scattered along the south bank of the watercourse. We approached one designated by Coco and dismounted as local men, women, children, and dogs came out to participate in the rare event of a visit.

That spot has quite a history. The Jesuits discovered it before 1730 and, noting its potential animal forage, founded a ranch and visiting station called San Pedro y San Pablo. Before long, the cattle herds here and at El Valle, eight miles south and over a high mountain, were the largest at any of the peninsular missions. Jesuit documents show that a stone chapel was built at each place. The ranches remained successful during the decline and closing of Misión de Guadalupe and the Indian population, dwindling from imported diseases, was soon replaced by the families of mission soldiers and cowherds, the ancestors of the present sierra folk.

At the home of Toribio Rojas, we were urged to come in and "take coffee," a typically depreciating sierra invitation that in practice means "coffee followed by a generous repast." Then, while we all waited for Toribio's wife to prepare a midday meal, Coco and Ramón got down to a serious visit with the family, and Enrique and I went out to learn what we could. The men had pointed to a mound when we asked about a stone chapel. Now we looked it over. Inside is a cleared area of 13 by 35 feet. Its stone walls are over three feet thick and still stand to a height of about five feet. Above that height, the walls had been built of adobe block, a section of which survives on the south side. The present moundlike condition outside was caused by the melting away and falling of the adobe. Although the ruin is not especially impressive, we were moved by our encounter with it. That modest little rectangle was probably built about 1735 at the direction of Padre Everard Helen, a German Jesuit. It stands today as the last tangible remains of the Jesuit dream in a lonely corner of their one-time realm.

During a welcome dinner we queried our host extensively about paintings, but the pickings were slim. Three local men were present and they could think of just one site, unimpressive and difficult to reach. The conversation did have an unexpected twist. Toribio's wife turned out to have been born and raised at San Tadeo. She was able to tell me what I had missed by electing not to visit the place. She could recollect perhaps half a dozen groups of paintings in caves and on low cantiles between the point where we entered Arroyo de San Tadeo and another point a short distance above the ranch of the same name. She was not so positive as to the kind or quality of paintings. "Regular paintings," she said, "monos, birds, deer, who knows what all?" All we could do was shrug it off and drop a card into our files for a future trip.

In mid-afternoon we started east again, passed the more prosperous looking ranch of another Rojas brother, and soon veered off to the south to start up a tremendous cuesta. By dusk, we had climbed to an elevation of about 4,500 feet and had reached Rancho El Potrerito, an abandoned Boleo construction with a spring from which water was still piped to a pila and a watering trough. We passed the night camped within the stone walls of the Boleo corral.

In the morning we set out to investigate possible painted sites. Coco and Enrique went to find the place described by the Rojas brothers. Ramón worked his way over to the head of a *salto,* a seasonal waterfall west of the ranch, and I wound down to look at its base. We were attracted to the latter sites by the combination of water and obvious rock faces that might have been painted. Because it was the first time we had split up over any considerable distance, each party carried half of Enrique's pocket-sized, two-way radio set. Ramón and I toiled separately for an hour and a half to reach the same conclusion that the steep cañada and salto had no paintings. Then we joined on the ridge below the ranch and, at the appointed hour, called Enrique.

In a few seconds we heard a weak but audible reply. Coco and Enrique had used their time to cross a series of rugged ridges and had found *El Barco* — The Ship — the rock formation described by Toribio Rojas. They had just arrived and were looking at paintings. Apparently these were small and in rather poor condition, but Enrique was enthusiastic. "They're different," he told me. "It's a new style and different looking paint, a lot of it yellow." I was tired but I didn't want to miss anything. We got directions and started out.

El Barco   The rock art site at El Barco is located on a rather hard, durable respaldo on the lower part of the north face of a conspicuous outcropping. Seen from the valley below, the whole structure looks like the prow of a ship, hence the name. The paint and painting style were indeed new to us; the outlines of animal images were still realistic, but the painting within those outlines presented had a new twist: The infill of the larger figures, all deer, consists of stripes or checkerboarding. The birds are more conventional, but the smaller paintings include a rare but unmistakable lizard and a deer with antlers immensely large in proportion to its tiny body. The colors are unusual, as Enrique reported. Half were painted in yellow ochre, heretofore a rare pigment, and the rest were done in a magenta cast of red. The paints have been dulled by exposure; here, as at La Puerta, the art has suffered more from poor protection than from a poor quality of stone.

The rock surface was also different from any we had seen painted: It is a hard, smooth-feeling stone as pitted as the moon, apparently from gas bubbles in the original melt. Enrique, having had much time to inspect the art, devoted himself to investigating the larger pits within easy reach. Shortly, he made a find. One, and then another, of these natural pockets contained accumulations of half-inch button-shaped pieces of the black substance we had seen exuding from crevices in so many caves. Here the find was especially odd. Since none of the stuff was present in its natural state, it must have been brought by human hands.

135

The Sierra de Guadalupe

By climbing up from El Barco we reached the trail linking Potrerito with the old mission community of Guadalupe that lies over the range to the east. That turned out to be an easier way, and we returned to camp without repeating the trials of the morning.

The next day we climbed, or I should say more accurately and gratefully, our mules climbed a thousand feet to a 5,500-foot pass. Then we came down Cuesta de la Palmita, the highest grade in the sierra, and very steep. When we arrived at its base, I measured the elevation at 3,000 feet. We, and certainly the animals, were so tired that we stripped off saddles and loads for a long midday rest. The exertions of both days so caught up with us that we went to sleep in the shadows of giant *datilillos*, the great yuccas of the region.

Sometime later we were aroused by shouts and the pounding of hooves. In a few moments we found ourselves in the center of a small cattle roundup. Half a dozen men were roping steers, tying them by the horns to trees, and then whooping off after others. In a few minutes they passed from sight, leaving us with a number of disgruntled bovines on very short ropes.

Our descent had taken us to the head of an unusually broad arroyo with the appropriate if uninspired name of *El Valle,* The Valley. Here, as at San Pedro, the Jesuits had cattle ranches and a visiting station at which monthly religious services were held. As I looked around I could see why the cattle industry had prospered and, no doubt, why it still endures. The arroyo, as mentioned, is very wide, unusually level, and carpeted with more low-growing herbs than I have ever seen elsewhere in the sierra.

As we began to pack up, the cowboys returned to collect their catch. They were curious about our unexpected presence. The men were not actual residents of El Valle, but were engaged in a seasonal roundup, an affair that drew them annually from the more populous eastern slopes. As a result, although we got little direction from them for our search of the moment, we did receive several leads to investigate during later parts of our trip. The cowboys were stopping at Rancho El Güéribo and invited us to join them.

The old trail down the arroyo lies along the east side of the broad wash. High mountains range around in a great horseshoe open at the south; on the skyline to the southeast is a large natural arch. As I rode along musing about El Valle, it occurred to me that the chapel ruins might be worth a visit and that we had not asked anyone about them. Despite my interest in mission literature, I knew of no modern account of anyone's visit to the place. Coco knew little except that it was behind us and across the arroyo. We backtracked and found it with no difficulty.

It was now late in the afternoon, too late for pictures, and we spent a scant hour at the site. Nevertheless, we saw enough to report that the remains of the chapel and compound of the visiting station at El Valle are extensive and, though fallen, are sufficiently undisturbed that they provide the best extant picture of a Jesuit visiting station and satellite ranch.

The original name of this visiting station was La Concepción, and it, too, must have been built in the 1730s under Everard Helen. We could believe, looking at the ruins, that it had been quite an establishment. The ruins are more extensive than those surviving at many of the missions themselves—certainly far larger and more complete than those at the mother mission of Guadalupe eight miles or so to the north. The ruins reveal that the central plaza was 108 feet square and that the chapel facing it from the north side was built of rock and adobe with an interior space measuring 18 by 60 feet. The remains of the walls, now about five feet high, are over three feet thick. They were built chiefly of large river cobbles weighing from 50 to 200 pounds. There had once been three windows equally spaced on each side. Facing the square from the west is a smaller building in better repair; it has three rooms, measures overall 13 by 60 feet, and its walls still stand to nearly their full height. We looked it over and judged it to be the priest's house. Facing the square from the east are the remains of a curious building 10 feet wide that extends along one side of the plaza for 80 feet. It was once divided entirely into small cubicles; we could only speculate that it might have been sleeping quarters for neophytes. Elsewhere, other piles of stone suggest fallen buildings. A ruined wall encircling the entire compound must once have kept cattle out.

That evening in camp we had a several visitors and finally succeeded in getting a clue about local rock art. Accordingly, we set out in the morning for a ranch located a mile or two downstream; its name, *El Cajón*—"The Box"—suggested that we should find it boxed, shut in by its surroundings. We followed what was obviously the old, broad mission road to the indicated turn and then went west to the edge of a bluff from which we looked down into a watercourse. The ranch occupies a scenic location on a shelf just above the waterway in a winding angostura carved from brown bedrock. The rancher greeted us in a friendly fashion and, upon discovering our purpose, led us down to the water, then across and up the steep rock of the other side. At a point a little higher than his home on the opposite side is a series of small cavelike depressions.

El Cajón del Valle   The paintings on the back walls and ceilings, both here and in another group a couple of hundred yards south, are chiefly of deer. Also visible are a few small monos of the fat striped sort, a bird, and an odd circular design. All are in about as bad a condition as such works can be and remain identifiable. The culprit responsible for their deterioration is a soft, friable rock; the caves have been heavily smoked as well.

The owner's next showplace is in a very different location and of a very different sort. We were led up the mountainside that towers above the little caves we had visited. After a lung-bursting climb, we came to a cave shelter with a well-protected ceiling panel decorated with several figures. However, from the first moment, I had eyes for but one striking image: a massive mono—brilliant red, vivid black, and beautifully preserved—that absolutely dominates the shelter.

Cyclops: a recurring theme

This lone, large, powerful human figure was painted on the ceiling of a very small, high, isolated cave—an unprecedented combination. His black face patch is rare as well, a decoration shared with only four other monos presently known.

El Cajón del Valle

The arresting aspects of the figure, besides its size and condition, are the presence of a vertical black rectangle in the "face" area and the absence of a left forearm; evidently, the limb was never completed. To the best of my knowledge, this unusual masklike facial infill can be found on only four other figures at four different sites. Two lie to the northwest in these same mountains at Los Monos de San Juan and El Carrizo; the others are found not in the Sierra de Guadalupe at all, but at Cueva del Ratón and Cuesta del Palmarito, over 60 miles to the north and in the heart of the San Francisco range. Food for thought indeed.

Eventually, my attention turned from the mighty mono and I became aware of other painted images: a faint ochre deer and a couple of small red monos—one of which has a delightful dancing mien and resembles a marionette.

A gallery such as the one high above El Cajón del Valle is rare. Minor painting sites in the greater Guadalupe area usually show only small figures, often of little artistic merit. Even the seasoned rock art hunter is amazed by an encounter with one of these isolated masterworks; a king hiding in a peasant's hut would not seem more out of place.

We resumed our journey by riding south from El Cajón until we reached the mouth of Arroyo del Valle proper and came to its junction with Arroyo del Rosarito. Here we turned east to visit Rancho Rosarito, located a short distance upstream. With that simple maneuver, I acquired a new role for several days. Two years before, I had come up into the sierra from Mulegé in the company of my old friend Guillermo Villavicencio. At that time, I was trying to visit historic and picturesque ranches, and Rosarito became the most remote prize. Of course, I had come by an entirely different route and now, joining a familiar trail, I found myself in an amusing situation. I was craning my neck to catch the first glimpse of an orange grove I knew would appear momentarily. For the next several days we would be traveling in country that I knew better than Coco. This resulted in a slight change of my status. I must have puffed up just a little, which was not lost on our legiti mate guides. I was welcomed to their ranks with elaborate deferences and frequent mock-solemn questions not unlike the sorts of things I had been known to ask of them.

Rosarito is an old ranch. I have found no record of its origin, but Elias Villavicencio, who was then eighty-eight years old, had lived there all his life and he was sure his grandfather had lived there as well. What is certain is that the place had been a magnificent orange ranch. Over 200 beautiful old trees, some 30 feet tall, still bore heavy crops of excellent Valencia-like fruit. In the old days, the oranges were hauled by burro to Mulegé, La Purísima, or wherever a demand dictated. Today, much of the fruit cannot be sold. Ferries now bring Sonora oranges to the peninsula and they are delivered to the markets for prices that make a three-day burro trip uneconomical.

The people of Rancho Rosarito were most attentive to our questions. They told us of at least three painted sites in the vicinity and one of Don Elias's sons volunteered to guide us. We walked to his first objective near the upper huerta, a second and larger fruit orchard a mile or so up the arroyo from the ranch house. He led us to a low, deep cave on the north side. This shelter obviously had long been used by the ranch people. For years it had been used to store crops; the floor was ankle deep in onion skins and stalks. Heavily blackened ceilings showed that it had also been the scene of many huge fires. Despite this, the ceiling near the mouth at the west end has several good survivals of paintings, one of which is the finest example of its rare kind that I know. The image of a large, unmistakable rattlesnake, rendered in red and outlined in white, appears to slither across an open space in the midst of a group of red and ochre deer. Heavily smoked figures of larger deer and some monos can be discerned elsewhere in the cave. The west wall, near the opening, retains a few figures more crudely executed. One, a mono with its body divided into six red-and ochre segments, has a clear indication of male genitalia.

139

The Sierra de Guadalupe

Survivors in a smoke-blackened cave

Few Great Mural sites have become the habitations or workplaces of present-day people. This cave is an exception; but despite its use as a shelter, a storehouse, and a smokehouse, several recognizable figures endure, including this rare painting of a rattlesnake.

El Rosarito

We finished the day with a fruitless trip up the arroyo to Rancho El Potrero. The tenants did not know the country well and were unable to tell us of any paintings. We returned at dusk to pass the night at Rosarito.

In the morning we left early to visit another promised site. Our path lay due north from the ranch house and involved climbing an extremely steep falda. After that, we were led on an intricate route through layers of cantil and eventually taken to a handsome slit cave that faces west and offers a view over the lower end of El Valle. Its elevation is over 3,000 feet, and we had climbed 1,000 feet from Rosarito.

The contents of the cave are different from any of the collections of paintings we had encountered to that point. Properly speaking, they could not be called Great Murals at all; the largest figures in the cave are less than two feet tall and most are nearer to one foot. The subjects are predominantly birds and indeterminable four-legged animals. We also found such exotica as a sunburst and a band of symbols in white suggesting written characters. Although I had seen dozens of figures in generally good condition, I returned to Rosarito in a state of disappointment. I had a sense that we had encountered a different people, or at least a different inspiration from that which produced Great Murals. I should emphasize that the scale of the works is not solely responsible for the poor impression: The figures do not seem to have been drawn with care; the degree of artistry seems low.

Our next objective required a short but very steep ride followed by a trying hike. High up amid the bluffs and peaks rising just north of the headwaters of Arroyo del Rosarito is a remarkably isolated cave—isolated even for a Great Mural site, among which considerable remoteness and difficulty of approach is more normal than not. The place is called *El Zotolar* because of its concentrated stands of *zotol,* a yuccalike plant growing to the stature of a small tree at elevations of 4,000 feet or more in most of the mid-peninsular sierras. Here, at a measured elevation of over 4,200 feet, hollowed out of a south-facing cliff, is a small, relatively deep cave with the double distinction of being the highest Great Mural site that I have ever seen, containing the least artistic Great Mural works that I have ever seen.

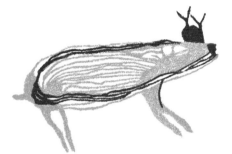

Seven figures—six deer and one mono—make up the collection. The predominant paint color is red, but there is also a striking display of a bright sulfur yellow that we would eventually encounter in relatively recent works at several sites. All the images look remarkably new and fresh and exhibit low levels of artistry. A deer, largely in this hue but with dashes of red, illustrates my points.

The mono at El Zotolar is puzzling. In another context it would qualify as a San Borjitas man, perhaps more ungainly than is typical of those stiff, bulbous creatures, but nevertheless having the proper form, longitudinal stripes, male genitalia, and even a characteristic impalement with arrows or spears. Yet this human representation is clearly in the same paint and style as the deer next to it. Could it be some decadent form of San Borjitas art? It may be recalled that few animals are found depicted at San Borjitas sites, and when they are found, these animals usually seem to be in another style. Are the misshapen images at El Zotolar related to San Borjitas somehow, or is the lone mono simply a copy of the apparently much older San Borjitas figures that El Zotolar's inexpert painter studied at another site? As with all other questions about the origin of Great Murals, the puzzle remains.

We returned to Rosarito and then rode down its arroyo to pass the night at El Rincón. We continued on to the beautiful Rancho Santo Domingo through one of the most scenic of all the sierra's arroyos, a complex watercourse twisting between high walls. Our one concern was time; the days were simply evaporating. We had now been gone over two weeks and had traversed only half of the Pacific side of the sierra. Our projection had been for a month's trip, but at the rate we were going it might take two or three extra weeks, and we realized that we would have to inform our families and get additional supplies.

141

The Sierra de Guadalupe

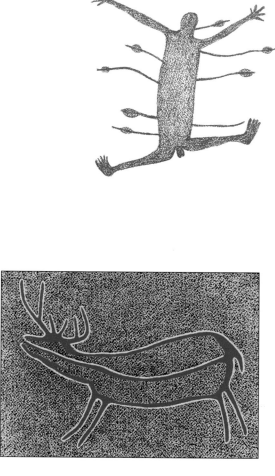

south, each subsequent rock art site presented us with subject matter, hues, treatment of areas within outlines, or other more difficult to define elements of style that we found increasingly foreign to the comparatively homogeneous artworks in the Sierra de San Francisco. Here at Los Venados, the break is total: Not one of the figures would seem at home in the northern sierra.

The subjects are commonplace enough—large and small deer, monos, and a bird or two. The omnipresent pinturitas depict strange little animals, possibly insects, and others too curious or eroded to identify. The most obviously new element is the method the artists used to fill in the areas within the outlines of the larger figures. These areas were never painted in solid colors; instead, they were decorated with internal patterns of red or red and white stripes. In some, these were given the form of crossed stripes or checkerboards, a technique we saw first at El Barco. A further strangeness is the frequent appearance of yellow chalk used for the original drawing. This would prove to be the only site where we saw a yellow material used this way.

The quality of the artistry is difficult to assess. On first impression, Los Venados seemed to be a place where very young artists had practiced. The monos are far more primitive than most of those we had examined. One agonized human figure, seven arrows protruding from its outline, was painted as if thrust violently into a pocket in the rock. Like the others, this tortured mono's proportions and attitude are most unlifelike. All the monos seemed to me to lack even the wooden charm of many San Borjitas figures.

The deer of this new school, however, have a real style to them. At first, I was merely curious because I was attracted to them and did not know why. I analyzed them. I grew accustomed to them. In time and through photographs, I have come to fancy them. I sense in them a vitality that I miss in many Great Murals; they show me a strong sense of design—an opinion no doubt influenced by my own positive response to crisp stripes and checks. Owing to the unevenness of the rock surface and the confusion of figures, I did not fully appreciate the most beautiful of the deer at Los Venados until I was home and able to analyze my photographs. Later at La Trinidad I saw what has become my favorite of the many deer in this homogeneous and recognizable style. As a token of my esteem, I refer to such figures hereinafter as "Trinidad deer."

We left Los Venados after an hour and a half of intensive study that left me with a growing desire to see what might happen next. Clearly, the Great Murals were evolving as we moved south.

We returned to the Casa Osuna where we sat around and talked at length. We were in no hurry because we could not go beyond Las Chivas that day. Not a drop of water can be found between Las Chivas and El Rincón Grande, a full day's ride, and the properly cautious Pancho Romero preferred not to make a dry camp. Osuna reminded us that we might find paintings in Arroyo del Pilo whose mouth we would pass en route. He had only heard of them but had a general idea of their location and offered some directions for finding them. Our map suggested that the

arroyo might be 10 miles long; our guide described it as little visited and virtually waterless. A search would require at least a day, plus a waterless night, and Romero would have none of it. Enrique and I discussed our limited options and decided to postpone the suggested detour. Finding a more willing guide might take days, and our trip was already a week behind schedule. The following day, we rode by the mouth of the painted arroyo with real regret—and that lost opportunity leads to a second digression in my story.

Events in the same area seven years later In 1980, Enrique Hambleton and I returned to pursue the leads we had not been able to follow up during our 1973 explorations. This time, we came into the sierra out of Arroyo de Mulegé by way of the old ranches of San Patricio and San Narciso. From a pass which is also the peninsular divide, we headed south-southwest up into the heights. There we found ourselves on the huge 3,000-foot-high mesa which, in place of the more usual peaks, forms the backbone of the south-central part of the Guadalupe range. We passed Rancho Zacatecas and, continuing on the same bearing, came to Arroyo de Nombre de María. Now we were about five miles east of the painted cave of Los Venados, discussed above, and Antonio Osuna's ranch. When we had ridden a mile downstream, we came to the first objective of this trip, Rancho La Vinorama, near which, we had heard, is a painted site.

La Vinorama The paintings at La Vinorama are located in a cave overhang 50 feet above the bed of the watercourse, and a couple of hundred yards from Rancho

149

La Vinorama. The unmolested condition of these readily accessible paintings stands as a tribute to the Aguilar family who have occupied and worked the ranch for years. Too many sites thus exposed show evidence of gunshots, scratchings, bonfires, and other acts of careless vandalism.

The natural contours of the shelter's ceiling divide it into two rather discrete surfaces, each of which has been heavily painted with images of Trinidad deer. These panels are very colorful because of their vivid paint and excellent preservation, but many individual figures are indistinct in the welter of overpainting. Some are difficult to trace in their entirety and virtually all are marred by the confusion of outline and infill paints. Despite this, several deer heads and their antlers are very apparent, and are fine examples of the best Trinidad style. A much rarer Trinidad borrego, in white outline only, sports a great set of horns that add spice to this collection. Rarer still, and astonishing in this area and among these works, is a large, handsome borrego executed in the purest San Francisco style—except for its deep ochre pigment, a rarity among all Great Mural paintings.

When we finished photographing the cave at La Vinorama, Señor Aguilar volunteered to take us a mile or two north to another painted cave. The site proved to be a rather open, low respaldo at a place called Los Toros. The material that forms the panel bearing the paintings is a rough conglomerate with a soft matrix. At one time this panel had been heavily painted with many handsome or at least interesting images. Now most are reduced to parts, and those quite degraded. Not surprisingly, the most common subject is deer in the style of Los Venados and La Trinidad. However, one surviving figure is eye-catching and different: a mono with a rectangular head, rectangular body, and sticklike lines to represent neck, arms, and legs. As will be told shortly, we had earlier found a better mono of this "school" at Loma Alta.

The next objective of our 1980 exploration was a rock art site in Arroyo del Pilo, the painted place that Antonio Osuna had suggested during our visit to his ranch in 1973. Accordingly, we rode 8 or 9 miles down Arroyo de Nombre de María until we came to Rancho El Reparito where we turned east into the broad opening of El Pilo. As I mentioned when describing how we bypassed this arroyo in 1973, El Pilo has no springs and no important tinajas. Therefore, it has had no modern occupancy except for herders rounding up stray cattle or goats. Not many know the area and fewer still know its paintings, but, when we returned, we were fortunate to encounter Melitón Aguilar, the owner of many cattle in the area. He was kind enough to guide my party to a remarkable painting site near a place he called La Gallina, about two-thirds of the way up the arroyo.

El Pilo The painted cave of El Pilo, like so many others, is almost invisible from the watercourse by which it is approached. Only a person who has had to seek the cattle that take shelter in caves would ever have been likely to stumble onto the place. This cave is a long, low slit on the north wall of the arroyo and not more

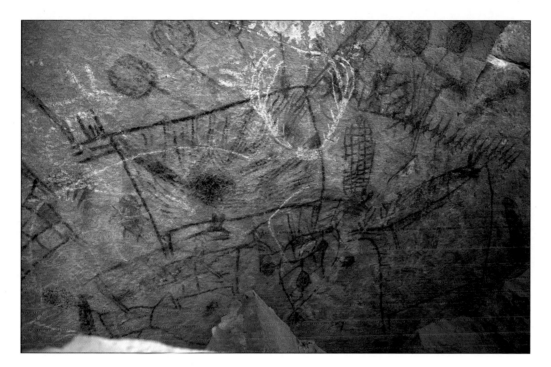

El Pilo

El Pilo is a transitional site on the southern perimeter of mid-Guadalupe styles. It shows a grand, rather eclectic deer in white outline, several Trinidad-style deer in black, and a few thoroughly unique deer depicted as large red rectangles, each with a tiny head, legs, and tail located at the appropriate corners. Another photograph of this beautiful rock shelter appears as the frontispiece of this work.

than 70 feet above the wash. The hard, smooth ceiling bears most of the painted work, although several figures, including a fine black Trinidad deer, survive on the much softer back wall. Other Trinidad deer, some black and some white, may be found on the ceiling, but they are difficult to appreciate or even to notice upon first inspection because of the radical and unexpected nature of other, more prominent figures.

El Pilo is the ideal site to describe as a transition from the school of Trinidad deer to that of the enigmatic abstractions found in this area and to the south. On its ceiling are located 10 or more large and small deer, each with its body depicted as a rectangle, and tiny head, tail, and legs neatly formed at the corners of the rectangular body. Most of these boxlike deer were delineated in red paint, but one appears in black and another in white. No words can describe the degree to which these representations break with the naturalistic Great Mural tradition. A small percentage of figures found in all parts of the Great Mural area are bizarre or unrecognizable, but most of those are either careless daubs or badly defaced. At El Pilo, neither of these conditions pertains. The rectangular deer are in splendid repair, were carefully painted, and could be said to have anticipated elements of 20th century Western art. All around and among the unique deer, there are other, lesser novelties like two strings of over 20 tiny fish, each eight or nine inches high, head up, tail down, and all as close together as strung beads. Also noteworthy are some interesting petroglyphs worked into relatively soft, white, rock fragments

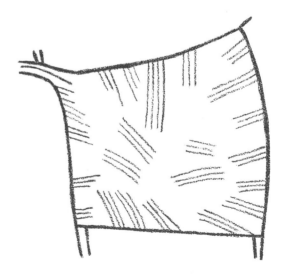

151

The Sierra de Guadalupe

strewn about the cave. One of these depicts a really handsome Trinidad-like deer with elegant antlers, while others decorate the flat top of a pedestal-like rock (see frontispiece, page vi).

We left El Pilo and returned to Arroyo de Nombre de María which we crossed in a northerly direction. We then headed northwest following a trail that is actually the local section of the peninsular camino real, or main road, of mission days, part of the route used by soldiers, padres, couriers, and packtrains going between Misión de la Purísima and Misión de Guadalupe. The section we were on goes to Cuesta de los Angeles by way of Rancho San Martín, but before reaching the ranch it crosses Arroyo de Rancho Nuevo, today unoccupied and rarely visited because modern trails follow different routes. We had been told of paintings in this gorge and we soon found a painted respaldo on the west wall of the arroyo. The immediate vicinity is called El Dipugón.

El Dipugón   I compare this rock shelter to La Vinorama which it resembles in many ways, including its form and the location and preservation of its art. It has a much larger ceiling than La Vinorama, more paintings, and despite much over-painting, less confusion in its art. Trinidad deer dominate the colorful exhibition at El Dipugón, but one large black borrego attracts attention because images of this animal are relatively rare in the entire Guadalupe range. El Dipugón also shows numerous red fish in the Trinidad style. Other fish, rendered in an unusual yellow pigment, are conspicuous at the east end of the painted ceiling and on the back wall. Two Trinidad deer, one red and one white, are notable for their great size and their odd relationship. They are painted in outline only, one over the other, with a 180-degree difference in orientation. If one is viewed as standing normally, the other appears to lie on its back with legs thrust stiffly into the air. Examples of this sort of confusion occur at sites like San Borjitas and El Dipugón where painting is on a ceiling rather than a wall, because each artist had a free hand in defining "up" and "down."

➤   ➤   ➤

The exploration of 1973 resumed   Once again, I return to our 1973 trip at the point where we passed the mouth of Arroyo del Pilo but did not enter. On that occasion, Pancho Romero, Ramón Arce, Coco Villavicencio, Enrique Hambleton,

Here, as at San Borjitas, artists could work in any direction they chose; invert this book to see the reversal of the two prominent images of deer. This ceiling panel is also notable for its heavy overpainting and excellent state of preservation. It exemplifies the many mid-Guadalupe sites that show few humans and are dominated by the images of Trinidad deer.

El Dipugón

and I rode down the arroyo until we came to the mouth of Cañada de la Purísima. We then turned to the southeast and ascended the cañada's steep course. We took our midday break at the *portezuelo,* the top of the pass leading to the next water-course, and then started down the long, direct arroyo leading to El Rincón Grande and beyond. Pancho Romero took his leave at the pass, assuring us that we had no further need for a guide. Off he went, intent on getting all the way back to his home in El Tule that night.

In late afternoon, we came to the broken edge of a prominent lava flow, a place where arroyo waters had undermined the basalt and created an abrupt palisade. Petroglyphs are scattered along this enticing slate of clean hard rock. We spotted images of animals and fish as we rode along.

We arrived at El Rincón Grande in late afternoon but were told we would find better water and fodder near the village of San José — once San José de Piadané, a visiting station of Misión de la Purísima. We rode on until dusk and camped near a stream of running water half a mile north of San José.

Isaias Mayoral

After we prepared our beds and ate dinner, Enrique and I talked over our next steps. My plan from the start had been to get to this place and then turn up Arroyo de Guajademí and head north toward Mulegé. That would require a new guide, since we would not be back in territory familiar to Coco until we were several miles north of Mulegé. We had also heard rumors in the sierra about paintings in the environs of San José and nearby Paso Hondo, and we agreed that it would never do to leave without investigating further. The more we talked, the more desirable it seemed to visit the village that night, since it would be impossible to anticipate when someone we needed might or might not be in. We took our flashlights and headed along an uncertain path.

At first we had no luck at all. We were told that the people who might guide us up Guajademí were all away for a day or more. Then, just as we were about to leave, a man finally comprehended my statement that I had ridden through six years before. He asked me if I had not ridden with Isaias Mayoral. When I told him I had, he informed me that Mayoral was visiting in a house down the street. In short order we were talking with a surprised Isaias, and he proved to be useful indeed: He knew a painted cave called Loma Alta in the mountains west of Paso Hondo. Moreover, he had access to a truck and could take us to see the place the following day. That was good news. Our animals certainly could use a day of rest, their first since our daylong hike to El Barco, two weeks earlier. We went back to camp and passed out.

In mid-morning, Isaias came and honked. We took our hiking necessities and left Coco and Ramón to rest, feed the animals, and, if possible, arrange for a guide. The ride to Paso Hondo was brief. We drove through the town to a point a mile or so beyond. There was no side road, so we simply parked and walked over a ridge, down a gorge of soft crumbling rock, and into a little valley containing a ranch. Crossing that, we started up a steep path and labored away, short-winded, in near-silence until we came out on a mesa sloping up to the mountains on the west. Then we hiked for an hour more up a steeper and steeper grade until we were looking up a final cañada at a large and obvious cave. That last stretch was the most trying of all, and it was a relief when we got into the shady chamber and looked around.

"Curiouser and curiouser." Alice's memorable phrase was the first thing that popped into my mind. The Great Murals were changing so rapidly now that they were difficult to recognize. The transformation was perfectly exemplified by an odd checkerboard figure made up of rectangles painted alternately pink and black. At first I had little notion as to what it might represent. Then, allowing for the strangeness and the vagueness of the other figures, I realized it might be a mono. Once seen that way, it became more obvious. The head is a block, the body is another. Neck, arms, and legs were reduced by the artist to simple lines. Nevertheless, this abstract pattern of rectangles stood before me as a man—a man with his arms raised in the classic salute of the Painters.

The most southern and abstract of the Great Murals

This pattern of rectangles and a similar one in yellow and black nearby are abstract representations of the human figure. So far, attempts to locate the origin of this style outside the Great Mural area have failed, but our searches inside the area revealed a growing emphasis on less realistic outlines and checkerboard infills as we moved south. At present, the trail ends at Loma Alta.

Loma Alta

A nearby painting initially defied literal translation altogether. We saw it as an , eye-catching and apparently abstract beehive form mounted, as it were, on a short pedestal. The hive is outlined in a pale yellow and filled in with vertical stripes, alternately black and yellow. Although we realized it was a misnomer, we dubbed it "the candelabra." Months later, while studying a photograph of this puzzling work, I stumbled onto its true identity. A large red deer had been rather sloppily painted just beneath it, obviously at a later period. In the photo, I found that I could see an older painting that was partially covered by the image of the red deer, a tall rectangular form divided into black and yellow blocks. Our "candelabra" is its head, and the whole figure can now be seen as a mono of the same abstract school as its more visible pink and black neighbor. Other figures are more abstract, no more than deliberate arrangements of lines. An amusing cartoon of a deer pierced by an oversized arrow is instantly recognizable, but drawings of several small animals are so generalized that they might equally well represent deer, rabbits, or coyotes.

The rock at Loma Alta is very hard — the surfaces show no sloughing whatsoever. Paintings like the abstract monos composed of rectangles are probably very old. Since they are somewhat faded in appearance, it is probable that the loss of color was due entirely to the weathering of the paint, a most unusual circumstance in a land where rock is usually the culprit.

155

The Sierra de Guadalupe

An association and a question popped into my head at Loma Alta. Paintings found in the Loreto region 60 miles south are almost entirely nonrepresentational. Were we seeing a gradual transformation of Great Mural forms into those of the smaller polychrome abstractions found in the south? Obviously more fieldwork was needed.

No sooner had we returned to San José than we literally bumped into Federico Arce Meza from El Rincón Grande, a man with whom my party had passed a night six years before. As soon as we mentioned rock art, he was eager to contribute. He said we must return to El Rincón Grande, where he would show us many figures painted and engraved on the cantil no more than 10 minutes' walk from his house. Off we went.

The painted site at El Rincón Grande turned out to be less exciting than Señora Arce's excellent coffee, which followed. The place is a wall of basalt, a continuation of the one on which we had noticed the petroglyphs on our ride down the arroyo. In various overhung locations we found small monos, a couple of nice turtles, a few simplistic fish, and a scattering of petroglyphs. Of the latter, one caught my eye sufficiently to record: two deer facing each other almost nose to nose, the curves of their necks and forelegs like two arcs of the same ellipse.

Later, after reviewing all I could learn about painting in this area, I decided that this modest little site is probably Diguet's number 17, "a cliff with paintings near Rancho San Jose, in Arroyo de Guajademí."

Back at our camp, all was in order and a reasonable arrangement had been made for the following day. Ramón had news of paintings at a place called Agua Puerca an hour or so out on our route, and of others near a ranch called Jauja, high in the sierra. A man named Esteban Romero was finishing his visit to town and would return to that region tomorrow. He would guide us to the first of the mountain ranches where presumably we could make other arrangements. Romero proved in practice to be the poorest guide of that or any trip. He also had the shortest tenure. We had been on the trail no more than an hour when we were joined by others headed into the sierra. A short while later I asked Romero if we were not near Agua Puerca. He told me we had passed it. Why had we passed it? Because, he said, it was not worth the stopping—there was nothing to see. I was not happy to hear that; we had discussed the purpose of our trip with the man at length. I stopped the caravan and said we were going back for a look. Esteban Romero continued with the other mountaineers. He had decided to go home, he said, and not to be a guide. They rode north as we turned around.

Agua Puerca was definitely worth the stop. The cave is well up the east wall of the canyon and clearly visible from the trail. We crossed the very broad arroyo on our animals, tethered them under trees, and climbed up yet another steep falda. The cave is large, complex in form, and has been heavily painted but, as with so many other sites, a large amount of the painted rock surface has deteriorated. Despite that, a few interesting figures remain. The most arresting, a vertically striped

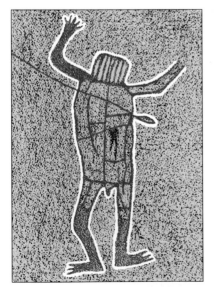

mono, looks as if it might have been stolen from the gallery at Boca de las Piedras, 24 airline miles to the north.

Agua Puerca also offers small paintings of birds and a yellow deer. While Enrique and I took photographs, Ramón was looking around the environs. He soon reported a find, a slit cave at a slightly lower level and just to the west. The cave is so low that we literally had to crawl under its shelflike roof and then lie on our backs to see the work. Once again Ramón found negative handprints, and this time there were many of them. The two most noteworthy handprints form a pair, thumb to thumb, one red, one white. Under a ledge, we found many pinturitas in the finest strokes we were ever to see. These elegant line paintings are of deer as well as other abstract or symbolic subjects. Perhaps most interesting was finding many four- to six-inch splints of pitahaya wood pushed into cracks in the rock. We were puzzled. Why had they been placed there?

We started up the great arroyo once more. Now we had a problem: It was not likely that we would get lost in that avenue-like wash, but it was also not certain that we would recognize the cuesta that would take us to Jauja, nor that we could follow the correct trail even if we got up the proper cuesta. Enrique and I kicked it around. Coco was gloomy. He seemed to worry about everything now that we were in country about which he knew nothing. Ramón, on the other hand, was cheerful and unconcerned. What was the worst that could happen? We could wind up on a trail to the wrong ranch. Perhaps they would have paintings of their own. Why not have an adventure, we decided. We rode on, knowing nothing but using binoculars on every respaldo and cantil we passed.

The Guajademí trail is ancient. It is the natural route between important food-gathering areas on opposite sides of the sierra and, therefore, a path alongside which we could expect to find art. Padre Francisco María Piccolo learned of this route shortly after he came to Misión de Santa Rosalía de Mulegé. In 1712, using Indian guides, he and a squad of soldiers came up out of Arroyo de Mulegé and entered the head of Arroyo de Guajademí. They then followed the arroyo to the Pacific. The ultimate result of that exploration was the founding of Misión de la Purísima, while Guajademí remained the road connecting the two missions. After my long association with El Camino Real, I was thrilled to experience another of its major links. Moreover, we would be taking a beautiful avenue into a remote and little-visited corner of the sierra. Come what might, I had a good feeling as we rode north.

As sunset shone in the sky far above our path in the shady depths, we came to a second great turn in the canyon a short distance beyond a place called Agua Honda. Here, we believed, would be the cuesta to Jauja. The suspense ended quickly; as we drew near the bend, the scar of the cuesta could be seen clearly as it snaked up a steep falda ahead of us. We camped on the ancón exactly at the foot of the cuesta. A few hundred feet up the hill to the east, we could see a cave. A mile

Different art forms share space in mid-peninsular caves

Layers of soft tuffs were responsible for the primary erosion that formed many painted caves. As this soft layer deteriorated, the rock above lost support and fell in scallop-shaped chunks, exposing the surfaces that would be used by the Painters. As a result, the tuff layer was found low in caves and became the favored medium for carvings, engravings, and drillings. All are common, but this is the most elaborate drilling site thus far reported.

Agua Honda

157

The Sierra de Guadalupe

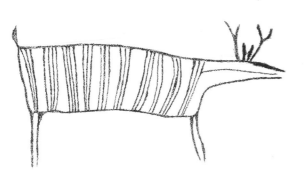

or less to the south, we had seen another, large and inviting. A storekeeper in San José had told us of paintings in the former. No one mentioned the other. We were always in a quandary in these situations. Was the large one ignored because it was known to be unpainted? Was the cave near us known to contain paintings simply because it is close to the trail and easy to investigate? It was so late that, for the moment, we chose the closer one.

We found crude paintings defaced by smoke and erosion. However, one stood out as a type, a huge deer over 10 feet long engraved deeply into the soft rock of the cave wall. After the outline was incised, the groove received a heavy coat of white paint. My photograph of this deer, taken in deep shade, has too little contrast to reproduce, but there is more to the story. Several years later, my friend Del Cover visited the area in his own search for rock art. About four miles south of the place where we found the engraved deer, he was directed to a small cave containing a painted deer in excellent condition. His photo shows that it is remarkably similar in outline and antlers to the incised deer we had found on the cuesta.

As we made our way down to camp, we arrived at the foot of the respaldo that contains the cave we had just visited. At its base is a layer of soft white tuff. The medium invites engravings, and the opportunity had been seized. The surface is heavily marked with a myriad of drillings: holes about half an inch in diameter and two to three inches deep are arranged into lines, loops, rows, crosses, boxes, and apparently random patterns. The pale gray panel also includes deeply carved petroglyphs of fish, vulva symbols, and parallel lines.

Since we had no water for the animals, we gave up the idea of taking time to visit the large cave. We climbed the cuesta to Jauja instead. At the top, we learned from my altimeter that our climb had been 1,500 feet and I had grateful thoughts about my uncomplaining mule. To the southeast, we had a magnificent view of the Sierra de la Giganta, dominated by a succession of massive peaks. Then our trail headed off to the northeast across a rolling mesa dotted with blue-gray *palo fierro* and leafless *palo brea,* two of the peninsula's many leguminous trees. In less than an hour we arrived at a ranch and stopped for directions. The place was called Tajo Viejo, no one knew of any paintings, and Jauja was to be found two or three hours farther on the same trail. We rode on. In half an hour or so we came over a rise and rode down to another ranch with a large water catchment. A woman told us the place was El Sapo. She knew of no paintings, but she pointed northeast and assured us that we were en route for Jauja. We skirted a deep cañada and after two more hours spotted a ranch in the midst of a large and level tableland. We rode up to it — Jauja.

The tenant rancher was Juan Mayoral Higuera. With him were two of his brothers and their families. They made us welcome, and after we broke down our things, we were seated in the kitchen. Juan Mayoral understood our quest with little explanation. Another Norteamericano, Eric Ritter, had come up from Mulegé the previous year and he, too, had wanted to see rock art sites. As for the sites themselves, well, what could he say about them? They displayed the same pictures that the Indians always made, neither more nor less. How large are they? Well, some are larger than others and all are *regular,* neither larger nor smaller than one might encounter elsewhere. All the Mayorales had an indirect and curiously lilting manner of speech, and, as our host went on with his entirely circular discourse on Indian art, I felt as though he would mesmerize us all, and that we might be turned to stones like those littering the Mesa de Jauja. Finally, coffee was produced. I looked at my watch and found that we had been sitting for almost an hour.

A boy came by with a yoke over his shoulders from which two five-gallon tins were suspended. Juan and his brothers rose languidly and found other containers. Come, we were told, it is time to go to the tinaja. We trooped off to the west along a well-beaten trail. In ten minutes we came to a drop-off at the very head of a cañada, a falls where, after seasonal rains, water from the mesa flows over into a gorge that would carry it 1,000 feet to the bed of the arroyo below. A steep trail had been worked into the rock south of the falls, and we picked our way down 100 feet to a murky tinaja that provided the drinking water for the ranch. The boy began to fill his cans while Juan and his brother motioned us onward. We climbed up to a cave at the base of the then-dry *salto,* or seasonal falls, and our host pointed to a spot above us on the rough overhang.

The rock is hard and smooth and has fractured into a maze of separate facets. Two of these are painted in a faded red. The subjects consist solely of several fish, a bird, and a tiny deer. Tears came to my eyes as I stood and looked. Somehow, I was not prepared; I was caught off guard by the beauty of the work. The group of fish on the lower rock face seems to move in water, such is the artistry. From stains running down the entire rock face, it was clear that after a rain, water washes directly over the fish and they would literally appear to be swimming in the stream. The tinaja and its little gorge bear the sad name "San Pedro Avíncolo"—a rustic version of *San Pedro Avinculado,* Saint Peter in Chains. I found myself wishing that the name commemorated that saint's association with fish rather than bondage.

I finally tore myself away. All the water cans had been filled, so we filed out. I looked back for a last time at the salto and its precious burden. It had a small collection, that gallery, but it was worth every step that brought us there.

Above the falls, a maze of petroglyphs is scattered about on large rocks. The subjects are animals and birds, and one especially caught my eye. On a large, rounded boulder a series of dainty deer prints had been engraved as if the animal had made them by walking across. All the petroglyphs look old because they are heavily patinated.

Later, another of the brothers took us on a long walk to the east across the stone-paved mesa. He began to point to metates and petroglyphs and soon we realized that we were seeing hundreds, which means that the greater area contains thousands. There is no apparent end to them; there are even petroglyphs on metates.

159

The Sierra de Guadalupe

Such legions of grindstones strongly suggested a sizable crop of seed to grind. The only candidate appeared to be *palo fierro,* a legume that does produce a heavy crop of seed-bearing pods.

We saw several examples of Baja California's rarest metate, those formed front, back, and edges into handsome stone dishes of rectangular outline. All that we saw were made of *tezontle,* a relatively easily worked type of scoria or vesicular basalt, and all were broken. Why had all of that type been broken? Could that have been a tradition? Señor Mayoral was amused at the question. He knew nothing of Indian traditions but he had his own answer to the puzzle: Such artifacts are handsome and useful, so whenever ranch people find them, they take them home to use. In time, they wear out. End of theory.

It was cold out on that windswept mesa. When I went to bed I pulled the flap of my sleeping bag over my face and shut out the chill and the stars as well. Sometime in the night I waked to the blare of a radio. I peeked out. Stars twinkled but there was no glimmer of dawn. My watch broke the unpleasant news: 4 A.M. In a few minutes pots and pans rattled, fires crackled, and I could hear the singsong of Mayoral speech. Presently, people began to pass me going to the corral with buckets for the morning milking. A girl passed, trailing the aroma of coffee.

"Coffee?" I asked.

"Come, I have a cup for you."

I crawled out and got my coat and boots. The wind had died, the stars were just beginning to dim, and I could see a beautiful profile of peaks etched faintly against the eastern sky. The coffee was beautiful also but it chilled quickly. There was chatter and laughter as everyone worked away with practiced hands and 20-gallon washboilers filled with milk. The coffee girl sang sweetly about love, but of what, I could not tell.

"What do you love?" I asked.

"I love to be warm."

In its time the sky lightened and the stars went out. The work at the corral was done and we went in for breakfast. Cheese-making was begun, and we who had no part in it feared that we might get stalled again in the slow rhythm of Mayoral ways. Tactful questions were put and by mid-morning we actually managed to extricate Juan and get away. Despite our impatience at times, we had been most fortunate to happen upon these helpful people when we did. In a few weeks the water of the *tajo,* an artificial catchment at a low spot on the mesa, would dry up, and then the herd of cattle and the people would leave.

We rode west down a 1,000-foot grade and entered a cañada just before it opens into Arroyo de Guajademí. During much of our descent we could see a large respaldo-cave on the other side of the cañada. The place is called El Zapote after a ranch just downstream. We crossed the cañada and pulled our animals up into the shade of trees near the cave.

The respaldo and the cave had once been heavily painted. The walls are speckled with vestiges of pigment, but not a single painted figure can be discerned. The villains, as so often is the case, are exposure and a soft, crumbly type of volcanic agglomerate. Nevertheless, remarkable works survive. Six figures of deer on the order of six to eight feet in length had been engraved into the rock surface in exactly the fashion we saw at the foot of the cuesta near Agua Honda. White, red, and yellow paints had been applied thickly to these recessed outlines—as we learned by inspecting some patches that remain in the carved grooves. All of the figures seemed rather awkward and graceless to me, but the technique is fascinating as a variation within the Great Mural region.

Shortly after our arrival we made an important discovery. In the cave at the east end of the respaldo, the numerous rock crevices have many pitahaya wood splints jammed forcibly into them. These continue up to the remarkable height of at least 18 feet. Furthermore, unlike those we had seen at Agua Puerca, each of these splints has been burned down until it is flush with the rock. This explained the unburned splints at Agua Puerca and gave us a sense of what might have been a beautiful ceremony in which these were tapers lighted for night vigils or religious services. This possible insight heightened my sense of empathy with the mysterious and long gone Painters.

Mayoral took us across the caja of the great arroyo. We rode for perhaps half an hour and turned west to approach rich pink rock formations. Passing the first of these, we rode up to the middle of the group and dismounted. Our guide called the place Cueva Colorada. He pushed a few branches aside and led us through the rocks to a little natural courtyard in the center of the area. We found ourselves facing a low cave and, on its bulging roof, a choice piece of art.

Using the rock engraving technique we had just observed at El Zapote, an artist here had created a pair of deer facing each other with their noses touching. The pose is so identical to the petroglyph described at El Rincón Grande that I am forced to conclude that one is a copy of the other. Oddly enough, they do not appear to be from the same hand; the work at Cueva Colorada has much surer lines, better proportions, and a sense of style quite missing at El Rincón Grande.

A great deal of the beauty of this work is derived from the artist's use of the rock form on which he did his engraving. The inspiration is reminiscent of Altamira, the famous Spanish Palaeolithic site, where rounded protuberances of the cave ceiling were painted and used to advantage as the forms of bison. Here at Cueva Colorada the effect is subtler. The artist designed the group to fit onto an oval-shaped rock convexity and also contrived to repeat the elliptic form of the rock in the lines of the lower front parts of the mirror-image deer. The result is a very sophisticated, cameo-like bas-relief.

A few other figures, including a fish and some smaller deer, were engraved in the same fashion but have not survived well in the soft rock. After I photographed everything, I lingered to look at the kissing deer. Once again I was held by a

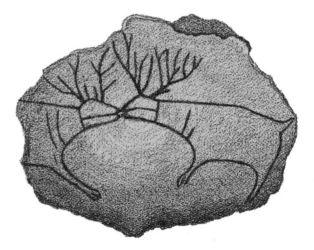

161

The Sierra de Guadalupe

sense of art transcending mere antiquarian or ethnological interests — truly, *ars gratia artis*.

We rode north once more and soon entered a narrows where the once wideset walls of the arroyo now closed in. In that place was Rancho Guajademí, a property also tended by *la familia* Mayoral. We rode into a huerta and dropped the saddles and loads to give the animals a rest. The orchard cried out for water. I hated to see large orange trees wilting, but Mayoral seemed as unconcerned about this as all else. "In its time," his manner seemed to say. We picked ripe oranges and harvested fresh mint for tea in the nights ahead.

After farewells we parted from Juan Mayoral and headed north. Our trail was steep but, in a mile or so, it took us to the prize vista of the trip. We quitted the last slope of Guajademí and, at the pass, a few steps put us on the brink of the gigantic amphitheater that is Arroyo de Mulegé. In front of us was a yawning, 2,000-foot drop-off and beyond that, a sweeping view of the shoreline, 25 miles away, and then the Gulf and its islands. Unfortunately, we had little time to enjoy the scene. It was growing late and the wind was howling. We scarcely wanted to get caught at that 2,800-foot pass and there is no stopping place on the dizzying cuesta we must descend. We moved, and although the entire descent is extremely lovely, we could not dawdle anywhere along the way. By dark we were camped just south of Rancho El Potrero, at the edge of the broad plain of Arroyo de Mulegé.

A mile or so to the east of us, a high hill — or small mountain — had attracted our attention. In the morning a man from El Potrero told us it harbored a fine collection of paintings, and he was good enough to cart Enrique and me over for a quick look. We stopped first at Rancho Horconcitos, nestled on the east side of the hill, and the rancher there joined us for such an early stroll that we reached the painted respaldo before the first rays of the rising sun.

Nothing could have better reinforced our sense of having quit Guajademí and, indeed, the sierra itself. Here we found pinturitas, or small paintings, mostly of fish and turtles, all done in the same red paint, and all in an excellent state of preservation. Remarkably, there is no overpainting although the rock face is crowded with figures. The artwork did not remind me of anything we had seen in the sierra; it did remind me of numerous pinturitas that I had seen around the nearby Bahía de la Concepción.

La Trinidad   On my list of hints and clues, I had several entries for Rancho La Trinidad. Leon Diguet had made it #13 on his list: "Paintings in a cañada near the Rancho La Trinidad, about 12 leagues from Mulegé." When we got back to camp and loaded up, I headed our little caravan due west to investigate the reports. The ride was simplicity itself over the levelest of level ground. The tenant family was at home in the ranch house, and we found them *simpáticos* in the extreme. The man interested himself in our quest and volunteered to take us for a look at the painted place.

A quarter-mile walk took us to the mouth of an unusually attractive cajón, a perfect miniature of some of the great sierra watercourses. Floor and walls alike are bedrock, a lovely pink stone that shines in the sun and glows in the shade. Scattered along the narrow corridor are huge blocks of the same material fallen from the vertical walls. It crossed my mind, as we walked along, that this place should be set aside, preserved as a park for all time. It also occurred to me that the art was unlikely to live up to its surroundings.

We came to a place where the little canyon is choked with house-sized boulders. Our guide took us up to the right out of the caja proper and into the remains of a cave whose roof had fallen. A single large rock face on the south side bears all the art of La Trinidad. My first impression was that I was standing in front of an aboriginal graffiti wall, a disordered array of drawings in several styles, sizes, and paints. Certain oddities add to the confusion. Several medium-sized deer are stiffly painted in stark white and completely upside down. Here and there are groups of handprints, also white. Some recent graffiti had been scrawled in charcoal across the lower parts. But the untidy and disorganized effect of the whole belies the charm of the parts. That wall bears several miniature masterpieces, and we spent a delightful time sorting them out and enjoying them.

A single figure serves as a prototype: the Trinidad Deer

For me, this simple panel is one of the most beautiful and affecting of all the Painters' creations. Vermilion paint consorts admirably with the rich rock of the canyon wall; the flaming colors contrast strangely with the calm and grace of the stately checkerboard deer accompanied by two fawns. The theme must have been very familiar to the artist, probably the same individual who created the impressive buck at Los Venados.

La Trinidad

163

The Sierra de Guadalupe

If one figure or group could be said to dominate, it is a large checkerboard deer high on the central part of the wall. This graceful, antlered form, rendered in a beautiful orange-red, is accompanied by three fawns created by the same hand. All move with unhurried purpose from right to left across the canvas. Something other than its beauty compelled me to make repeated inspections of the single large figure, the graceful checkerboard deer. It looked familiar, but none of us could place it. Later, at home, I found the answer while looking through my photographs. A large deer at Los Venados, 13 miles to the south, resembles this one in every line and nuance.

Several other graceful images in the same paint, and apparently from the same hand, appear below the enchanting group of deer: to the right a delicate fawn, to the left some extraordinary fish. The largest of the fish looks like a corvina and is unusual on several counts. First, the image of this fish, like those at San Pedro Avíncolo, was not placed with head up and tail down in the manner of most others in the Great Mural area. Second, it was drawn with an internal pattern suspiciously like bones; it presents an x-ray vision of a fish. And last, it was transfixed by a nicely fletched arrow, a common enough device with four-legged animals or monos, but quite rare with fish.

Besides those highlights, the wall at La Trinidad displays a strangely skeletal mono and perhaps a dozen smaller figures — fish, deer, monos, and a rabbit — drawn with various degrees of artistry in red, white, and black paint.

During my preoccupation, Enrique, who has a penchant for examining every crevice, came up with evidence that the entire cave had once been painted. By getting down on stomach or knees he inspected the rock pile that had resulted from the fall of material from other walls and the ceiling. He pointed out parts of other paintings visible in the rubble. I looked back at the surviving wall, not sure whether to be elated at its survival or sad at so great a loss.

Across the way is another cave, a deep cave, looking within like an amphora lying on its side. But its lovely walls of warm pink rock bear no paintings; the inner surface has sloughed off in scales. We noticed an interesting phenomenon there and elsewhere in the cajón. Deposits of a pure white solid appear wherever water has percolated through the rock above and evaporated as it seeped out. It seems likely that this was the pigment used in the unusually large number of white paintings in the vicinity.

After returning to the ranch, we transferred our operation to a spot just below Rancho San Patricio, a scant mile away in the same cañón. This was not quite as simple as it sounds. La Trinidad is so choked with fallen rock that there is no passage for loaded animals, and we had to go by a steep roundabout to the north. Nevertheless, by dark we found ourselves back in the same sort of lovely surroundings. The tenant at San Patricio came down to our camp to offer his help. He was a young man and he professed to know the whereabouts of several painted sites in the area. He confirmed what we had heard at La Trinidad: There were paintings here and they were almost under our noses. It was dark, but we were curious. We all had flashlights and he was willing to guide, so we set off, stepping with care to avoid the spines and rocks of an uncertain trail.

The cajón, at just that point, makes a spectacular hairpin turn that we avoided by climbing a ridge. We crossed the caja and climbed up to a low cave. It was a strange sensation, something entirely new, to be poking around a painted cave at night. As our flashlights scanned the rough ceiling and walls, painted figures seemed to leap when struck by the beam. The first thing I found was a small ceiling panel with several dazzlingly white handprints. However, we soon tired of the novelty and picked our way back to bed.

The morning light conveyed a better picture of the place but, unlike La Trinidad, the art here really is no match for its beautiful surroundings. The paintings are small, inconsequential, and damaged by numerous instances of vandalism. In a fairly short time we departed and reported in at San Patricio.

Our guide of the flashlight tour repeated his story of two other rock art sites. A long discussion convinced us that they must be visited on a side trip because no one knew whether we would be able to continue our journey directly from the places he wanted to show us. We cooked up a plan. Coco had no interest in going, so we left him to make sure the unused animals ate well, and the rest of us headed east to see what could be seen.

The less said about that day the better. The young man proved to be entirely sincere but possessed of a poor memory or poor judgment. He took us first to an arroyo named *Tata Dios* — The Arroyo of Grandfather God — the second one with this engaging name that we had encountered on this trip. Then he took us to Arroyo de Los Zalates. Our entire finds for the day included one line of extremely weathered handprints, a nice wall of petroglyphs, and a small painted panel so eroded that the images literally did not emerge in our photos. We got back to San Patricio late in the day and set out for Rancho San Dieguito on the trail indicated by our guide. When we arrived at dark, we learned that the ranches are joined by another route only half as long.

Our next rock art lead directed us to San Sebastián in the upper part of Arroyo de San José de Magdalena, an area 25 miles distant by air but much more over rugged ground. Our route would bear northwest and generally cross arroyos rather than run up or down them. The great Cueva de San Borjitas lay almost directly on our projected path, but we had received no information about additional sites in its vicinity. Our plan, therefore, was simple: We would cover the ground and get what news we could along the way.

We started up the arroyo of San Dieguito and followed it until high hills turned us west. Skirting these we found and used an ancient and overgrown cuesta to cross a high arm of the sierra. On the other side, a gentle, grassy cañada led us down to a point where we encountered the wheel tracks of a primitive auto road. We followed the tracks downstream until they joined a larger road that soon looked familiar to me. Two years before when visiting San Borjitas, I had come up this road, but I did not remember the spur we had just descended. A short while later, spending the night at Rancho Las Tinajas, I learned why I was confused. The Gorosave family had recently constructed that spur to bring tourists to the famous painted cave. I had not realized we were passing within half an hour's ride of the cave. Since my companions had looked forward to seeing San Borjitas, I was not soon allowed to forget my guiding gaffe.

Riding up Arroyo de San Baltazar, we passed Rancho Las Tinajitas and shortly quit the arroyo altogether by way of a pass to the north. While descending a cañada on the other side, I made one of our few independent discoveries. In the deep shadow of a gorge to the east, I saw a cave. Although binoculars showed nothing of interest, I was determined to investigate, so we detoured and made a brisk little climb up a wooded waterway.

The cave is made of good hard rock and contains several paintings. None, however, could be photographed or easily appreciated. I have often recounted the forces and the odds that oppose the survival of painted rock art, but here was a new hazard: Water had percolated through the massive crown of rock over the cave, flowing out of cracks in the hard roof and leaving a mineral deposit all over ceiling and walls. The paintings are now heavily glazed by a layer of insoluble salts; their colors can be seen to some degree, their outlines less so. Despite this, we could detect a strange limbless figure pierced by arrows and the forms of at least two deer. An hour or so later when we arrived at Rancho Las Cañadas, we learned that the place we had found is called El Salto. The local people apparently did not know that it contains paintings.

From Las Cañadas, we proceeded west over a pass to San Isidro. We could get no reports of rock art there, so we rode on toward San Sebastián, stopping for the night a mile or two beyond San Isidro. The next morning we soon came to Rancho Las Bebelamas. Coco's spirits were up; he was now back on familiar ground and he remembered talk of paintings nearby. We rode in to ask and encountered two women drawing water from the well. Our questions amused them. Yes, of course, it was well known that they had paintings. Where? One of them pointed to a rock outcropping 50 yards away. We walked around a corral and looked up at a tiny respaldo-cave.

A profusion of little figures done in red-brown and black, none over 18 inches in height, adorn the ceiling. They include two bicolored monos, a deer, a probable crab, and several others with an uncertain but zoological look. Many rocks had fallen from the ceiling and carried away all or parts of paintings. All those that remain are obscured somewhat by lesser forms of the same water stains we had seen at El Salto.

Another short ride took us down into the main arroyo of San Sebastián near Rancho San Javier. Within minutes we saw a series of caves up a cañada to our left. Enrique and I were trailing at the time; we yelled ahead that we were stopping and then turned up the cañada. We quickly came to a point below the caves and dismounted. As we did, a man on a white mule came along behind us and saluted us politely. A brief exchange introduced us all and explained our mission. The man was Melchor Villavicencio González and his ranch was San Javier in that same cañada. As for the caves, yes, they were indeed painted. And the good señor insisted on filling the totally unnecessary office of guide to those small nearby places. No matter—we enjoyed his enthusiasm. We scrambled up and had a good time inspecting what is chiefly a varied collection of pinturitas ranging from the most ordinary to some inspired and stylish originals. One of the rock shelters is in itself a handsome curiosity. It appears to have been formed as an immense bubble in basalt, and rock layers had formed around it as if it were an onion. This whole formation is now exposed in cross section and makes quite a display on the hillside. The smooth concave facets within exhibit paintings of a striped mono, a red mono, and a very fine but faded borrego. This last is especially interesting because the borrego, such a common subject in the San Francisco region, is much rarer in this sierra.

The cave nearest the main arroyo might well be called "The Cave of the Hands" since it contains many handprints and, more unusual, painted depictions of hands. The principal feature however is a spritely compound figure, a tiny red mono with outsized hands and feet superimposed on a fat, black-banded deer reminiscent of a striped watermelon.

To the north, across the broad main arroyo, we spotted one last cave. Señor Villavicencio had gone home so we could not ask him about it. We crossed and hiked up quite a hill. The paintings inside the cave are crude and childish. Daubed on broken rock outcroppings are monos and animals painted in unbelievably gaudy shades of mustard yellow and orange-red. At first I suspected a hoax, but close inspection suggested the work had some antiquity. In any event, I feel sure it was created by hands other and later than those of the Painters.

Finally, after all those diversions, we rode on the last mile to San Sebastián. Here we found Guillermo Villavicencio's father, Jesús, who took us in and gave us a hand in unpacking. Later we sat around and discussed rock art. In the course of the conversation, he mentioned a Doctor Villalpando from Santa Rosalía who had visited several painted sites in the area of San Sebastián. We paid close attention because Jesús Valenzuela had also mentioned this man's name at Los Monos de San Juan. In addition, Tacho Arce had known him casually and remembered that the doctor had visited San Francisco and seen Cueva del Ratón and perhaps other painted places in that sierra. It was now obvious that Dr. Villalpando had visited many sites and perhaps could contribute to everyone's knowledge of the Great Murals. When we returned to our homes, Enrique was able to get a current address for him in Mexico City. I wrote and found a willing and helpful informant.

Dr. Cuauhtemoc Villalpando Mexía practiced general medicine in Santa Rosalía for 16 years during the 1950s and 1960s. Whenever his calls necessitated visits to the sierras, he made it a point to ask about and see paintings and petroglyphs. As a result, he saw not only Cueva del Ratón in the Sierra de San Francisco, but also La Natividad and Cuesta de Palmarito. In the closer Sierra de Guadalupe, he was able to visit a dozen or so sites. These explorations certainly made him a leading authority at that time on the artworks and their locations. When the doctor read of Gardner's discoveries, he wrote to him and, in an ensuing correspondence, sent color transparencies of some of what he had seen. Dr. Villalpando's knowledge was briefly recognized in an article in *Life en Español* in 1962. Apparently he never attempted to publish his discoveries, but he deserves a place in the history of the Great Murals.

As Jesús Villavicencio rattled off the names of places Dr. Villalpando had visited, he included San Javier. We stopped him to say that we, too, had visited San Javier. When he asked what had we seen, we told him. "Oh, below the ranch," he said, "but what of the ones above the ranch? They are more important." What could we say? We explained that we had met Melchor and that he had showed us the works at Boca de San Javier. We said he had not mentioned a thing about paintings above. The upshot of our talk was that our host would accompany us in the morning to two places he knew well, Las Cruces and the upper San Javier.

So, the next morning bright and early found us going down the arroyo to a place called Pozo Viejo just below Rancho Las Cruces. This is probably the "el Pozo" to which Leon Diguet referred, but did not otherwise describe, in his item #14, a probability reinforced by the relative proximity of Guadalupe and Santa Isabel, the other two sites that Diguet mentioned in this item. In any event, the rock art site consists of a large collection of rather badly weathered paintings on a very unprotected respaldo. Over a run of perhaps 50 feet, we found small, attractive petroglyphs of fish, several badly faded monos and deer, and an especially good borrego with handsome horns. Alas, he, too, is fading.

When we had turned around and were backtracking to San Javier, I began to feel uncomfortable at the thought of facing Don Melchor. Perhaps he did not want us to tramp through his place. The visit might also be embarrassing to Jesús Villavicencio: Perhaps it was he who was confused, and there was no art above San Javier.

The problem of diplomacy did not present itself immediately. At the ranch, the dueño was out and we were met by his daughter. Guillermo's father told her what we were about and led us on through. In minutes, we were in a narrow and steep little cañada. We climbed its south bank and scouted around. Jesús Villavicencio seemed confused and apologetic. He pushed ahead to check out a high respaldo far above us. Enrique and I were amused. We thought the matter had been settled, but to be safe we prospected on.

We soon found a small, deep cave, hidden by brush, that opens onto the steep slope. Inside not a flake of paint could be seen, but what a find it was.

A *symbol common to many ancient peoples*

This small cave is engraved with hundreds of oval devices nearly identical to those created by virtually every culture to evolve in the past 20,000 years. Anthropologists consider them vulva symbols and speculate about their meaning. It has been suggested that they were created during fertility ceremonies, puberty rites, or as calendrical notations (thus making use of the regularity of the menstrual cycle and its similarity to the lunar month). Whatever the reason, this is the most common symbol found engraved in soft rock within shelters in the Great Mural region.

San Javier

Every square foot of wall is covered with engravings, hundreds of deeply carved symbols. And they are all alike: vulva symbols. Of course, I had seen these before; there are a few at several San Francisco sites and an area of San Borjitas Cave was devoted to them, but this—this was truly amazing. I called Enrique. He came in, turned around once, whistled, and politely inquired, "The Playboy Cave?" The name stuck.

169

The Sierra de Guadalupe

We could hear our would-be guide thrashing around far above us but, since he gave no word, we continued our own search. The slope became impassable, so we went down. In the caja, I quickly found two caves exactly opposite each other. The one on the south side was clean of paint. The one on the north was the jackpot, or as close to it as we were going to get. Inside are a number of large, handsome monos in red and black divided vertically. All are in the most lamentably flaked and washed-off condition. We pored over them for a while. Our guide rejoined us and, having found nothing more, decided this must be the art he remembered. We returned to the caja. Just below the cave we found an open wall of rock decorated with a group of giant monos arranged shoulder to shoulder in the manner of those at Boca de San Zacarías. They are, if such a thing is possible, in worse condition than those within. We started back to the ranch in low spirits from our encounter with such losses.

Don Melchor was waiting for us in a jovial mood. Had we had a good tour? How did we like the paintings? His daughter had coffee waiting for us and we rested for a while in his pleasant corredor. Why had he not mentioned these interesting places when he first heard about our quest? We will never, never know.

The painted place at San Sebastián itself is so obvious that the people merely pointed to it and Enrique and I set off by ourselves. Our goal was a cave we could see clearly as a dark spot on the brow of a hill to the west. We soon came to the foot of the hill and labored up several hundred feet to what proved to be a wide, shallow rock shelter rather than a cave. The back wall was formed from two different rocks, neither of which has satisfactorily supported paintings. The upper rock is a softer material with a surface that crumbles as it weathers. A virile black borrego is fading away as small bits of his essence are lost.

The lower rock is much harder, a mosaic of small fractured domains of basalt that weep with groundwater and accumulated caliche along every crack. On this surface are a black *aura* and the best survivals in the cave: a row of five small whales. These last are indeed iconoclastic, lined up from left to right in order of increasing size with their tails up and their heads down. "Heads-down" breaks with the conventions observed in the depiction of fish or any other sea animals.

Enrique and I expended a good deal more energy and the better part of an hour visiting a much larger cave north of the one just described. It is deep, so deep that a flashlight would have been needed to explore its recesses. It is complex, with large openings in front and on top as well. In short, it is such a fascinating place that it had not attracted a single painting, not even a trace. That surprising absence illustrates an important point: We can make a strong argument for the ritual nature of the paintings because we know the mountains in the Great Mural area offer so many inviting places, often near painted ones, that remain unpainted. It seems certain that some authority designated the places to be painted, and that they were not selected simply on the basis of availability or practicality.

Enrique and I returned to headquarters just in time to arrange a move to Los Gatos, a ranch up the valley. We hurried and completed the short hour's ride just before sunset; in fact, the proximity of that sunset created an amusing tableau. We pulled into the ranch and met the owners, the prosperous Villavicencio López brothers. We told them what we were seeking and they told us we must hurry. They had paintings to show us that could scarcely be seen except in late afternoon. We grabbed our cameras and, with the enthusiastic brothers bounding ahead, literally ran up a very steep falda and a high one at that. We got to a cave front with about three minutes of sunlight left and hastily snapped pictures of large, handsome deer. Then we trouped at a leisurely pace down the hill and enjoyed an evening of warm and generous hospitality. Later, when our transparencies were processed, we learned that all those taken on that mad, lung-bursting jaunt had been spoiled by strong shadows. Late afternoon is probably the only time of day that presents this problem. ¡Así es la vida!

For the record, this site is north of the ranch and directly up the slope, a long slit cave facing west. The paintings are on the exterior face and the inner ceiling and consist of six deer, four in very good condition. Several other figures may be found on various parts of the ceiling, but they are too deteriorated to analyze.

In the morning we began a more serious study of the Los Gatos area. We started very early with a huge cave on the other side of the arroyo and downstream a quarter of a mile. From a distance it looked as if it would be extremely simple to reach; not so in practice. The route, though no more precipitous than a hundred others, was guarded by a legion of garabatillo shrubs whose long, wandlike branches are armed with nasty hooks. We approached this cave at a very dignified pace, a dignity marred by our frequent resort to progress on hands and knees.

The cave itself is the largest we investigated on this trip. Its general dimensions are on the order of 60 feet wide, 20 feet high, and 80 feet deep. In addition, it has galleries that run even deeper. In its day this cave — unlike the deep cave near San Sebastián — was heavily painted. The remains of about 20 deer figures can be seen on the east and back walls, and despite advanced deterioration, they exhibit an interesting feature: They range in height from two to four feet. This is an oddity since, in our experience, figures of this size are rare, and when they do occur, they are found in groups with larger murals.

We visited a third Los Gatos site as we rode out of the area, an impressive ceremonial center located in a cave near the mouth of the second cañada west of the ranch. The cave is long and rather shallow. The ceiling and back wall are both heavily painted, almost entirely with heroic-sized monos. Sadly, the entire mural is in an advanced state of decomposition. It has degraded to the point where a viewer has to puzzle out each figure and try to visualize missing parts.

As we left Los Gatos and headed northwest, we were once again on El Camino Real, the route I had traveled six years before. Riding up Arroyo de San Venancio, I was fascinated by the interplay of familiar and strange elements. I suppose that my attention was selective in the first place, and my memory stored only a part of what met my senses. At any rate, riding along, I had the sensation of watching a familiar film heavily intercut with another that I was seeing for the first time.

We rode up to the top of San Venancio and came to a point where the trail divides. El Camino Real proceeds northwest down a remarkable cuesta that I rediscovered on my previous trip. Modern traffic goes down another longer and poorer grade to Rancho El Rincón to the east. Having done the first already, I was inclined to try the other. Coco and Ramón clinched the decision by pointing out that the family at El Rincón, known to both of them, could be helpful if there should be paintings in the area. We stopped for a few moments at the portezuelo to savor one of the peninsula's more beautiful views. Before us was the broad arroyo of Santa Agueda, basinlike here and six miles wide. Beyond rose the Sierra de Santa Lucía, a ragged line of broken hills, and behind that, towering over all, the serene cone of Cerro de la Vírgen, trailing its usual wisp of clouds.

Down we went, on a descent long and tiring for the animals. At El Rincón we were unfortunate to miss the dueño, because his wife and daughters were not knowledgeable in the matter of paintings. Ramón, however, was philosophical about this matter as we rode away a couple of hours later. The dueño, he pointed out, could hardly have cooked the meal we had just enjoyed.

Our route lay across the slopes that separated us from El Camino Real. We were heading in a direction few people now traveled and we found no real trail for an hour or more. Eventually, however, we had to cross a route that comes up the valley from Santa Agueda. When we did, we got our bearings and were soon following the old mission trail as it makes its remarkably direct northwest passage over and through the broken terrain.

Late in the afternoon, I was able to point to the west and show Enrique an important place in my own history. Clearly visible a couple of miles away was the huge tumbled boulder of La Candelaria where I had seen my first Great Murals. We toyed briefly with the thought of visiting the shrine but opted instead to save the time for new discoveries.

On my first pursuit of El Camino Real, our party got sidetracked just here and went by error over the Cuesta de la Candelaria in order to get out of Arroyo de Santa Agueda. We discovered the mistake after several miles, but did not feel that we had time to backtrack and do it over. We had to assume the whereabouts of the road in that short but troublesome stretch.

This time we stuck to a more northerly route that passes over a lower and less trying pass. In doing so, we were able to observe a beautiful piece of Boleo road-building, a truly impressive and well-preserved cuesta that leads absolutely nowhere. Its construction was interrupted and there it remains, spiraling up a steep hillside to an abrupt end. Ramón remarked on its pristine condition. He called it "unworn" and said it was a pity we could not find the wrappings and the sales slip so that it could be returned for credit.

When we reached the top of the old cuesta, I was happy to discover that El Camino Real did just what we had assumed it would six years before: That pass essentially put us once again on the plain of San Ignacio. Though we faced a long ride down an arroyo, we would not have a single cuesta to traverse in the two days it would take us to get back to our starting point at Rancho La Esperanza.

That night, in order to reach Rancho Santa Cruz, we rode in the dark for the first time. The moon had not risen and I discovered that mules apparently depend on starlight to some degree. When we passed under canopies of trees, they became more hesitant and had a few small footing problems. Out in the open, they seemed to move at much the same pace employed during the day.

The family at Santa Cruz was large and lively. They were also relatives of Coco, so we had no trouble enlisting their attention and help. The young men had herded cattle around there for years, they were observant, and the mention of paintings brought prompt response. They described several places that lay along our next day's itinerary.

Thanks in large part to this unusually good local information, the following day unfolded as one of the most efficient and productive of the trip. We started down the arroyo of Santa Cruz and came to the ruins of Rancho San Antonio, our first signpost, within an hour. Continuing for a quarter of a mile, we looked along the top of the falda south of the trail as we had been instructed to do. The directions were perfect; we found our objective easily on a respaldo 100 feet off the trail and perhaps 50 feet above it.

The first view of this site forcibly reminded me of the relationship between geography and the Great Murals. Now that we were back at the north end of the sierra and not more than 30 miles from the Sierra de San Francisco, the art was assuming the very familiar look of San Francisco work. Here we were looking at a wall with over 20 large monos in the pure tradition of the Great Mural heartland. Most follow the traditional red and black vertical division pattern, and they are ranged across the respaldo shoulder to shoulder, or actually superimposed on one another, so closely are they spaced.

Having established their traditional character, it should also be noted that this mural exhibits one unique aspect: Three monos were painted over the heads of the others and exactly inverted, feet up and heads and extended arms down.

As the morning wore on, the simplicity of our ride began to sink in; the terrain presented no real ups or downs. We were so comfortable in the warm sun that it was almost possible to doze in the saddle. Less than two hours from San Antonio, we came to the second place on our list—a cave near the top of a small hill on the north side of the arroyo.

The paintings there are small but curious. One red figure looks like a large worm or eel, but the other two command even more attention. The first is a miniature red and black mono, about 18 inches tall. His right arm is ex-tended into a circular, netlike appendage over half his size. The other figure is similar except that

173

it is all red and inverted. Its net is an extension of its left arm. We were given no name for this site, just its location near Cuesta de las Tunas.

Another hour brought us to a great bend in the arroyo just south of the historic ranch of San Borjitas del Norte. There, precisely at a right turn of the watercourse, we found ourselves riding toward a high bank containing many caves and sheltered overhangs. We dismounted and, within minutes, found paintings within at least seven of them. These rock shelters gave us two hours of pleasure and frustration. We were treated to many, many works, among them several appealing compositions including a group of small deer frolicking across the wall of a cave. Unfortunately, the entire complex of caves and rock shelters has eroded out of a hill of yellow-beige volcanic agglomerate. This makes an attractive background for the works and a very effective color contrast to the predominantly black paint used at this site, but because the rock is soft and crumbling, not a figure survives without substantial damage.

In the end we shrugged it off; we could not allow ourselves to be downcast by encounters with irremediable losses. Enrique and I—who had reminded each other many times that we should rejoice at any survival whatsoever—put into practice what we had preached. We concentrated on studying and photographing everything from which we might be able to restore images.

The total material at San Borjitas del Norte is very large and a shelter-by-shelter description would be wearing; the salient features are better suited to a summary: This site was painted in at least two different periods, with a lot of over-painting, and the older layer of paintings is conspicuously more deteriorated. That condition argues strongly that much time passed between the two periods of painting activity. In my opinion, the paintings present two different styles corresponding to the different periods.

Although most of the painting is in black, a few figures are red and a number of monos are black and red. A showing of ochre paint remains where it was used to outline deer, but these works are in very poor condition. Several groups of paintings seem to have been made at one time by one artist. Three such are parades of very small deer, two in black and one in red. Others are pairs or threesomes of larger black animals, probably deer.

When we finally quit the hillside, we rode on a short distance to a very fine petroglyph site Guillermo Villavicencio had noticed during my trip with him six years earlier. On a high rock is a group of five deer by the same hand. They are large for petroglyph figures, ranging from one to two feet in length. They are arranged in a vertical design and all face in the same direction. They attracted my attention because they appear to be stylistically related to the nearby paintings. I believe this is truer of petroglyphs in the larger San Ignacio area than in any other region I have studied.

Enrique pointed out a second noteworthy fact: The basalt cantil and boulder pile on the east side of the arroyo, the formation that bears all these petroglyphs, was engraved during two widely separated periods. Most of the figures have a light but definite golden patination. A few, including a mono over four feet high, appear much older; these engraved figures are so heavily patinated that they no longer contrast with their backgrounds. Such works are difficult to detect without the help of side lighting to throw shadows into their incised lines. That older mono, incidentally, bears a striking resemblance to the "rectangle" men of faraway Loma Alta.

The area proved to be a maze of petroglyphs and pictographs. At the mouth of a cañada across from the old San Borjitas ranch site, there is another large batch of engravings and below the ranch, on the west side, there is a wall of rock with both engravings and paintings. The pursuit of all this was exhausting. It is a temptation, heretical of course, to admit that we were tired of the chase after more than 40 days on the trail.

However, the survey which ended that day had served our purpose well: We observed that Great Mural art extends, in one form or another, throughout the relatively large Sierra de Guadalupe. Since our single pass took us only to sites near our route or known to inhabitants whom we chanced to encounter, it was obvious that we had seen only a minor fraction of the total art in the vast, mountainous expanse between San Ignacio and La Purísima.

In following years, Enrique and I were able to make additional explorations and add significantly to our first impressions of Guadalupe's rock art. More important, we added several major sites and broadened our knowledge of the already impressive range of styles and expressions found in those mountains. As the reader knows by now, I have interpolated descriptions of some of these finds into this account. I draw on all my experiences in the region in offering some concluding observations about the rich art of the Sierra de Guadalupe.

Regional Rock Art   Paintings in the caves and rock shelters of the Sierra de San Francisco remain the most admirable expression of the Great Mural phenomenon. Cumulatively, their numbers, sizes, condition, and artistry exceed the corresponding attributes of the painted artworks in any or all of the other Great Mural regions. Most of San Francisco's painted works seem closely related. While many individual artists can be recognized (sometimes in works at several different sites), their artistic conventions and styles appear very homogeneous. Their works appear, in short, to have been executed by different students of the same academy. Each pupil may have developed a different talent and degree of craftsmanship, but all were inspired by the same masters.

In Guadalupe, the paintings are greatly varied, although most adhere to the same basic conventions observed in San Francisco (e.g., humans were drawn head on, animals in profile; outlines are literal, infill patterns fanciful; all anatomical features are revealed in outlines even if distortions of perspective were required, etc.). In Guadalupe paintings, several different "schools" seem to be represented,

San Juan San Juan Agua Fría II La Huertita

**Human figures
in the style
of Los Monos de San Juan**

and each seems to have a geographical center or area that it dominates. Some sites, it is true, display two styles, but these usually lie along the borders between two schools' areas and seem to occupy an overlap zone.

For the sake of identifying stylistic distinctions, it seems desirable to name each school for the site that preserves or imparts its best or strongest examples. These sites will be treated, for reasons that will soon be apparent, as a progression from north to south.

Los Monos de San Juan   No student or even casual observer of San Francisco rock painting could fail to perceive its strong relationship to the art at most sites in the northwestern third of the Sierra de Guadalupe. The kinship is so apparent that it invites a hypothesis: The same groups who painted the more northern of the two sierras also painted in the adjacent part of the more southern sierra.

The figure that unifies and exemplifies northern Guadalupe art is the large, half-red, half-black, usually headdressed human figure, or mono. These monos dominate all other representations at sites located at Agua Fría, El Cajón del Valle, El Carrizo, El Muerto, La Puerta, Los Gatos, La Huertita, La Matanza, San Antonio, San Javier, San Zacarías, and, preeminently, San Juan.

One clear difference between Guadalupe art and its apparent mother lode in San Francisco is the ratio of monos to deer and other animal figures. San Francisco sites usually present a mixture of human and animal forms (with perhaps an overall majority of animals), but in the above-named Guadalupe sites, human

San Borjitas   Agua Puerca   San Borjitas   El Arrepentido

forms overwhelmingly outnumber all others. In fact, at San Antonio, El Muerto, San Zacarías, San Javier, and Los Monos de la Matanza, virtually all discernible figures painted in the shelters are monos. The great upper panels at Los Monos de San Juan, despite single strong representations of deer and mountain lions, are dominated by dozens of the life-sized monos that typify the northern Guadalupe style.

Despite this emphasis on human figures, it would be a mistake to dismiss San Juan animal forms as less related to San Francisco traditions. Although sparser in proportionate numbers, their style suggests a tie to San Francisco as strong as that of the monos. San Juan men and beasts differ from those observed in San Francisco no more than some figures at the various San Francisco sites differ from each other.

San Borjitas Men   Seventeen miles west of Mulegé is the very important rock art center of San Borjitas. There, an impressive cave ceiling displays more than 50 large monos—and no other major figures. This emphasis on human representation seems to continue the trend observed in the north among San Juan figures. In most other respects, however, the highly stylized San Borjitas men are totally different from those of San Juan and form the basis for recognizing a separate "school" of Guadalupe art. Since they have been pictured and described, it need only be noted that these monos are characterized by can-shaped heads, stiff, slightly bulbous bodies, limbs thrust out at awkward angles, legs spread wide,

177

The Sierra de Guadalupe

and arms horizontal rather than in the classic "hands up!" position of most other Great Mural humans. In addition, many are longitudinally striped rather than divided into red and black zones.

Clearly identifiable San Borjitas men are known at present in only a handful of sites, but the area in which they are found has been poorly prospected. The characteristic monos of this school are painted on the walls or ceilings at Agua Puerca, El Arrepentido, El Muerto, La Angostura de San Juan, Boca de las Piedras, and, obviously, San Borjitas.

San Borjitas monos have several distinctions other than their odd, unnatural forms. Many show prominent male genitalia, a feature not found in San Francisco or San Juan figures. Furthermore, according to the sites I have been able to observe, most of the Painters responsible for creating San Borjitas men seem to have painted no accompanying deer, borregos, birds, or fish. This is not to say that no animals are painted at the same sites—though they are rare—but rather that few animals can be attributed with confidence to the hands of those who painted the San Borjitas monos. Finally, it should be noted that San Borjitas monos show no artistic relationship with San Francisco figures. In that respect, they represent a clean break from the adjacent Los Monos de San Juan style. This is not, however, a unique attribute; the remaining Guadalupe schools also are detached from San Francisco. Nevertheless, all Guadalupe schools truly deserve to be placed under the Great Mural heading because all exhibit a high percentage of the naturalistic figures that, regardless of artistry, style, or school, adhere to the underlying Great Mural traditions in attitude, perspective, infill patterns, and so forth.

Trinidad Deer   A marvelous group of painted figures decorates the lone surviving wall of a collapsed cave in the small bedrock cañón above Rancho La Trinidad in the upper part of Arroyo de Mulegé. Three deer, perhaps a doe and two fawns, appear to move from right to left—slim, graceful figures elegantly outlined and infilled with a large, bold checkerboard pattern, all done in a vibrant vermilion paint against a rich red-ochre-colored rock. I have chosen to use these figures as the stylistic prototype for dozens more found in numerous caves and shelters in a 20-mile-wide swath that cuts all the way across the sierra to the west. The choice of La Trinidad's deer, of course, is arbitrary; no one knows which of these splendid images was created first, or even if the original survives. However, the beauty at La Trinidad serves as an ideal model because it shows the features that define the style. Notice the carefully executed antlers, the tongue extended into the body, the relatively short but graceful legs, and especially the odd, rounded rump and the method of depicting the tail. All of these serve as guides in identifying what I call Trinidad deer. Less universal is its checkerboard infill; other examples have no infill, or instead have the tongue line extended through the body to conclude at the tail.

La Trinidad   Los Venados   La Trinidad   Fl Dipugón

Images of deer
in the style of
La Trinidad

Trinidad deer paintings tend to dominate the sites where they are found, but they are not the solitary product of their creators as San Borjitas monos tend to be. Images of fish, birds, and humans are also found at sites that display deer in the Trinidad style. These were done in the same paint, survive in the same condition, and ostensibly were created by the same artist or artists. However, with the exception of fish, the other figures suggest a surprisingly low level of interest or inspiration on the part of their painters. They seem clumsy, even ugly when compared with the deer. Repeated observations of this phenomenon reinforce the conviction that, among the Trinidad painters, there was a strong deer cult. Deer were paramount and were painted with care and feeling; most other subjects got relatively perfunctory treatment.

Southern Semiabstract Styles   The rock art found thus far in the Sierra de la Giganta, just south of the Sierra de Guadalupe, is almost entirely abstract. The best known site, Cuevas Pintas, is located in Arroyo de las Parras just south of Loreto, but a fine painted wall south of Rancho Canipolé is not only the most northerly Giganta site, it is also just a few miles from the foothills of the Sierra de Guadalupe. The art at Canipolé is in wonderful condition, similar in style and content to the art at Cuevas Pintas, and equally abstract. Because of the persistently abstract nature of prehistoric art to the south, it is a temptation to speculate that—in the the southern reaches of the Sierra de Guadalupe—these abstract/symbolic traditions combined with Great Mural traditions to form an artistic union that accounts for the curiosities found in that region.

At Loma Alta, we saw a strange new form of mono with a rectangular head, rectangular body, and sticklike lines representing neck, arms, legs, and digits. Later we found a similar figure at Los Toros, a cave near La Vinorama situated at a point about midway between Loma Alta and Mulegé. Paintings of deer found south of the area dominated by the style of La Trinidad also show a tendency to become

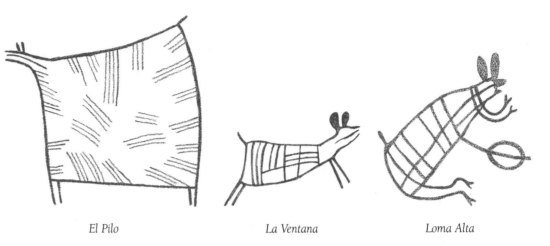

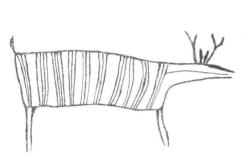

near Agua Honda   El Pilo   La Ventana   Loma Alta

**Images of deer
in southern
semiabstract styles**

more abstract — that is to say, stiffer and less lifelike — and to exhibit even more severely geometric infill patterns. The progression is fascinating: First, one sees the fluid outlines characteristic of La Trinidad. Then, to the immediate south and west, one sees images of deer that have Trinidad-like heads, with open mouths and prominent tongue lines, but increasingly rectangular and unlifelike bodies. Tongue lines, instead of proceeding to the tail as in Trinidad deer, now butt into some form of internal geometrical obstruction and terminate. The final step in this remarkable progression produces the boxlike deer at El Pilo — which still retain heads in the manner of La Trinidad!

My earlier suspicions seemed increasingly justified as we moved along and examined ever more paintings: Great Murals seemed more abstract the farther south we encountered them. The number of these increasingly aberrant sites that have been discovered is still small, but their art consists of major works — large, striking, and artistically vigorous. Since my visits, paintings have been reported in the watercourses leading north from the upper parts of Arroyo de la Purísima. I feel confident that explorations on those slopes and in the greater south of Sierra de Guadalupe will reveal much additional semiabstract art.

Tantalizing Links between Guadalupe and San Francisco   Modern interest in the Great Murals began with the discovery of noble examples in the Sierra de San Francisco; my first impressions of this extraordinary artistic phenomenon were formed there as well. I find, in looking back, that I easily assumed the viewpoint that San Francisco was the cradle of this art. I have speculated that similar work in the northern end of the Guadalupe range was influenced by or actually done by nearby San Francisco inhabitants, and that the increasingly different schools of Great Mural art encountered as one moves south might represent the steps by which the influence of the pure northern form faded as the Painters became more distant from their source. In fact, such an idea is no more appropriate than the reverse. It is equally logical to propose that various schools, following Great Mural conventions, developed in different areas of Guadalupe and that the bands which created the San Juan school, being nearest to San Francisco, carried their art north to that range where they flourished in a golden age of rock art. One or the other of these propositions will probably fit the facts — but those facts remain to be unearthed.

The Sierra de Guadalupe

Rancho Santa Bárbara

Sierra de San Juan

CHAPTER 5

The
Sierra de
San Juan

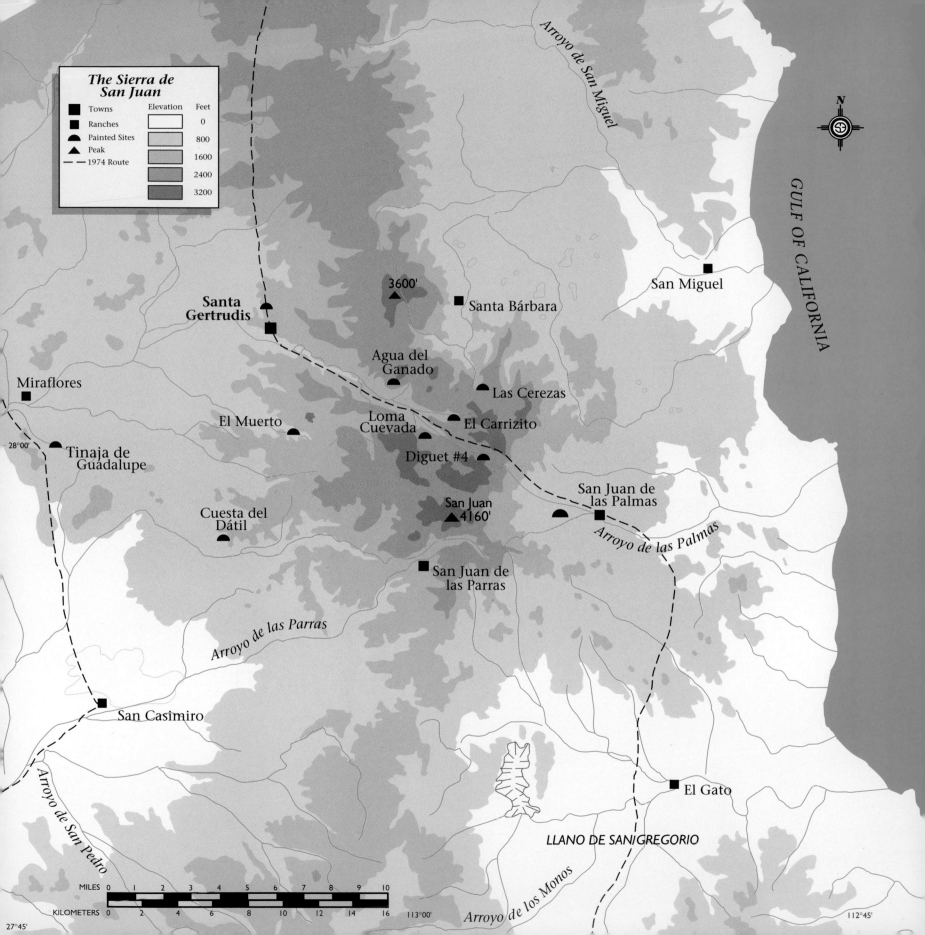

The Sierra de San Juan

Towns
Ranches
Painted Sites
Peak
1974 Route

Elevation	Feet
	0
	800
	1600
	2400
	3200

Arroyo de San Miguel

GULF OF CALIFORNIA

3600'

Santa Bárbara

San Miguel

Santa Gertrudis

Agua del Ganado

Las Cerezas

Miraflores

El Muerto

Loma Cuevada

El Carrizito

28°00'

Tinaja de Guadalupe

Diguet #4

San Juan de las Palmas

Cuesta del Dátil

San Juan 4160'

Arroyo de las Palmas

San Juan de las Parras

Arroyo de las Parras

San Casimiro

El Gato

Arroyo de San Pedro

LLANO DE SAN GREGORIO

MILES 0 1 2 3 4 5 6 7 8 9 10

KILOMETERS 0 2 4 6 8 10 12 14 16

Arroyo de los Monos

27°45'

113°00'

112°45'

A stride the 28th parallel, which divides the states of Baja California, is the smallest of the painted sierras—the remnants of a single volcano whose flows and bedded ash covered a triangular area measuring twenty miles on a side. Its central peak, the twin-spired Cerro de San Juan, rises to an elevation of 4,160 feet due north of the Sierra de San Francisco and only 12 miles from the Gulf shore. The aboriginal people knew this place; their trails lead to its meager springs from every point of the compass. Catholic missionaries tried building roads over several routes while searching for the best of a bad lot. Today this rugged, broken place is quiet and deserted. Because it is so far from major settlements and so poorly served by roads, a newcomer to its inner recesses can feel like the first man. It is a shock to stumble onto a labor from mission times or a cave painted by the ancients.

My first encounters with traces of the Painters in the Sierra de San Juan occurred by pure chance. After my 1967 pursuit of El Camino Real from Loreto to San Diego, I was left with much uncertainty about the route of the old road in the rugged San Juan region. Later, I returned to investigate and, in the course of doing so, stumbled onto a number of rock art sites. They actually displayed little, but their very presence held out the tantalizing possibility of more.

After several excursions into the Sierra de San Francisco and one long survey of the Sierra de Guadalupe, I was finally able to get back to San Juan. A trip was organized at La Esperanza in the spring of 1974 based on an itinerary that would go north through the Sierra de San Juan and then circumnavigate the uplands of the Sierra de San Borja.

It was late in March when Tacho Arce, his son Ramón, Enrique Hambleton, and I rode north. We chose a course lying along the east or Gulf slope of the Sierra de San Francisco; for the first two days, we would be on the more easterly alternate of El Camino Real in that area. At the Llano de San Gregorio, we would have the opportunity to explore a route that deserves a footnote in U. S. history.

In 1849 and 1850, several parties of American gold seekers, as a result of ignorance or necessity, landed at points in the south of the Baja California peninsula and undertook overland trips to Alta California gold fields. Some survived the ordeal but many, without guides or adequate animals, did not. Food was scarce, but lack of water was the most crucial element. The diaries of survivors recount excruciating hardships; local lore dating at least as far back as 1853 tells of roadside burials of hapless 49ers all along the route from the Llano de San Gregorio to Misión de San Fernando.

By turning north at El Piojo on the southern rim of the Llano de San Gregorio, we were able to follow a well-defined trail across that flat expanse and on into the small but rugged Sierra de San Juan which lay between us and Santa Gertrudis. At first, this version of El Camino Real stayed on the Gulf side of the sierra and crossed only low ridges. But, at Rancho San Juan de las Palmas, the indicated route crossed a high arm of the sierra by the thoroughly precipitous Cuesta del Obispo which appeared in the bitter accounts of 49ers.

The Sierra de San Juan

At San Juan de las Palmas, we were directed to a small group of caves about 100 yards above the ranch house. There we found a few small artworks in the final stages of deterioration.

Our mules climbed the cuesta slowly to a high pass; just beyond, the trail started down a large brush-choked cañada. After an hour's ride, our sharp lookout produced results. Several layers of high respaldos rose just above a very steep watercourse entering the cañada from the south. We could make out prominent paintings on two of them.

The upper level in particular is interesting for its typical San Francisco style of art, a group of larger-than-life monos and three borregos. One of the latter is bicolored, which is common enough, but the colors are divided in a way that is unique in my experience. The head and forequarters were rendered in red and the hindquarters entirely in black. In general, we were disappointed at the poor condition of the art. We felt deceived because the view through our binoculars had suggested better things. Before long, we became familiar with this phenomenon. In such small, highly magnified images, the scattered bits of partially disintegrated paintings tend to coalesce and appear to be in better condition than they prove to be when seen at close range. Later, working with a map, it was possible to place the site at the head of the Arroyo de Santa Gertrudis drainage. From its location near the pass, it could be deduced that this site was Diguet's #4, "Between Santa Gertrudis and Puerto Trinidad, about the highest point of the cuesta of San Juan."

When the cañada in which we had been riding opened into a larger waterway, we spotted a second site on its west wall. A stiff climb took us to a respaldo displaying a sun symbol, rare in the Great Mural region, and a number of very badly decomposed paintings of animal forms.

At nightfall we came to as curious a group of caves as may be found on the entire peninsula. In the middle of the arroyo, which at that point is very broad, there rises an "island" of beautiful reddish-pink cantera, a relatively soft type of volcanic agglomerate rock. This height is stepped with caves shaped like eye sockets and so numerous that the whole eminence looks like a strawberry jar.

A laborious search of the many caves and depressions disclosed that two of them have been painted. One, higher and more southerly, displays three monos side by side like a needlework sampler. The first is divided vertically between black and red, the second is black, and the third is red. The second painted cave contains a large red and black animal identified by Tacho as a borrega, a figure depicted with all the grace, skill, and color usual to the best artworks in the nearby Sierra de San Francisco. Below and to the left of this familiar type of work are greater novelties, a fascinating maze of small figures a foot or two in height. These depict people, animals, and birds, but the majority are fish, an unusual occurrence.

In the morning we photographed this *Loma Cuevada,* or "Cave-covered Hill," as we facetiously dubbed it. Then we rode for an hour and a half before encountering another painted site at Agua del Ganado, a striking setting. A grand bluff, very

steep and made up of many layers, towers on the east side of the arroyo. By using binoculars we were able to see paintings on a respaldo near the top. By now such evidence was suspect and we were impatient to reach Santa Gertrudis and continue to the Sierra de San Borja. Somewhat reluctantly, we left the bluff behind.

In Santa Gertrudis we contacted an old friend of Tacho's, Victor Aguilar Zúñiga, and had a long discussion of the area's Indian past. Victor knew a number of painted sites, but his time estimate was discouraging: Five or six days would be needed to see them all. In the end we compromised on two days and Victor took us to the three nearest places.

The first morning he led us on foot from his home up a steep trail to the northeast. A brisk 40-minute walk took us to a small shallow cave overlooking a minor cañada about a mile north of the old mission center. Every inch of the back wall of the shelter had once been painted and repainted. The rock is soft; much of it has deteriorated and released its paint. Despite that, the place fairly glows with color and the wall retains the air of a faded tapestry or Persian rug.

Individual figures are extremely difficult to distinguish, but we could make out monos and deer. The rich colors and the few recognizable drawings were familiar: The art in this cave reminded me strongly of Cuesta de San Pablo I and IV as well as of two sites in Arroyo de la Cuesta Blanca. Significantly, all of those are on the north end of the Sierra de San Francisco, the part closest to the San Juan region.

It is very frustrating to report a site such as this. It is possible to say that in its prime it was a gem, a place magnificently decorated in the pursuit of the Painters' ends. However, it can be enjoyed today only by those with a feel for the art and a knowledge of what it can be. No photograph can show its past glories.

Oddly, Victor knew no name for the cave's location, nor for the cañada below. When we found no better knowledge among other Santa Gertrudis people, we named the site, for convenience, Santa Gertrudis Norte.

By riding back up Arroyo de Santa Gertrudis for an hour and a half and leaving it by a cuesta to the south, Victor brought us to a high, open cave overlooking the arroyo. The art of this place is also very faded. The walls of the shallow shelter display a few deer and rabbits in very pale colors, but the most interesting remains are those of a turtle and a well-drawn, heavy-bodied fish.

After we crossed a pass, our guide led us into the headwaters of Arroyo del Muerto, the next drainage system southwest of Arroyo de Santa Gertrudis. A curiously overhung shelter can be seen on a hillside at the upper end of the arroyo. We approached it from the east along the top of the falda and tied our animals in the shade, literally overhung by a ceiling mural.

A soft layer of rock some eight feet high has weathered away to a depth of a few feet, leaving a massive, harder overhanging layer. The ceiling of the shelter displays the painted figures of about a dozen monos and a great turtle in one rather crude style easily distinguished by its orange-red paint. A large black bird, a vulture or a hawk, may be of this school as well.

Victor Aguilar Zúñiga cutting Tacho's hair

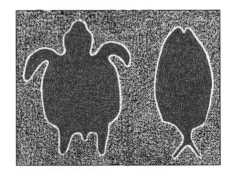

187

The Sierra de San Juan

A notable curiosity of this group of monos is the treatment of their legs. All the bodies whose lower parts can be discerned taper to a point and display no separation into distinct limbs. As an additional oddity, one of them seems to have been drawn first as a fish complete with small fins. The subsequent addition of arms converted the figure to a mono not markedly different from the others. This was not simply an overpainting—it was clearly a deliberate change in the identity of a figure, a very rare occurrence among the Great Murals.

To the right of the group of orange-red images, another sizable area spans both wall and ceiling and bears paintings in the style and colors of Santa Gertrudis Norte and the similar sites at Cuesta de San Pablo and Arroyo de la Cuesta Blanca. Deer predominate in these more faded figures, but the prize survival is a handsome pair of five-foot-long red and black fish. Their condition is bad, but by good fortune their elegantly crafted tails are quite clear and enough paint remains to reconstruct the remainder.

El Muerto is not, in the larger scheme of the Great Murals, a particularly well-preserved site. But in the San Juan area, where the rock is apparently very soft, the place is outstanding. Its paintings are in the best condition of any so far reported from this region.

Victor mentioned other paintings known to his brother, Manuel, who lived at Rancho Santa Bárbara east of Santa Gertrudis, but we had no time for such a detour. Instead, we rode to San Borja.

As we returned from our northern excursion about four weeks later, our route took us near the western fringe of the San Juan eminence. On that occasion, we visited a site reported at the Tinaja de Guadalupe near the ranch of the same name. The entire area shows extensive signs of human habitation; numerous caves exhibit modest midden deposits and an abundance of metates. Open clearings called *rancherías*, onetime aboriginal seasonal encampments, are likely to be found on any level piece of ground. Near the center of all these artifacts is a high hill, the Pilón de Guadalupe, which has a regular conical form that can be identified from great distances. A small watercourse runs from the east side of this pilón around to the south. We visited a large cave shelter just above the caja and on its south side.

Reports had described extensive painting in the cave. Our visit disclosed a sad development similar to what we had observed at the painted cave at La Trinidad in Arroyo de Mulegé: A large part of the roof had recently fallen, and most of the paintings had fallen with it. Parts of figures could be seen on the undersides of fallen blocks but only five faded monos and a small deer survive on less painted but still intact surfaces.

In the fall of 1974 I returned to the Sierra de San Juan with William Price, a former student and longtime friend with a degree in anthropology. We prevailed on Victor and Manuel Aguilar Zúñiga to take us into the Santa Bárbara region east of Santa Gertrudis. The brothers took us eastward out of Arroyo de Santa Gertrudis and onto a mesa. For an hour, we rode parallel to the arroyo until we came to a point just above the great bluff that we had left uninvestigated in the spring. The trail then turned northeast and started down the impressively steep Arroyo de Santa Bárbara leading to the Gulf coast. Far below in the caja we came to a fork in the trail. The left branch led down to the ranch; we took it and spent the night with Manuel's family in an extremely beautiful setting replete with palms, red rock canyons, and a sweeping view of foothills and the blue Gulf.

In the morning we returned to the fork, ascended heights to the south, and spent the following two days investigating a series of small painted sites near the peninsular divide that separates Santa Bárbara from the Pacific-bound drainage of Arroyo de Santa Gertrudis. The character of the geology and the forms into which it has eroded created a rather odd pattern in our travels and in the locations of the painted sites. Cañadas leading toward the Gulf cut the spine of the sierra in an alternate pattern with cañadas leading toward the Pacific. The first painted site is on the Pacific drainage, near the head of Cañada de las Cerezas.

Las Cerezas consists of a respaldo and cave combination about 100 feet long. The respaldo, at the east end, has been painted with large, well-defined red and black monos and deer. Enough survives to show good craftsmanship. In addition, various small figures persist in better condition. They include monos, as well as a more notable angular black bird and a conspicuous group of three red birds. The cave at the west end was once filled with paintings, but the rock is now so deteriorated and heavily smoked that not much can be made out.

An hour's ride to the southeast put us in a cañada called La Joya that runs toward the Gulf. On the east side, a large cave opens wide in plain view of the trail. In spite of its high ceiling, which must be 16 or 18 feet off the ground, the entire interior is smoked to a deep black relieved only by patches cleaned by the deterioration of the rock surface. These smoked caves are common in the sierras of the mid-peninsula. For want of a better term, Tacho, Ramón, Enrique Hambleton, and I had fallen into the habit of calling them "kitchens," the implicit idea being that these were places used selectively for cooking. It also occurred to us that, during cold weather, people might have built fires in these shelters to warm occupants while they slept. Bill Price and I discussed all this while examining the big smoked cave at La Joya. He considered the explanations I have just suggested and immediately offered two objections that had also crossed my mind: Cook fires are rarely large enough to heavily smoke even a low cave roof; fires to warm people are usually kept small and fed often. Price proposed a third and, I think, more probable explanation: When the first Europeans met the people of this region, they discovered that the local people cremated their dead and presumably had done so for a very long time; human burials were virtually unknown. Might these smoked caves be crematories? The idea is plausible. Most arroyos and cañadas offer a large supply of dry wood. A cave would conserve the heat of a fire so that it would better desiccate and then burn a cadaver and calcine the bones. Such pyres would indeed

189

smoke the interiors of even large caves, and repeated use would produce the dense blackening seen at many sites.

Above the large cave and ranging up the hillside, several smaller caves and shelters have eroded out to create a complicated sculpture in the dark red volcanic rock. Several are decorated with fairly crude figures, all rendered in red paint. We saw a borrego and possibly a berrendo in bad condition. In better shape are a four-foot-long turtle, unusually large for this subject, and a bird. A group of small monos painted in a low hollow is the most artistic of the remains. A couple of hundred yards away, in some narrows of the cañada, we came upon a large tinaja with good water. This could easily explain the extensive aboriginal activity in the neighborhood.

Five minutes' walk to the west from the tinaja, a pass leads to an abrupt drop into a cañada that empties into Arroyo de Santa Gertrudis. Victor took us down a very poor trail into that cañada. After a rough and twisting ride, we got out of its steepest, narrowest part and entered a long regular waterway heading northwest, Cañada del Carrizito. As we rode down, we saw a large cave high on the south slope of the canyon. Victor knew nothing of it, so we gave it the binocular test and found several readily visible but faded paintings. We stripped packs and saddles off our animals and started up the high slope.

This cave in Cañada del Carrizito is about 80 feet long and 20 feet high, and it was once heavily decorated over much of its rather large inner surface. The left third of its length is a real cave perhaps 35 feet deep; the middle third is an alcove raised off the ground so that a climb is necessary for a close view of its works; and the right side is a pure respaldo, a fairly flat wall protected only by an upper over-hang. The entire covered space bears a remarkable resemblance to the cave at La Candelaria in the Sierra de San Francisco, but this near-replica is a smaller mirror image.

In the true cave at the left is a large black borrego, very faded. All the other artworks in this section are reduced to vestiges except for those that were painted in whole or in part on hard included rocks. Entire birds and rabbits appear on two such surfaces. In the central part of the shelter, a five-foot piece of basalt exposed as part of the cave wall bears an astonishing collection of small painted figures. Rabbits, birds, deer, a turtle, and a couple of rotund monos leap with startling color and clarity from the flat side of this durable fragment embedded in a soft matrix. And all around it the pale agglomerate has shed its painted burden without a trace.

At the point where Cañada del Carrizito intersects the main arroyo, we spied a familiar sight directly ahead of us as we emerged: the tall bluff towering above Agua del Ganado, the same pilón whose paintings we had spurned in our haste six months before. Now we stopped for a full investigation.

After a thorough survey, it was decided to attack that many-layered tower from the southeast side. We began what proved to be a stiff climb. In 30 minutes, however, I had arrived at the highest layer and found the paintings my binoculars had picked up during the earlier excursion. All proved to be very faded, although most of the figures can be made out. Humans are the principal subjects; large red and red and black monos predominate, but we also found two or three large red birds. The prize of this collection, as at El Carrizito, is a single included rock that stands well out from a wall and bears on its hard, smooth surface a number of neatly executed red and black monos less than a foot tall. This beautiful work has suffered an inexplicable act of vandalism. Someone has used a pointed object, perhaps a sharp stone, to pound the face area of the central mono, the only one with a headdress. This site is so high and so remote it would seem safe from any wanton act. The damage could represent personal or tribal rivalry, almost as old as the painting.

On the level of the respaldo below, Victor prospected about and shortly found more art, a pair of crudely realized red and black deer, as well as other faded deer and monos. As we climbed down, working along the edge of a tiny cañada heading east, Victor and I both spotted paintings on its other wall. So, following the long scramble down the hillside, we immediately began the ascent of the opposite slope. After a wearying climb, we stood in front of three monos. Two are very tall, red and black, and one of them represents a woman. The third is small and black. All are crude and childish in proportion and technique, as artistically negligible as anything we were to see in the area.

The return to these high paintings at Agua del Ganado ended the survey of the Sierra de San Juan. The area initially offered much promise and it did in fact prove to contain a number of Great Mural sites. Some of its art must once have been fascinating and very beautiful; remnants at Santa Gertrudis Norte and Arroyo del Muerto attest strongly to this. But in this sierra, the important element of survival is missing from the known works of the Painters. No one site — not even the accumulated experience of all the sites we saw — imparts a strong sense of art alive. I am no stranger to a depression that sets in after discoveries of losses that far outweigh survivals. This reaction is common after visits to painted places throughout the four-sierra range of the Great Murals. More sites than not show only vestiges of once important painted works. But San Juan is the only region within those sierras that has failed to provide a single real survival, a single place where the art lives and breathes and the hunter experiences the joy of knowing it for its own sake. Nevertheless, these San Juan paintings and their locations are worth examination. They are the northern frontier of the San Francisco style, so they add a critical dimension to our understanding. No time was lost in their pursuit; the exploration is not finished, but — so far at least — there is an almost tangible void.

The completely different art north of the Great Murals

Examples of this fanciful, multicolored, abstract style of art can be found to the northwest of San Borja over a range nearly as extensive as that of the Great Murals.

Montevideo

CHAPTER 6

The
Sierra de
San Borja

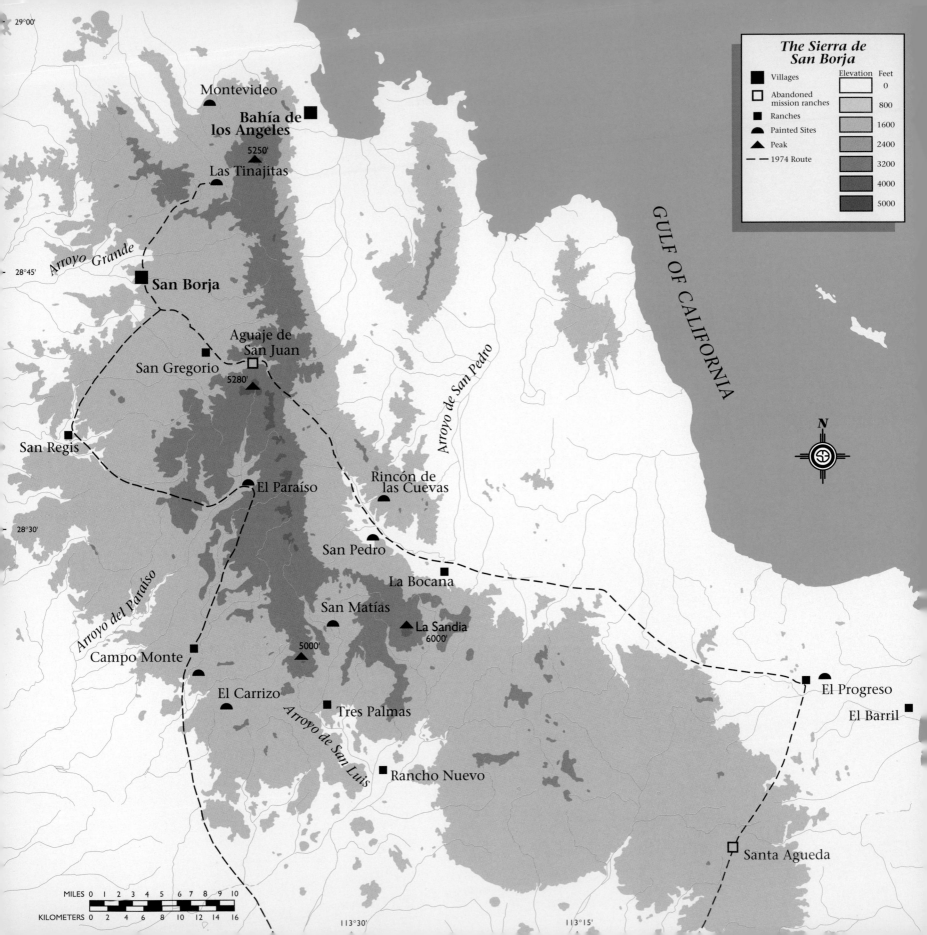

The Sierra de
San Borja

■ Villages
□ Abandoned
    mission ranches
■ Ranches
◗ Painted Sites
▲ Peak
-- -- 1974 Route

Elevation   Feet
              0
             800
            1600
            2400
            3200
            4000
            5000

29°00'

Montevideo
**Bahía de
los Angeles**
5250'
Las Tinajitas

Arroyo Grande
28°45'
■ **San Borja**

Aguaje de
San Juan
San Gregorio
5280'

San Regis

El Paraíso

Rincón de
las Cuevas

28°30'

San Pedro
La Bocana

Arroyo del Paraíso

San Matías
▲ La Sandia
  6000'
5000'

Campo Monte

El Carrizo
Tres Palmas

Arroyo de San Luis

Rancho Nuevo

El Progreso
El Barril

Santa Agueda

Arroyo de San Pedro

GULF OF CALIFORNIA

N

MILES 0 1 2 3 4 5 6 7 8 9 10
KILOMETERS 0 2 4 6 8 10 12 14 16

113°30'   113°15'

F rom Bahía de los Angeles on the north to the hamlet of El Arco on the south and dominating the whole lower end of Baja California's northern state is a range of mountains and foothills that resembles a geology sampler. The underpinnings are granite interspersed with pockets of metamorphic rock. Millions of years ago those were overlaid by volcanic flows. It is not unusual to see a pile of granite boulders weathering from its parent mass while still wearing an outlandish cap of lava. Despite its mixed parentage, the range as a whole is more unified in form than most of its peninsular neighbors, presenting a continuous wall toward the Gulf and a gentler decline of long, arroyo-cut slopes leading to the west. A generation or two ago, a score of families lived at widely spaced locations in every corner of this sierra, but drought and economic changes swept the heights. Lore and guides are now in lamentably short supply.

Explorations of the Sierra de San Francisco and a long expedition through the Sierra de Guadalupe raised tantalizing suggestions. The art of San Francisco had proved to be very homogeneous with only a scattering of eccentric works. The art of the adjacent northern end of the Guadalupe region had turned out to be similar, but increasing differences were observed as the inventory was carried farther south. This suggested the possibility that the San Francisco mountains were the homeland of the Great Mural phenomenon, and that the phenomenon had spread through movements of its parent culture or by the acculturation of neighbors. If that were indeed the case, we might expect a corresponding spread into the adjacent mountains lying to the north. That last frontier would be the Sierra de San Borja, a challenging row of peaks clearly visible from the uplands of San Francisco.

History offered little encouragement for a pursuit of Great Murals north of Santa Gertrudis. Leon Diguet listed a site north of Calmallí but neglected to specify whether it presented petroglyphs or paintings, a vagueness which suggests that he may have been reporting hearsay. The paintings that I had seen documented from regions north of the Sierra de San Francisco are on a smaller scale and of another school, a school characterized by polychromatic groupings of abstract symbols. Only a few rumors suggested that the tradition of large realistic paintings established in the Sierra de San Francisco might extend in that direction.

In the fall of 1973, after the month long exploration of the Sierra de Guadalupe, I planned a spring venture to include San Borja — if solid clues could be found. I asked Tacho Arce to make inquiries among all his extensive acquaintances.

When the spring came, a surprise was waiting for us in Tacho's home at Rancho La Esperanza: Manuel Flores, a member of a large family of vaqueros working as tenant ranchers in the Sierra de San Borja. Years before, I had given antibiotics to Manuel when he became ill in a remote place. When he heard we were looking for paintings, he hitched a ride down to tell Tacho what he knew. By a fortunate accident, Enrique Hambleton and I walked in at the time of this meeting.

Manuel, with his brother Ignacio, lived at Campo Monte, northwest of El Arco. Their ranch was surrounded by large paintings of monos, deer, borrego, and so forth. If we could visit his ranch he would show us everything.

The Sierra de San Borja

Our plans fell nicely together. We were set at the time to embark on a survey of the Sierra de San Juan, an exploration described earlier in these pages. That trip ended at Santa Gertrudis in the company of our guide for that region, Victor Aguilar Zúñiga. Victor did not know the Sierra de San Borja. However, both he and Tacho knew the several Villavicencio brothers living in the general area of El Barril on the Gulf coast, and everyone agreed that they were the authorities on San Borja. Their father had been born at El Paraíso in the heart of the sierra and they had all run cattle in the region for years. In the end, Victor agreed to guide us across the little-known stretch from Santa Gertrudis to the Villavicencios' ranches.

The trip to El Barril required two days. We found no appreciable rock art along the way, but on the afternoon of the first day we entered a valley called Santa Agueda that was littered with innumerable Indian remains of other sorts. According to Victor, the place had been a ranch of the Santa Gertrudis mission, an idea supported by several old stone corrals in the area. Earlier, it had served as a seasonal Indian encampment, a fact made obvious by a large tinaja and, within its environs, dozens of rock circles and literally hundreds of metates and manos scattered over level ground. Also, the place is thickly grown with *dátilillo,* the giant yucca, the fruit and seeds of which were important to the Indian diet.

We were disappointed at El Barril, a place apparently without rock art. A resident, José Rosas Villavicencio, the man who had guided Erle Stanley Gardner to the great painted complex in the Sierra de San Francisco, proved to know far less about San Borja. The best he could do was to suggest that we visit two of his brothers at Rancho El Progreso, less than 10 miles to the west. These men, Higinio and Lorenzo Villavicencio, were able to show us three painted sites in the area around El Progreso, sites quite different from anything farther south.

The plain around El Progreso is dotted with piles of huge granite boulders, some as much as 20 feet in diameter. With stones of such dimensions the voids between them could be equal to small caves. Two of the rock art sites actually consist of paintings on the undersides of such great boulders, bottoms exposed because the rocks lean or rest irregularly on others. The paintings in these poorly protected rock shelters are relatively small, eight to 24 inches, and depict fish, turtle, deer, and perhaps rabbits, all in various shades of red paint.

The third site, and the most impressive, consists of a pair of small interconnected caves weathered from in situ granite that forms the base of a sizable hill. One of these contains a group of figures in the same colors and dimensions as the paintings at the first two sites, but in a style that suggests a different art tradition.

In sum, the art in the region of El Progreso seems to bear out the tradition that places the Great Murals to the south. However, we were encouraged to proceed into the uplands. El Progreso is in low, level country and we knew that, elsewhere at least, the giant figures were painted in more mountainous settings. And, of course, we felt secure because we could rely on Manuel Flores's report of six-foot-high paintings in the San Borja foothills far to the west.

Despite his years of cattle herding in the San Borja uplands, Higinio Villavicencio could not remember a single painted site. He was an intelligent and generally observant man, so this void in his knowledge of his own area embarrassed him. However, he did not dodge the question; he simply admitted that the subject had never interested him, so he paid little attention to rumors about the finding of any sort of antiquity.

We headed northwest following a wheel-track auto road and in a day's ride came to the mouth of Arroyo de San Pedro, the largest watercourse on the eastern slope of the sierra. There, at a ranch appropriately called *La Bocana,* or The Mouth Place, we found the tenant rancher, Ignacio Murillo. "Galo," as he was universally called, was delighted to see Tacho. The two were childhood friends who had not met for 40 years, although they had kept up with each other's activities through the inevitable peninsular grapevine. Indeed, Galo even knew something of what we were about. As Tacho had imagined, Galo was willing to guide us and, after a day of preparation, we headed up the arroyo identifying remains of the eastern alternate route of El Camino Real as we went.

Galo was honest in his report on paintings. He personally knew only one site in the entire San Pedro region, but he enthusiastically endorsed the method we had developed. He promised to take us to each inhabited ranch to ask for local information.

Two hours out of La Bocana, we came to the spring and the ruins of historic Rancho San Pedro. We also came to an abandoned stamp mill that had been used by an American for years in a small gold-mining activity. The water, which would be our last for a day's ride, made us suspicious that paintings might be near. However, the immediate area around the spring consists of hills formed from a soft fractured metamorphic rock shot through with quartz veins which must have been the source of gold. Enrique noticed higher hills of granite half a mile or so to the west and he was determined to explore. As he started up a rough cañada, I followed his

Galo Murillo

197

The Sierra de San Borja

progress with my field glasses. A few minutes after he entered the steep-sided watercourse between the high hills, he turned and raised both arms aloft to mimic a mono. That was a thoroughly exciting gesture in a place so far north. I hurried to join him.

Enrique had found a site in that cañada which yielded, in a run of no more than a 100 yards, five large painted figures and a number of smaller ones. In a few minutes, we were photographing images of three deer, each about one and a half times as large as life, and two monos about four feet tall. One of the monos breaks entirely with previously noted tradition because its arms were painted extending downward.

That difference aside, these paintings adhere to most Great Mural conventions, but look subtly different from the many examples we had studied in sierras to the south. The paint is exclusively red, but in several shades ranging from rust to maroon. None of the figures is solitary; they are arranged in groups of three to five. Each such grouping was painted on a separate, nearly vertical granite surface. They are all unusually exposed to the elements compared with most Great Mural groups found to the south.

After the briefest inspection, I offered my companion hearty congratulations: He had just established the existence of large naturalistic paintings substantially north of the 28th parallel.

The next day, Galo showed us his site, significantly called *Rincón de las Cuevas,* the boxed-in or out-of-the-way place of the caves. Three hours' ride north of San Pedro, we were directed up a cañada to the northeast of the main wash of the arroyo. According to Galo, this box canyon had long been used as a place for cattle roundups and its caves often served the vaqueros as shelters.

We were now looking at different terrain. In the decidedly mixed geology of the Sierra de San Borja, we had arrived at the eroded edge of an ancient volcanic formation about 2,000 feet above sea level. The caves are smaller duplicates of those typical in the entirely volcanic San Francisco mountains, and in the first cave we found an array of paintings that might have come directly from San Francisco. We saw the remains of carefully and beautifully painted representations of deer, rabbits, and people—remains, and only remains. Fires, apparently of rather recent origin, had been built against the painted walls and they had caused the surface rock to expand and flake away in sheets. Higher up, the paintings are badly smoked. On the floor near the back wall, partially obscured by the fallen debris, we found a maze of those enigmatic cuplike pits we had encountered at several sites in other sierras.

We pored over the polychromatic patches of paint, trying to interpret them. We photographed the small areas that were reasonably intact. Later, when our trip was done, we felt the sense of loss even more keenly. By then we realized that all the other San Borja Great Mural sites present a distinctly parochial aspect: Style, paints, and the surfaces on which the Painters chose to paint would define a "Red-on-Granite" school of painting, of which our recent find at San Pedro was typical. But that little cave at Rincón de las Cuevas demonstrated with finality that the familiar tradition of the San Francisco style of Great Mural art extended well into the Sierra de San Borja. And, for the moment at least, that is the only evidence.

Our journey continued with a spectacular crossing of the 4,400-foot pass between Arroyo de San Pedro and Arroyo de San Gregorio that leads down to San Borja. From the pass, we had a sweeping view of the Gulf dotted with islands as large as the 60-mile-long Angel de la Guarda to the north and ranging down through assorted shapes and sizes to mere rocky pinnacles. A panorama of bays was also apparent; we could see the bahías of Los Angeles, Las Animas, and San Rafael. After those vistas, it was wrenching to turn west and plunge into the narrow confines of another cañada. We arrived at the Aguaje de San Juan in the gloom of evening and camped among the ruins of a ranch and visiting station of the San Borja Mission. During this ride we saw no promising caves or respaldos and, indeed, saw just one piece of rock art: a badly-faded white painting on a vertical basalt surface. The form resembled a string of beads or perhaps a section of intestines.

At Rancho San Gregorio, the dueño, Armando Villavicencio, assured us that there were no paintings in that region. He did, however, know of artworks a few miles north of San Borja. We immediately asked him to guide us and, to save time, Enrique and I went with him in his truck while Tacho, Ramón, and Galo took our caravan on to San Borja itself.

Armando drove us to Arroyo Grande, a very broad watercourse at an elevation of about 2,100 feet that is studded, like so much of the Sierra de San Borja, with countless tall tapers of *cirio*, the giant, single-stemmed member of the ocotillo family. There, on the south side of the arroyo, around the mouth of a small, open cañada called Las Tinajitas, is a set of bluffs literally honeycombed with tiny caves; the formation looks for all the world like a miniature of Loma Cuevada in Arroyo de Santa Gertrudis. For two hours, Armando, Enrique, and I poked through an enchanting maze of over 20 painted caves decorated with hundreds of abstract forms in an unusually broad palette of colors: white, ochre, and orange are common, as well as the more usual reds and black. Most of the painted works are in poor condition, but enough was visible to show us images like nothing we had seen during our long pursuit of Great Murals. These are small works, most under a foot in diameter, and appear to be allied with paintings of symbolic character found throughout the region to the north as far as Cataviña near the southern flanks of the Sierra de San Pedro Mártir.

We returned to San Borja and passed the night. Early the following morning, I noticed that the high hill just east of the village is crowned with cantilería in a way very reminiscent of what we had seen at Las Tinajitas the previous day. I got out my binoculars and was able to discover numerous caves and shelters too shaded to see into effectively. The local people were no help; not a soul seemed to have made the climb. Off I went. Twenty minutes of stiff hiking took me to the level of the shelters at the base of the cantil. I made my way along for 100 yards or more and examined half a dozen promising places. Not a vestige of painting or drawing was to be seen, so I returned to the village.

Meanwhile, the other members of our group had found no one who knew of paintings. We saddled up and took our caravan to San Ignacito to no avail, then headed south to traverse the western drainage of the sierra. At Rancho Santa Ana we stopped to query Amado Villavicencio, who had lived in the region all his life. He, too, could offer no help, so we continued south over high hills.

The character of the country changes dramatically at this point. From volcanic scapes covered with cardón and cirio, we passed into a region of metamorphic rock like that of San Pedro on the other side of the sierra. There are many signs of gold-seeking here as well—little shafts and tiny mills for reducing ore. The plant cover also changes; we now found ourselves riding among the heaviest stands of *copalquín,* the elephant tree, I had ever seen. These trees with their contorted forms and swollen-looking trunks and branches are bizarre enough in themselves, but all those in this region were heavily infected with dodder, a parasite resembling strands of orange hair. The scenes through which we rode had a nightmarish quality— ragged hills bristling with grotesque leafless trees, each of which sprouted a tangled head of flaming hair.

We came to Rancho San Miguel and found it abandoned; its large huerta had died off except for a few hardy olive trees, and the substantial adobe casa was be-ginning to tumble. In a way, San Miguel characterized the problems we and anyone else attempting research in the Sierra de San Borja would have. Most of the ranches were abandoned, most of the knowledgeable old-timers were dead or scattered. We were rather sad as we turned east to go up the arroyo to San Regis, which, like San Miguel, had been an agricultural center since the early days of the San Borja mission.

San Regis presented a more cheerful picture. Part of the large huerta was being watered and tended, and a sizable vineyard was leafing out strongly. Two widely spaced casas were occupied, each by a single old man. We had come specifically to see one of these men. Back at San Borja, we had been told about Antonio Rios, the caretaker at San Regis. Rios was reputed to be the last pure-blooded Cochimí Indian in that quarter of the peninsula; he was also supposed to know the western slopes of the sierra better than anyone else then resident in the region.

We found Rios clearing irrigation ditches. He was a quiet, shy little man in his sixties, wiry of build and with skin like tanned leather. We outlined our quest and asked for his help. Without committing himself, he laid his hoe aside and sug-gested we sit down and have coffee.

We sat under a shady mezquite in front of Antonio Rios's tiny house and told him what we had done and where we had gone. He knew Galo Murillo from some distant year and apparently liked him. He warmed to Tacho and Galo's obvious good humor; he even contributed a few stories of his own. Gradually, he began to tell us what he knew about Indian remains. In the end, he agreed to guide us from

Antonio Rios

San Regis to Manuel Flores's ranch at Campo Monte and to take us to the one painted site he knew in the intervening country.

In the days that followed, we got better acquainted with the gentle Indian, but we were disappointed in our expectations. His family descends from neophytes of the San Borja and San Ignacio missions but, at San Regis, they were isolated from other Indians for so long that Antonio had never learned a word of Cochimí. As we rode along, it was obvious that the ancient trails, rock circles, metates, and, eventually, paintings, though familiar, were as alien to him as they were to Tacho, Galo, or Ramón.

We crossed from Arroyo de San Regis to another called Catarina. Antonio told us that these two join farther west near a ranch called El Cardonal, and that he knew of a painted rock near there. His description sounded familiar: two deer painted in red on the side of a granite boulder. Since there was an auto road to El Cardonal, we decided to return by car and save the two days the detour would have cost.

On the cuesta leading out of Arroyo de Catarina, another abrupt change in plant life occurred. The giant agave, or *mezcal,* had been rare or absent from the terrain we had covered in coming from San Borja. Suddenly it became one of the most common plants of the slopes and mesas. That observation recalled Dr. Homer Aschmann's hypothesis, put forth in *The Central Desert of Baja California,* that the Indians of the San Borja mission had used mezcales as food during famine periods until finally these plants were gone for up to two days' travel in all directions from the population center. Our encounter with them in this lonely region seemed to bear out that idea. Other observations were thrust upon us. The cardón obviously favors southern exposures while cirio prefers northern. Riding south, we descended from mesa to arroyo by way of cuestas surrounded by cardón and climbed out through equally thick stands of cirio.

From Arroyo de Catarina, our trail crossed the Mesa del Corral Blanco and descended the Cuesta de San Bartolo into El Paraíso, the largest arroyo in the sierra. The drop from mesa to arroyo floor is over 1,300 feet — from volcanic palisades above to a place of trees, water, and huge blocks of granite below. Antonio Rios led the way past the abandoned ranch of San Bartolo to a sandy flat near a pool thickly ringed with rushes. He pointed across the pool to a vertical face of granite that towers above. It was his painted site, a place he called *Los Venados,* the deer. The scene was simple but impressive. The granite provides a large clean canvas for the painted representation of a single large deer in a maroon shade. The animal showed very clearly even in the late afternoon shadow — only its head is badly faded.

We crossed the watercourse and clambered up to the painted area. Essentially, we had seen it all. Once there had been the image of another animal to the right of the great deer but the same flow of water that had so faded its head had virtually obliterated the second figure. Only a pair of legs remain to show where it was.

201

The Sierra de San Borja

The Red-on-Granite School defined

The Great Murals in the Sierra de San Borja consist almost entirely of paintings in various shades of red applied to the sides of large granite boulders. This was a notable departure from Great Mural practices in sierras to the south, where polychromatic works were painted on the walls or ceilings of caves. A further break with the predominant tradition can be seen in the downthrust arms of these three linked human figures, *Los Tres Reyes,* The Three Kings.

Campo Monte II and Campo Monte I

That was the extent of Antonio Rios's contribution to rock art knowledge: a single great deer in a totally remote place. It was symbolic of both the difficulties and the grudging rewards that await any visitor to the vast rock pile that is the Sierra de San Borja.

Just north of the campsite and several hundred feet up the steepest sort of falda, we saw a marvelous array of cantilería. In the morning Enrique explored it and found a small shelter containing crudely painted works. One very badly worn mono appears to be a duplicate of the odd, arms-down figure we saw at the first site in Arroyo de San Pedro. As nearly as I could determine from so faded an image, it has bowed legs and male genitalia like some monos we had seen in the Sierra de Guadalupe.

We left Arroyo del Paraíso by way of the Cuesta de las Cruces which climbs to a mesa 3,000 feet above sea level. As we broke onto the mesa, we startled a large deer, causing it to flee across very broken ground in a series of heroic leaps. One posture froze in my mind as I watched the succession of bounds: At the top of each leap, the forelegs went back and the hind legs were brought forward in a startling recreation of the deer painting that we had just seen in El Paraíso. Obvi-

ously, the ancient painters were observant and knew their animals. It is probable
that most paintings that appear to portray animals in awkward or unlikely postures
were actually modeled from life.

A long day took us south to Campo Monte, a region of unrelieved granite outcroppings. By good fortune the Flores brothers were at home and, within a few
minutes of our arrival, the paintings were being pointed out. Manuel Flores had
not exaggerated; we could see two paintings from his doorstep, and he indicated
the way to four others nearby. We hurried for an inspection. The first group faces
the ranch from the opposite or east side of a wash. On a single granite boulder are
life-sized deer, a borrego, and a turtle, as well as smaller monos, birds, and fish, including a manta ray. There is a great deal of overpainting, the first we had seen in
the entire San Borja area.

The second site is farther south, back across the arroyo, and hence facing east.
After climbing up to a row of huge, in situ granite boulders, we had a commanding
view of a large stretch of the arroyo from our position high on a point that forces a
bend in the waterway. Here, a group of paintings is dominated by one very large
mono. To the right, three others, smaller and nearly identical in shape, stand side

by side with their arms in the unusual downward position that seems to be limited to the Sierra de San Borja. Manuel Flores called the latter figures with linked arms *Los Tres Reyes*, The Three Kings. These striking monos are accompanied by paintings of birds and several small deer that seem to move as a herd before them.

The other painted sites offered distinctly less. One consists of two large monos with a tiny mono like a child at their feet. Another shows three giant monos so faded that they have lost all individual features. A third is no more than a single large deer, which appears to be almost a replica of the survivor at San Bartolo as nearly as we could tell from its disintegrated image. The fourth and last site is curiously different. As we walked back to the ranch we saw a small, clear painting that might have come from Arroyo Grande. It consists of purely abstract designs and looks entirely out of place in the company of the naturalism consistently painted on nearby rocks.

The painting locations are instructive. Each group is on a rock face visible from and facing the bed of the arroyo. It seemed almost certain that they were placed this way to expose them to the view of people using the caja of the arroyo as an avenue. To test this hypothesis, we walked up and down the 200 yard stretch in which the paintings are located and found that they occupied all the best places in terms of the size and conspicuousness of the available rock surfaces.

We left the Campo Monte area with one last find. Not more than two miles from the principal concentration of paintings, Ramón spotted a handsome borrego above a small wash near the trail. It, too, is red on granite, the common currency for painting over a very large area.

All the paintings around Campo Monte are in red and all are on vertical faces of granite. The significant features of this collection are numbers, quality, and condition. In all of these matters, Campo Monte outshines not only any individual Great Mural site we saw in the Sierra de San Borja, but all the others combined.

Our three-week exploration of the Sierra de San Borja ended at Campo Monte, but the San Borja story was not quite over. In the fall of 1974 I returned to the sierras of San Juan and San Borja with a list of all the clues and suggestions picked up in the spring but not pursued. My companion was William Price, whom I mentioned in the previous chapter.

Around the village of San Borja, I had heard many references to paintings in Arroyo de Montevideo, just off the road to Bahía de Los Angeles. Antero Díaz at the Bahía gave us precise instructions. A comparison showed that his directions matched others given to me years before by Dr. Reid Moran at the San Diego Natural History Museum and by William Weber Johnson, author of *Baja California,* in the Time-Life series *The American Wilderness.* Further coincidences were apparent when we came to the actual site. We immediately recognized the paintings as those published in Mexico by Ingeniero Ernesto Raúl López and located at "Volcancito." In short, it was clear that these must be among the peninsula's best-known works of rock art.

204

Chapter 6

The site consists of a 50-foot-high cliff of solid volcanic rock lined with small caves and shallow depressions. These are characterized by generally smooth interior rock surfaces. Many are painted and the school of art seen here is identical, or at least closely related, to that of nearby Arroyo Grande. However, these figures on the whole are somewhat larger and more skillfully painted. It is the finest and most extensive display of the abstract, symbolic type of prehistoric painting yet reported in Baja California (see photo on page 192).

The Montevideo figures contrast strongly with typical Great Murals: Besides the obviously different subject matter, these figures are smaller, display a wider range of colors, and are more precisely worked. The last of these traits was probably due in part to their smaller size and the unusually smooth surfaces on which they were painted.

Despite the almost universally abstract character of the Montevideo designs, two natural forms stand out. One is a stiff, long-bodied mono about 40 inches tall, similar to those at San Pedro or Campo Monte except that it is divided vertically into red and black zones in the San Francisco fashion. Another realistic work almost certainly represents a flowering plant. This beautiful painting adds to the petroglyph from Cuesta Blanca and the identical leaf paintings at San Gregorito and El Parral to form the very short list of plant depictions encountered during my explorations.

Next, William and I drove to El Arco and entered the sierra from the south via Calmallí and Rancho Nuevo. At Rancho Nuevo, Jesús Aguilar, whom I knew from my search for El Camino Real, was able to provide animals, so we rode north to Tres Palmas, the ranch of Francisco Romero, who had guided me before. Our goal was to find the paintings at San Sebastián and San Matías reported by the Flores brothers and other cowboys I had quizzed. Romero proved familiar with the San Matías work only. Although he knew the San Sebastián area intimately from cattle roundups, he had never seen paintings or heard them mentioned. He hesitated to undertake a blind hunt over an area of several square miles, so we settled for San Matías.

As we approached, the region had a thoroughly familiar look. The arroyo winds through an increasingly high and narrow channel between walls of in situ granite blocks. The way is littered with boulders derived from the same source. All of this is reminiscent of both San Pedro and Campo Monte. We rode for hours past rock faces that it seemed must be painted, but our constant surveillance produced no results.

Finally we turned north into Cañada de San Matías, and before long the waterway became too boulder-choked for mule travel. We unsaddled the animals, tied them, and proceeded on foot. Within 10 minutes Romero was able to show us what he called *El Rey de San Matías,* the King of San Matías. He pointed to obvious paintings in a shallow depression high on the west side of the cañada and, with difficulty, William and I made our way up and into the shelter. We found two painted figures, a five-foot mono in red in extremely faded condition and another of similar size, El Rey, that is still sharp and bright. The principal features of El Rey,

El Rey, the King of San Matías

In the southern Sierra de San Borja, humanity seems to have left a record of long effort and desultory success. Aboriginal remains are scarce, abandoned mining camps abound, and ponderous stone corrals mark deserted cattle ranches. Now the area is quiet; days of searching for ancient art produced little more than this figure known as *El Rey* to the few people who live in the region of San Matías. Gold is where you find it.

San Matías

like its location, were familiar from previous San Borja experiences: The Red-on-Granite style of mono shows in the elongated, formless body and the short arms. Less usual are the elaborate representation of hair or a headdress and the large number of apparent arrows with which the body fairly bristles.

Below us, Francisco Romero had found other paintings and we descended in response to his call. Under an immense fallen and fractured slab of granite are about two dozen small red paintings, mostly of deer. Apparently, they were done when the slab was in a more vertical position. Subsequent movement of the fallen materials left the paintings visible only in a narrow slit or from peek-through crevices beneath the slab. As a result of the changed position, the art is almost impossible to photograph, but it also is superbly protected from the elements and in generally good condition.

A search of the area produced only one other painted figure, farther up the cañada. A mono about 40 inches tall has been made faint by weathering but, surprisingly, its hands and scrotal sac remain clearly delineated.

During our return to Tres Palmas, Romero said he knew of similar rock art near Rancho La Huerta, half a day's ride to the west. We extended our tour accordingly and shortly after noon of the following day, we arrived at that ranch. In fact, we discovered that the actual site is over another cuesta to the west and nearer the abandoned Rancho El Carrizo.

We found the paintings in two locations a little over a quarter of a mile apart. The first is on an exposed granite rock face just south of the trail. Two large figures are in evidence, a borrego with marvelous horns and a deer with heavy antlers, both in poor condition but clearly visible.

The second is immediately south of the huerta at the abandoned ranch. There, literally within a pile of granite boulders, are small monos and a two-foot-tall fish, all in the usual red.

These minor discoveries marked the end of my efforts to find ancient art in the Sierra de San Borja. The small number of sites we had discovered in the four weeks we devoted to the area is not indicative of its potential. Compared with similar studies in other sierras, our efforts were hampered by the need to examine a vast, poorly watered area while handicapped by a distinct lack of local information. Despite these obstacles, it is certain that dozens of additional sites will eventually be located. In the meantime, the few reported here demonstrate the broad distribution of large naturalistic paintings north of the 28th parallel and offer considerable insight into their special character.

Useful generalizations can now be made about Great Murals located in this new area: The works are executed in shades of red on granitic rock. The surfaces chosen are either on large freestanding boulders or blocks weathering out of their mother formations. While large, the painted figures are smaller on the average than those in other Great Mural areas. Human figures, especially, tend to be approximately life-size or smaller. Subject matter in general is limited to deer, borrego, and humans.

The style of the paintings is conspicuously homogeneous and discernibly different from artworks elsewhere in the Great Mural area. Wholly apart from the similarity of their paint and rock surfaces, these Red-on-Granite works compel one to think of a regional "school" of art. For example, elsewhere among the Great Murals, monos have more natural proportions and, usually, upraised arms. In the Red-on-Granite realm of San Borja, human figures are represented less realistically. They are stiff, with long torsos and short limbs, and their arms are occasionally thrust down and out instead of up and out.

Painted panels are small and generally display few figures. Overpainting, practically a hallmark of the sites to the south, is extremely rare in the Sierra de San Borja.

The condition of all the Red-on-Granite artwork is remarkably similar. The paint has adhered unusually well to the granite; the hard but finely checked surface provides an excellent basis for an enduring mechanical bond. Offsetting this positive survival factor is the element of exposure. Most of these Red-on-Granite works are on the vertical faces of rounded boulders. Such faces are washed by every rain of consequence even if the paintings are on the rolled-under surfaces at the bases of the boulders. In contrast, most of the surviving Great Murals to the south are in rock shelters well protected from rain. The result of this exposure in the Sierra de San Borja is a rather uniform fading coupled with occasional vertical streaks where greater damage has occurred due to specific flows of water. Nevertheless, it is important to reemphasize the striking sameness in the condition of all known Red-on-Granite sites. This, taken with their stylistic homogeneity, leads to a preliminary opinion that they were created by members of a single cultural group during a relatively brief period of time.

This exploration extended beyond the Red-on-Granite area and apparently established the general location of an interface between two cultures with markedly different rock-painting traditions. The abstract works around the village of San Borja seem to derive from a common culture and relate to similar sites stretching for 100 or more miles northward. The Red-on-Granite works may be distinguishable from the Great Murals to the south, but they were created in adherence to most of the same artistic conventions. They share nothing with the polychromatic abstractions that make up the large majority of the art in the adjacent region to the north.

The ambience in many painted caves
encourages a modern viewer to see
retreats devoted to spiritual activities.

Cuesta de San Pablo

CHAPTER *7*

The
Practices
and
Puzzles
of the
Painters

*T*he meager archaeology of the mid-peninsula suggests an occupancy of many thousands of years. San Dieguito Man left his telltale artifacts on his way to the Cape. La Jollan-like tools suggest the passing of that people as well. Early splinters of Yuman folk followed at some undetermined time and added to the growing assemblage of human discards. Europeans found the area populated by a single, far-flung, loosely organized group. These first historic people were still working stone and contributing to the archaeological record, but they had no bent for painting. Sometime during the latter part of this long human presence, a culture with organized, even institutionalized artists invaded this ground or evolved from its occupants. They painted as few on this globe have done, decorating hundreds of locations with thousands of images, great and small. They left no other obvious clues to distinguish themselves in the parade of peoples. Who were the Painters? How, what, why, and when did they paint?

Traditions Define the Great Murals   Paleolithic rock art depicting humans and animals survives on every inhabited continent. Apparently all peoples, as they passed through the hunting and gathering phase of their cultural development, responded to a common impulse to create long-lasting art and to celebrate some now-forgotten sense of relationship to their fellow creatures and their deities. The rock paintings of central Baja California are very much a part of this ancient tradition. Much about them — subject matter, materials, and locations — hauntingly resembles artworks found on other continents, paintings separated from them by thousands of miles and thousands of years. Although the creation of art on the California peninsula has no history and the painted sites have been subject to little archaeology, I have no hesitation in associating them with religious practices. This connection has been assumed by most scholars of ancient rock art in general and, in Baja California, it is supported by a persuasive argument: All evidence suggests that the Painters were organized into small bands that occupied discrete territories. Their art, however, adheres to overriding principles; it seems to celebrate something greater than the power of a tribal leader or a band. If that sort of petty aggrandizement were its main objective, we would expect to see many truly individual statements. Instead, the artworks of all bands seem designed to make more universal statements. I cannot imagine a unifying force more likely than religion.

Despite its marked resemblance to ancient rock art in Europe and Africa, the rock paintings in central Baja California constitute a separate, distinct art form with its own unique set of characteristics. After viewing, photographing, and studying hundreds of sites and thousands of painted figures, I coined the term "Great Murals" as a collective title to distinguish art that meets the following criteria:

1. Artistic images painted on the walls or ceilings of caves or rock shelters, or even on unprotected rock surfaces, at elevations above 600

feet, on the Baja California peninsula between 26° 20' and 29° north latitude.

2. Images derived from observations of creatures in the natural world — humans, deer, mountain sheep, antelope, rabbits, hares, mountain lions, bobcats, various birds, fish, turtles, snakes, whales or pinnipeds.

3. Painted figures, life-sized or greater (and placed high when painted on a surface displaying figures in a range of sizes).

4. Painted figures, smaller than life sized (and placed low when painted on a surface displaying figures in a range of sizes).

5. Outer boundaries of painted figures rendered as recognizable but formalized line drawings of the subjects, the formality demanded that the perspective be altered to allow the representation of features in the outline that would be invisible in a completely realistic silhouette.

6. Internal or field area of painted figures rendered as devoid of natural details, but filled in with arbitrary artistic devices: i.e., the entire field in a single color; the field divided into two areas with two colors of paint; the field filled with stripes, a grid, a checkerboard pattern, etc.

An analysis of the myriad of figures that meet the Great Mural criteria demonstrates forcefully that their creation was neither casual nor the product of individual inspiration or self-expression. This list of criteria shows conclusively that the Painters adhered to a remarkably rigid code. In spite of their obviously representational character, we find that the seeming "naturalism" of the Great Murals was actually subject to a number of formal and arbitrary rules. For example, nearly all the Painters gave each creature a characteristic and invariable aspect. Humans were presented head-on with arms extended upward in a gesture suggestive of the classic "I surrender" pose. The upraised arms and flat view of the extended hands are natural enough, but the feet are turned outward and then rotated spatially so that they alone appear as if seen from above — that is, as a flat foot with toes extended. This display of the feet and toes presents a twisted perspective that is not possible in reality — a formal manipulation which suggests that these figures are ideographs of men rather than lifelike sketches. In addition, other features that reasonably could have been depicted in the generally realistic outline are conspicuously missing — as in the case of ears — or are usually missing — as in the case of genitalia.

Several different subjects were regularly portrayed in accordance with criteria specific to them:

≫ Women were distinguished from men only by the addition of rather long, pointed breasts which appear as if in double profile and hence seem to issue from each armpit. This convention is analogous to the treatment of the similarly oriented feet.

The Painters invented their own skewed perspective

The hoofs of most animals were painted in a curious four-digit pattern that gives their feet the appearance of hands. This photograph of the hoof of a peninsular mule deer shows the reason: The Painters depicted not only the cloven hoof, but also the dewclaws splayed to the sides to make them appear in the outline. This spatial rotation was consistent with their treatment of human feet and women's breasts. Every aspect of anatomy was portrayed as part of the outline — or not portrayed at all.

211

>> Four-legged animals were given active profiles as if running or leaping. Yet these are not true side views. Heads were drawn as if slightly turned in order to show both ears and both horns (where applicable). The dewclaws on deer were swung out so that both appear above each hoof.

>> Turtles and manta or bat rays were depicted in dorsal view. Other fish were usually drawn from the same viewpoint, but sideviews are not rare.

>> Birds were drawn as if seen from below while in flight, yet their heads were turned in profile, probably in order to display the beak.

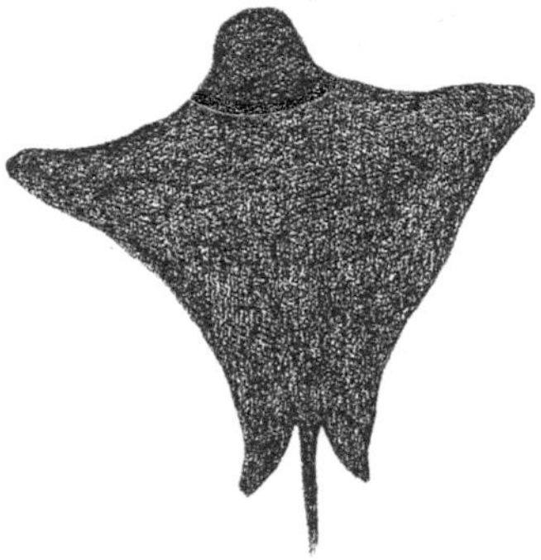

Sexual distinctions in animals seem to be limited to those that can be indicated by the presence or absence or differences in horns or antlers. Some paintings seem to suggest pregnancy. However, the observable spread of body types in each species ranges from slender to heavy, so it is impossible to say which ones might have been intended to represent pregnancy.

Conventions governing the creation of Great Murals called for another departure from reality more profound than twisted perspective. Only the outlines or silhouettes of the painted figures clearly relate to their subjects. All anatomical features that could have appeared within the diagnostic outlines are missing. For example, human figures never display eyes, noses, or mouths. Animals portrayed in profile, or with only their heads in profile, like birds, do have mouths and noses, or their equivalent, but they never have eyes. All of this follows a rule: Only the outline drawing is representational; everything that lies within is some sort of conventional abstraction.

In the majority of painted figures, the characteristic and formalized outline is simply filled in with a layer of paint undifferentiated in hue or density. However, a large minority of figures are bicolored, with the areas assigned to the two colors painted in a variety of traditional patterns. Some of these patterns are so rare that only the perusal of many dozens of sites proves that they have precedents. It is in the infill patterns that we see the greatest differences among the works of the Painters in the several sierras. The reader may wish to consult the table that follows to see examples of the infill characteristics encountered in different parts of the Great Mural range.

Despite adhering with remarkable consistency to certain rigid practices, Great Mural art does vary a great deal from one end of its range to the other. I think of these differences as regional styles that still belong under the Great Mural umbrella. I conclude — quite subjectively, in the absence of science — that the style of art employed at a given time or place was dictated by the customs of the immediate culture rather than by the personal choices of the individual artists. Thus we wonder less at styles that vary from region to region than at those that vary from figure to figure on the same wall. The former speak to us of people operating within their own homelands. The latter, as I see it, represent work done at different times.

The dissimilarities between artworks in different regions include virtually every aspect of style except the underlying conventions that led me to call the paintings, collectively, the Great Murals. For my own convenience, I have coined terms for what I perceive to be the major "schools" found under the Great Mural umbrella. They are summarized here, as closely as possible, in a north to south succession.

> ≫ Red-on-Granite: a style of painting found almost exclusively within the confines of the southern half of the Sierra de San Borja. Figures are usually life-sized or somewhat smaller. Almost all were painted in a uniformly solid dark red, so outline and infill are virtually indistinguishable. Human figures often have arms extended out and down rather than out and up.

> ≫ San Francisco: a style found in the Sierras of San Juan and San Francisco as well as the northwest third of the Sierra de Guadalupe. The painted figures are usually larger than life and depicted in outline with recognizable, classically realistic proportions. These outlines were typically infilled with solid or sketchy red or black, or in bicolor, with the red and black areas determined by rules that applied specifically to the animal that was painted. This is the predominant Great Mural style in terms of public perception.

> ≫ San Borjitas: a style found in the northeast third of the Sierra de Guadalupe. Human figures predominate. They usually display bulbous

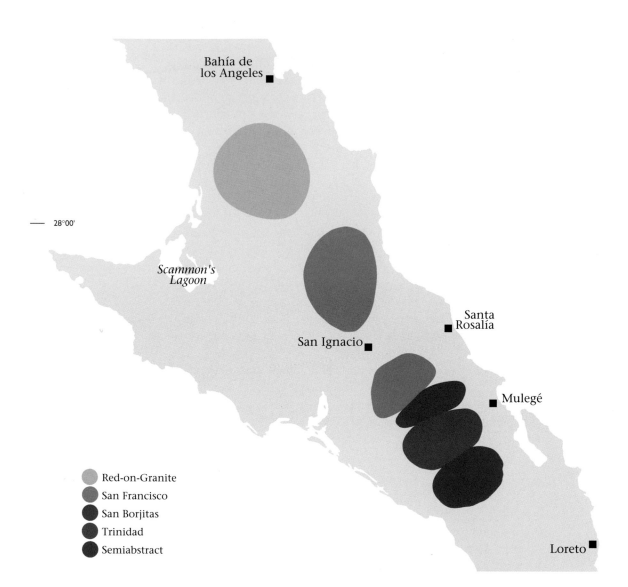

Bahía de
los Angeles ■

— 28°00'

*Scammon's
Lagoon*

Santa
Rosalía ■

San Ignacio ■

Mulegé ■

● Red-on-Granite

● San Francisco

● San Borjitas

● Trinidad

● Semiabstract

Loreto ■

bodies, legs straight but spread, arms thrust directly outward, no neck, and heads that are flat-topped and often resemble cans. Most frequently, these figures are infilled with vertical stripes, but instead may show horizontal stripes, vertical bicolored areas, or, occasionally, spots.

≫ Trinidad: a style found in the southeast part of the Sierra de Guadalupe. The characteristic images are deer, the drawings of which often suggest a graceful walking motion. They range from much larger than life to somewhat smaller. They are very realistic in outline and typically more delicate than comparable San Francisco images. Infill patterns vary widely, but the more common ones are longitudinal stripes, checkerboards, or a line connecting an apparent tongue with the tail.

≫ Semiabstract: a potpourri of styles found in the most southerly part of the Sierra de Guadalupe. Characteristic images include deer and humans with boxlike bodies, stick legs (and arms, in the case of humans), and very arbitrary, often unrealistic proportions. Infills range from stripes to checkerboards to scattered daubs of paint. The area dominated by this school—or these schools, as some may prefer—has been little explored and should provide many new discoveries that could clarify our rather murky perception of this school's characteristics, range, and influences.

This simple review of the elements of the Great Mural phenomenon falls far short of answering many of the questions these paintings raise. Archaeological research and a great deal more study of these artworks may very well increase our knowledge of their origin, development, or decline, but there is no imaginable way that we can reconstruct the Painters' thoughts or motivations. We have no evidence that explains or even suggests why their painted figures have realistic outlines and fanciful internal details. Or why they froze each kind of creature in a particular attitude. We cannot account for the presence or absence of arrows or spears in different figures at different sites.

But these paintings are the only message we have from the Painters, and that message is not so cryptic that it cannot be read at all. The elements of tradition and discipline are strikingly evident. The fact that so many conventions were observed over a considerable period of time argues that these people knew how to exercise and obey authority. The painted record also betrays a degree of tribal organization adequate to support a class of artists, probably not full-time, but certainly for significant periods. This support apparently extended beyond the mere feeding of a materially nonproductive group. Long trips were made to gather special colored rocks, a great deal of labor was expended grinding them into suitable pigments, and other large outlays of labor were required to collect construction materials and erect scaffoldings.

The fact that similar but not identical paintings are found over large areas bespeaks a high degree of rather specific communication, but the mechanisms remain obscure to us; we do not know if the Painters' traditions were transmitted by word of mouth, by means of sketches, or by visits among groups who actually viewed each other's art. But whatever the mode, complex communications did take place, and the resulting works have a codified relatedness reminiscent of what is seen in centuries of Russian icons or millennia of Chinese brush paintings.

215

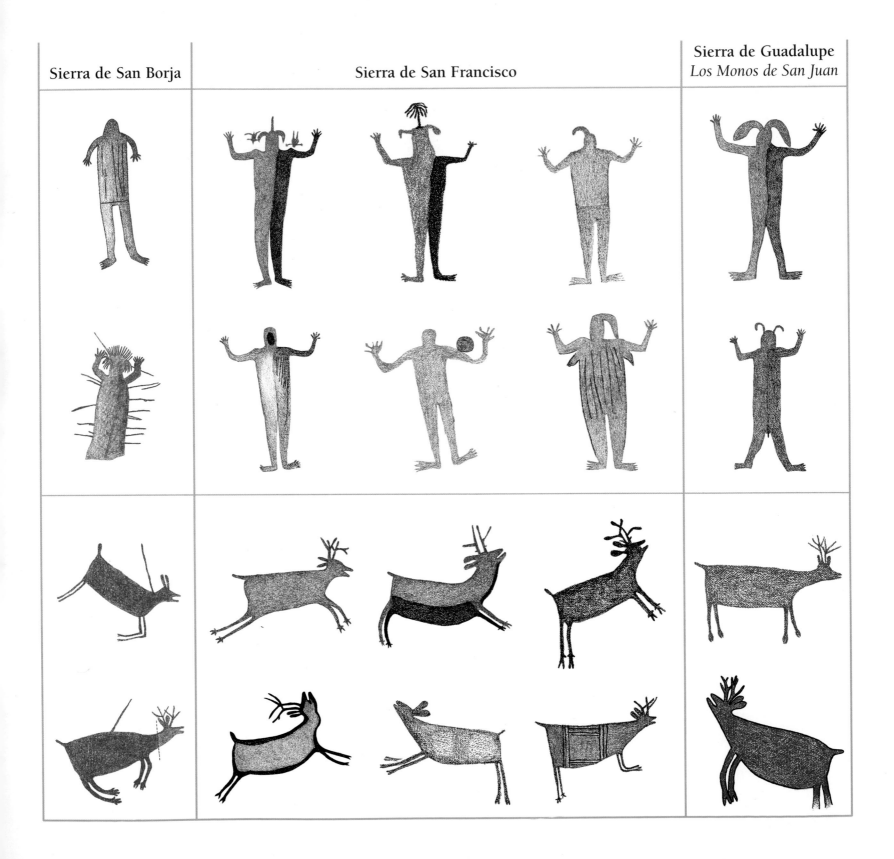

| Sierra de San Borja | Sierra de San Francisco | Sierra de Guadalupe Los Monos de San Juan |

| Sierra de Guadalupe | | |
| San Borjitas | La Trinidad | Southern Semiabstract |

The Scope and Geography of Great Mural Styles

"*The Great Mural Phenomenon consist of thousands of prehistoric rock paintings found at hundreds of sites located in the middle of the Baja California peninsula. Although the geology and morphology of these sites vary widely, most of the painted places are caves or rock shelters situated at elevations of 1,000 or more feet in the three ranges of mountains listed here from north to south. [Note: The Sierra de San Juan has been omitted because its small showings of art are indistinguishable from those of San Francisco.]*

As the table shows, these ancient artworks adhere consistently to certain formal artistic conventions, but they also have characteristics peculiar to their own regions.

If you rotate these pages clockwise about 45°, the table forms a crude map of the entire geographic range of the Great Murals, with the most northerly style—that of the Sierra de San Borja—at top left and the most southerly—the Southern Semiabstrasct—at bottom right."

21/

Much of what we see and feel as lofty aspirations and esthetic accomplishments in the Painters' art seems inconsistent with the poverty of their other material remains. No doubt we see this as a paradox because of our own technical bias. We in the West have always tended to evaluate other cultures on the basis of their material achievements. But the Painters were not lacking in the human determination to engage in dramatic and conspicuous offerings or representations to their gods and to leave their marks on the world they inhabited. If we consider the probable sizes of their bands, the enforced simplicity of their economy, and the sparse materials they had at their disposal, their Great Murals emerge as impressive — even monumental — achievements. And they remind us that humanity at its simplest is still a complex proposition.

The Painters at Work   The galleries of the Great Murals are so hushed and deserted today that it requires a real effort to imagine the activity that must have accompanied their making. The serenity of these sunlit gorges lulls us into supposing that they have always been quiet, and that the art treasures they house were as much a part of creation as the warm-toned rock or the rustling palms. But that feeling passes soon because the paintings exercise a more active fascination: They impart a sense of our own kind calling out to us. In our minds, we populate the places and imagine the scenes as they might have been during the busy ceremony of decorating these walls.

The season was probably fall. The summer rains would have filled the tinajas to provide water in every corner of the sierras. For a few weeks, the pitahaya crop could provide the abundance of food that would allow a few helpers to feed themselves and the artists with ease. Temperatures during that season are moderate. The caves, especially with fires, would provide better night shelters than most of the stops on the seasonal rounds that dictated the rhythms of Painters' lives.

When a group met to enact the painting ritual, the needs of its members extended beyond food, water, paint, and brushes. As we stand today and admire the murals in the larger shelters, we are acutely aware that lofty constructions were an indispensable part of their production. Some of the painted figures have been rendered at heights over 30 feet above the shelter floors; this implies the use of very tall ladders or scaffolds.

Interested people who know these places only from photographs have suggested other means by which the artists might have reached such high places. One common thought has been that the floor level of the shelters might once have been higher. Another has suggested that the Painters let themselves down from above in slings and worked while suspended. Local people did make excellent cordage from long, strong fibers of agaves and yuccas; we know this from missionary reports and remnants of just such cordage found in local caves. However, inspection of the sites invalidates both hypotheses at a glance. The painted shelters were not formed by a gradual wearing down of their floors, but rather by the erosion of their walls and the collapse of their ceilings. In addition, much evidence involving style and preservation indicates that the highest works are usually the newest, not the oldest. The suspension idea is equally infeasible because all the painted walls are topped by rock masses that extend up and out at great distances from the paintings.

The construction of ladders or scaffolds would have been a difficult project, but the materials and technology were available. Most of the shelters containing high figures are found in or near palm-lined arroyos. The trunks of the palms grow to more than 50 feet in height. In addition the entire area is liberally supplied with cardón, the giant cactus whose skeleton consists of a bundle of straight wands of a light but fairly strong fibrous wood. Hunting produced hides from which thongs could have been cut. Using these materials in conjunction with cordage, it would have been possible to construct an apparatus to facilitate work on a high part of a respaldo. Cardón stakes could have been leaned every two or three feet against the desired wall and then converted to a continuous or broad ladder by having more cardón wands bound across them to form rungs. This mesh could have been made as wide as desired and up to heights of about 20 feet. To climb higher, the Painters could have used palm trunks rather than cardón stakes as vertical members.

With ladders, another problem presented itself. Try to visualize an artist attempting to draw a freehand picture of a man or an animal ten feet high and with natural proportions. Imagine that he had to stand on a ladder which placed him so close to the wall that he could not step or lean back to see his entire sketch. Such obstacles obviously were not beyond the Painters' ingenuity. The problem must have been solved by frequent descents of the ladder for inspection, or by long practice, or perhaps by constant communication with a collaborator standing at a vantage point below.

However speculative our view of these preparations may be, we are on firm ground as we approach the actual creation of the art. Ample evidence indicates that many, if not all, artists started by sketching figures in chalk or paint. Many painted figures retain vestiges of chalk outlines, and, in at least a few cases, sketching and then painting was clearly the sequence of events. At El Brinco V, in a closely spaced group of four nicely delineated rabbits, two have been painted black while two more, with identical outlines, remain only as sketches in white chalk. The same site has an unpainted chalk sketch of a medium-sized human figure with an elaborate headdress.

Visible remains of chalk outlines are easily confused with painted outlines. Many Great Mural works were finished with fine bands carefully painted in white, black, pink, or orange. Weathering sometimes reduces these painted outlines to the superficial appearance of chalking. A close inspection, however, will readily show the difference: the painted work, even when eroded, retains flakes of solid paint too thick and regular to result from even a heavy chalking. The right end of the grand cavalcade at El Batequi appears, on close examination, to show both sorts of outlining. Paintings that retain no vestige of chalking or outlining may well have been sketched preliminarily with charcoal, an effective but short-lived drawing material.

Examples of chalks used by the Painters may exist to this day. Three men in the Sierra de Guadalupe and one in the Sierra de San Francisco have given me similar plausible accounts of finding chalks. Each found a small ball or stick of a white or brightly colored chalklike substance that, when tried on rock, produced a good colored line. Each identified the stuff as man-made, evidently a powdered rock loosely cemented with water and perhaps a binder.

We can learn some things about the painting process as we inspect the course of the paintings' decomposition. As these works eroded, each painting technique came to exhibit its own pattern of disintegration. Some of what evidently were once solid colors have eroded evenly and retain the look of a wash of color until they are finally reduced to extinction. These paints appear to have been applied originally as a slurry that produced a thick, even coat with good adherence to the rock.

Some eroded works display streaks of color. The simplest are probably no more than the deterioration of areas that were once chalked solid. These are betrayed at times by a surface that is scratched as well as colored. The chalk strokes show quite clearly and are usually parallel. Another variety of streaked surface seems to have resulted from the erosion of paint that was applied sparingly with a fairly dry brush. A few heavy strokes were probably used to get paint on the area, where it was then worked around to cover. Erosion has apparently removed a good deal of the latter and left a pattern of only the first, heavier brush strokes. By and large, the streaked works of either type appear to be among the last painted of the Great Murals.

Painted outlines give much evidence of having been done with great care. At many sites there are figures in which white or occasionally pink outlines have survived better than any of the larger colored areas. On close examination, these outlines prove to be composed of a heavy layer of paint, probably applied as a thick slurry. In addition, the excellent survival of white paint in general suggests another factor: The Painters may well have learned some of the properties of lime, collected limestone, and burned it in simple beehive kilns built by piling rocks. They were not lacking for materials: Rock is everywhere, the arroyos are littered with dry wood, and there are small pockets of limestone scattered all over the Great Mural region.

Whatever the reason, some of the surviving white paint has a remarkably plasterlike character. In several instances, it survives literally intact on a heavily eroded surface and bridges over small voids in the honeycombed rock beneath. At a number of sites, including El Carrizo and Santa Isabel in the Sierra de Guadalupe, there are figures whose white-painted outlines survive virtually entire, while only the barest vestiges of the interior paint can be detected.

The longevity of all the paints and hence the works as a whole may be purely accidental. The idea that the Painters intended their works to endure is difficult to reconcile with their almost universal willingness to paint over the art of their own forebears.

Who Were the Painters?   The concept of the Painters as a cultural entity is based solely on spectacular artworks confined to limited mountainous regions of the mid-peninsula. The greatest problem in knowing more about them lies in making the short but difficult step from paintings on cave walls to the array of other remains buried or lying about below.

Artifacts of many kinds are widespread and abundant in the Painters' region. Trails, hunting blinds, rock circles, fire pits, smoked caves, cleared areas on level ground, metates, manos, cores, flakes, projectile points, choppers, scrapers, other stone implements, seashells, worked bone and shell, basketry and other woven or braided fibers, bows and arrows, fire sticks and hearths, and other miscellaneous by-products of human toil are found throughout the painted area, many of them in and around painted caves. With adequate archaeological research, this great pool of material probably could be stratified as to both time and cultural levels, but the process has barely begun.

Among the scant studies of the peninsula's prehistory, the work of Dr. William C. Massey seems most relevant. In the 1940s, Massey collected surface artifacts and conducted cursory excavations at a few sites just south of the Great Mural area. He dubbed his aggregate finds "the Comondú cultural complex" after the major town in the area. The term was descriptive of the work of a postulated group of Native Americans whose long occupancy had produced a poorly differentiated succession of artifacts. Massey assumed that the Cochimí encountered in the area in historic times represented the last phase of this culture.

The Jesuits, however, found the Great Mural area occupied by Cochimí, who told the Jesuits of a legend widespread among their people which related that the Cochimí were not the Painters, or even their direct descendants. Thus, from the outset, we seem to be denied the simplest assumption of the Painters' identity.

Several Jesuit missionaries left ethnographic writings describing the people who lived in the Great Mural area in historic times. These works are full of references to cultural traits, crafts, rites, costumes, and even art; matters which tempt us to all sorts of speculation about possible ties to the rock paintings. Consider the reports penned by Sigismundo Taraval in 1732 while he was stationed at San Ignacio. He remarked that the *guamas*, the shamans of the Cochimí, piled their heads so high with all sorts of objects that they made ludicrous figures of themselves. Elsewhere he notes that these same medicine men had the people placate, or moderate, the sun by raising their arms to it.

It would be exceedingly simple to accept these firsthand accounts as explanations for two features found in the Great Murals: Many monos certainly have headdresses that could be silhouettes of manifold objects worked into a head of hair; all the monos in two of the sierras have raised arms, and it is tempting to conclude that these are paintings of obeisances to the sun just as Taraval described. Regrettably, available facts do not permit such conclusions. The only secure link between the Painters and the Cochimí is their occupation of the same terrain at different times.

Despite the probable lapse of centuries, the Painters faced an environment much like that of the later Cochimí. When we study the economy of the Cochimí, we learn about that of the Painters in the process. In visiting the shores for marine food, the Cochimí must have trod their predecessors' trails. And when they collected the seeds of the same trees, what could have been more natural than to kneel at the same grindstones that their predecessors had left at hand?

The great pool of artifacts in the region may show no radical layering of styles or techniques precisely because of the continuity or commonality of the peoples involved. My choice of the name "Painters" is designed to circumvent controversy. Whether archaeology eventually shows that they were indeed an alien group intruding from the north or merely an earlier phase of Cochimí culture, the name serves equally well to designate the people from whom the Great Murals sprang.

If the succession of mid-peninsular inhabitants cannot yet be accurately distinguished, they can, as a group, be compared through their artifacts with others in the greater continental area. The total of the peninsula's prehistoric remains, to which the Painters clearly contributed, can be sifted for factors conspicuously present or absent.

What is missing in the Great Mural region is perhaps more striking than what is present. From the cumulative record, we know that the Painters lacked a number of rather fundamental cultural attainments otherwise common in the greater Southwest. For example, they did not have permanent buildings. They practiced no form of agriculture. They made no pottery. They did not have the domestic dog.

The array of artifacts as a whole is that of a society of hunter-gatherers more primitive in terms of durable remains than most other Southwest groups. Apart from the paintings themselves, their artifacts range from poor to commonplace in design and craft. But long-lived remains do not tell the whole story. Paleolithic people in an environment like this created a great deal more than is suggested by their meager durable remains. Such nomadic cultures concentrated on the production of light, portable, and, hence, ephemeral artifacts. Products crafted of wood, hide, and fibers almost certainly were more sophisticated and differentiated than the less portable products worked from stone.

Movement was the key to life for people inhabiting the central desert of Baja California at any time. No area could support numbers of people throughout the year, not even the seashore. There are few permanent springs along the coasts, so most people who used marine food sources must have done so in short forays, especially after rains had filled temporary water catchments.

Peoples' lives were passed in making seasonal rounds; they were completely dependent on seasonally available fruit, seeds, stems, and roots. In the summer and fall they occupied the foothills and margins of the plains where cactus produced copious fruit. Later they moved to the washes for the ripened pods of seed-bearing trees. In late winter they were probably forced to the intermediate mesas to gather giant agaves, whose hearts they roasted as a staple of their diet.

Missionary accounts show that deer hunting was still an economic necessity at some missions. In aboriginal times, the chief pursuit of Cochimí men was hunting deer, sheep, and antelope—their only sources of meat, leather, gut, and bone. Here, as elsewhere in both time and geography, these hunter-gatherers appear to have ritualized an activity that involved their males and all the large animals in their universe.

At some time during the people's annual rounds, the sierra upland figured as either a pass from plain to plain or as a focus of interest in itself. Most of the hunting must have taken place on the mesas, where the thickest accumulations of edible agaves could also be found. Strategically placed hunting blinds, circular walls of stacked stones, can be seen today in many places in the sierras. Several trails cross each of the mid-peninsular sierras and, in the heights, they branch to enter mesas and cañadas. These trails also pass numerous smoke-blackened caves and shelters, tinajas, and rings of rocks on the ground that are often called "sleeping circles." The age and importance of these trails is indicated by the quantities of stone artifacts and seashells scattered along them.

But, if a succession of cultures occupied the sierras, just one left convincing proof that it did so for reasons other than simple economic necessity. Only the Painters made these places holy ground: places where they came to practice the higher human pursuits of magic, ritual, and symbolism. And, although they might never have thought of it in this way at all, they left us with a vast museum of unexpectedly sophisticated primitive art.

Dating the Painters   The Great Murals exhibit a characteristic that allows any patient observer to fix the relative ages of many painted figures. Overpainting is almost synonymous with the Great Murals. Each generation of ancient painters, unmindful of our interests, buried much of what had been painted before; but that act of overpainting is a curse that may prove to be a blessing in disguise. Overpainting is obviously sequential; that is, the work on top is newest, and so on back to the one that is painted on bare rock or at least is the oldest distinguishable work.

223

As stated earlier, I believe the destruction of Great Mural art has resulted far more from disintegration of rock surfaces than from decomposition of paints. Therefore, I find a site like El Batequi a powerful argument for the relative antiquity of the Great Mural phenomenon. There we see remarkable differences in the erosion of successive layers of painted figures. We see a dramatic contrast between the newest, which are in quite good condition, and the oldest*, which are about to vanish. If the newest are over 500 years of age, as I believe, then a logical argument could be made that the oldest have been on that rock face for 2,000 or more years. Similar observations can be made at several other sites.

Relative dates are interesting, but it is the question of absolute dates that intrigues everyone. Most techniques capable of providing solid evidence for absolute dates require high degrees of scientific skill, elaborate equipment, time, patience, and money. Even without these, we do have before us a good deal of evidence to help in determining at least the end of the painting era. For this, we turn to the writings of the pioneer Jesuits (1683–1720), the same missionaries who provided us with nearly all we know of the peninsular natives' culture and living conditions at the time of their contact with Europeans. These Jesuit reporters included intrepid travelers and explorers, men like Padre Francisco María Piccolo, who knew the Cochimí living on the land as well as those who occupied the missions. The Jesuits left several ethnographic documents of some depth, but none of these mentions rock painting as a contemporary activity. Later in the Jesuit Period (1750–1767), Padres Consag, Barco, Linck, and Ducrue left extensive reports on their Cochimí contemporaries. These missionaries lived and worked at missions surrounded by many kinds of rock art sites, yet they made no reference to contemporary artists practicing in that medium. Neither, for that matter, do we find any rock art on the peninsula that shows evidence of a missionary presence. In many other parts of the world, including Cambodia, Australia, South Africa, and the American Southwest, various forms of rock art were still being created at the time of contact with Western culture. In each of these places, depictions of European people or their animals, garb, or implements soon followed. Among the Great Murals, however, not one such example can be found.

It will be recalled that two Jesuits, Joseph Rothea and Francisco Escalante, actually visited Great Mural sites and became interested enough to write reports of their observations.** Both made inquiries among their Cochimí converts concerning the origin of the rock paintings, and both reported folkloric accounts of a giant people from the north who had painted in the sierras. Each must have accepted the Indians' legend as a reasonable indication of age, because neither made any comment indicating disagreement. Additionally, each divulged a private opinion

*By "oldest," I mean the oldest observable. We have no idea how many layers of paintings may have preceded those now visible.

**See Chapter II.

that the works were old. Since these eyewitness accounts document the earliest examinations of Great Murals of which we have a record, it is worth examining their pertinent parts.

Rothea:
> The durability of these colors seemed notable to me; being there on the exposed rock in the inclemencies of sun and water where they are no doubt struck by rain, strong wind, or water that filters through these same rocks from the hill above, with all this, *after much time,* they remain highly visible. [Italics are mine.]

Joseph Mariano Rothea was a remarkable figure in the history of the San Ignacio area. He worked unusually closely with the headmen of the various rancherias that formed the population of his mission. Under his direction, several stone chapels were built at *visitas,* the visiting stations at satellite ranches. He also supervised the construction of the great dike, La Muralla, in the wash of Arroyo San Ignacio. He planned and partially built the grand church of that mission. In the course of these labors, he came to know the environs, the climate, and the people as few others have. For example, he discovered, no doubt with native guidance, the sources of such stones as cantera and tezontle that were needed for the walls, vaults, and tower of his church. Significantly, his tezontle quarry lies on a mesa in the Sierra de San Francisco. The clearly marked mission trail to that area passes within sight of rock art concentrated in Arroyo del Parral. When this man commented on durability, it is clear that he felt that the quality had been tested. Even without his subsequent and unequivocal time reference, "after much time," it is evident that Rothea was referring to something he regarded as remarkable for its age.

> Escalante (as quoted by Miguel del Barco): "These paintings are well preserved, clear, and perceivable."

Once again the author's intent is clear. One does not flatly refer to something as well preserved unless he assumes that it is also old.

As further evidence, if the reader takes the time to re-read these quotes and then compares them with the photographs in this book, he or she will find that, although more than 200 years have passed since these descriptions were penned, the words apply to many works in their present state with perfect aptness. It should also be recalled that a comparison of Diguet's photo of Los Monos de San Juan with the actual site some 80 years later showed no apparent change. These observations can certainly be used as arguments for the antiquity of the Great Murals.

Yet even if we can satisfy ourselves with the validity of their opinions, the Jesuit chroniclers could scarcely provide absolute dates. We can only guess at the age that would have so impressed them and elicited such remarks. To be on secure ground, all we can do is fix the latest possible date for any of the Great Murals at a time shortly before the missionaries arrived. This puts the creation of the newest of them

225

back over 500 years if we allow them two or three centuries to have acquired the appearance of age.

In the pursuit of absolute dates, broad surveys of rock art in the American Southwest might provide us with a clue to dating the Painters' epoch, or at least to dating two pieces of Great Mural art. For this, however, we must start with astronomical data.

On the fourth of July of 1054 A.D., as reckoned by the Julian calendar, a brilliant object appeared in the heavens in the constellation Taurus. It was visible in broad daylight for 23 days and by night for over 600. The event was reported by Chinese astronomers of the Sung Dynasty in a record called the Sung-Shih. That record, by a fortuitous chain of circumstances, may be instrumental in providing a date within the epoch of the Great Murals.

During the '20s and '30s of this century, the American astronomer Edwin Powell Hubble conducted his renowned studies of celestial nebulae. In the course of this research, he proposed that the great Crab Nebula had originated about 900 years previously in a supernova explosion. He noted the coincidence in time and location suggested by the Sung-Shih, and further studies and calculations by others strengthened his hypothesis. It is now well accepted that the Chinese saw and recorded the birth of the Crab Nebula.

Another American astronomer, William C. Miller of the Mt. Wilson and Palomar Observatories, later calculated that just before dawn on July 5, 1054, the brilliant supernova and the crescent moon appeared in spectacular conjunction. The event was visible only in western North America. In 1955, Miller published his work in a paper that also called attention to at least two examples of Indian rock art in northern Arizona which apparently recorded the remarkable astronomical occurrence. Miller advanced a number of circumstantial but intriguing arguments: The paintings did appear to show just such an occurrence in graphic detail, the appearance of crescent symbols used in any other way was rare or absent in the area, and archaeologists had already proved that both sites were occupied during the time in question. Subsequently, a third American astronomer, John C. Brandt, and his coworkers extended Miller's research, confirmed his calculations, and added examples to the list of painted representations of the event.

In the fall of 1971, I noticed a small painting on the roof of a slit cave in Arroyo del Parral of the Sierra de San Francisco. It showed a circle, with rays like a conventional sun symbol, close to a larger moonlike object (see pages 35, 36). I was immediately struck by its uniqueness. Even at that rather early date in my investigations, I was aware of the rarity of abstract symbols in the Great Mural heartland. Knowing the Painters' propensity for depicting real objects such as men, animals, arrows, and spears, I at first assumed that the painting represented the Sun and the Moon or, even more likely because of their relative sizes, Jupiter or Venus and the Moon.

El Parral, Baja California   White Mesa, Arizona   Navaho Canyon, Arizona   Chaco Canyon, New Mexico

Later, reading a newspaper account of Dr. Brandt's work, I was struck by the similarity of the art he described and illustrated to what I had seen. All the pieces seemed to fit. In the geographical region I was studying, as in his, such symbols were rare — rarer, in fact, than in most of those places where the other "supernova" paintings had been found. If the Painters had been inclined to depict ordinary celestial events, surely there would have been other pictures of the Sun, Moon, and Stars. All my searches turned up no such works; even the simple circle appears rarely among the Great Murals. It is tempting to suppose, along with Miller, Brandt, and others, that only the sudden apparition of a body so brilliant that it shone by day and may well have been seen first in the company of the Moon could have moved the Painters to the unusual act of picturing the event. When I sent Dr. Brandt a photograph of the painting in El Parral, his response — "The painting to my eyes very clearly resembles the other representations of the supernova" — encouraged the supposition.

If we accept, for the moment, the hypothesis that the figure in El Parral really represents an event observed in 1054 A.D., then this small painting takes on extreme significance and deserves a closer examination.

The work is quite faded and deteriorated. At first glance, any observer would be inclined to judge it as relatively old, at least in comparison to the strikingly well-preserved deer painted nearby on the same surface (see page 36). But there is other evidence. This cave has a classic formation; its roof was once a hard layer of rock in intimate contact with a soft layer below. That soft layer has weathered away almost entirely to a depth of 15 feet or so; hence the cave. However, the roof of the cave still has some rather extensive flakes of the softer rock adhering to it. All of the "Moon" and part of the "supernova" are painted on this softer relief from the harder and flatter true ceiling material, so it is these parts of the painting that have suffered the deterioration. At times in the history of the painting, water has percolated through the roof and been held by these flakes of more porous material.

227

The Practices and Puzzles of the Painters

Here it evaporated, leaving a deposit of its dissolved solids. This residue, called caliche, has also affected the color of paint on this surface. Fortunately the remainder of the "supernova" is on the harder, unstained part of the ceiling. There it is in excellent condition and its true color—a rather brownish-red as opposed to the rose-pink of the stained area—can be seen.

Once we understand some of the factors that have affected this painting, it can be compared with others in the same shelter and perhaps, by a less reliable extrapolation, with paintings at other sites. Many such comparisons suggested to me that the work is neither remarkably older nor newer than the average of the Great Murals.

The physical sciences offer more precise methods for fixing dates, but their demands cannot always be met by materials available for dating. The relatively old Carbon14 method, "radiocarbon dating," requires significant quantities of carbon of organic origin for isotopic analysis. Unfortunately, the paintings prove to contain very little; the black pigment surviving so well at some sites is not carbon at all, but rather a complex of metallic oxides. Another potentially applicable dating technique involves quantitative measurements of amino acids that undergo time-related changes. Dr. Jeffrey Bada of Scripps Institution of Oceanography in La Jolla made such a study on paint from a Great Mural site, but the results were frustrating; the amino acid content of the paint was too low to register in even a sensitive test.

Dr. Clement Meighan was responsible for the first reported radiocarbon determination from the Great Mural area. During his 1962 visit to Cueva Pintada, he gathered many artifacts, a collection to which I have referred. Among these was a wooden peg which was submitted to testing for C^{14}. The age of the wood proved to be 530 years, ±80 years. But how are we to interpret this with reference to the paintings? The peg was taken from below the floor surface of a heavily painted cave. No paint or debris connected specifically with the paintings was associated with the peg. Meighan pointed out that the artifact assemblage as a whole was quite homogeneous and fitted well with Massey's Comondú cultural complex. In Meighan's opinion the radiocarbon date placed this assemblage in time and indicated a period when the cave was occupied. He was comfortable with the assumption that the people who had lost the peg had also painted the walls, and he placed paint and painters in the Comondú complex and their time at 1432 A.D. ±80 years. Meighan then indulged in a bit of unexplained conjecture when he chose to regard his C^{14} finding as the probable end of the painting period and to place its beginning 500 years earlier.

➤　➤　➤

Since about 1980, when I concluded my study of the Great Murals, and especially in the past few years, several teams of researchers from Mexico, Spain, and the United States have conducted fieldwork at Great Mural sites and subsequent laboratory work designed to learn more about the Painters by making on-site observations and by studying all recoverable artifacts. In the Afterword that follows this final chapter, Enrique Hambleton tells the story of this research and other activities launched in concerted efforts by local, regional, national, and international authorities to know and date the Great Murals, and to preserve them and their fragile environment.

**El Cartucho near the headwaters
of Arroyo de San Pablo**

Sierra de San Francisco.

CHAPTER 8

Afterword

The Cave Paintings of Baja California *is a timeless account of exploration and discovery. It stands as one of the seminal works on Baja California's rock art and is responsible, in no small measure, for an exponential growth in interest by professional and avocational researchers worldwide.*

When Harry Crosby and I undertook the expeditions described in the previous pages, little was known of the extent and number of rock art sites in the mid-peninsula. The sphere of influence of the Great Mural tradition and the boundaries of the territory it occupied had scarcely been guessed at. Our project took some of the first steps in attempting to answer these and other puzzling questions. Since the publication of the first edition in 1975, a number of other projects have continued the quest for knowledge about this extraordinary cultural manifestation. My own book, *La Pintura Rupestre de Baja California,* published in Mexico in 1979 by Fomento Cultural Banamex, was my initial effort to create awareness within Mexico of the importance of the Great Murals. In the years since, scientific interest has grown to involve individuals and institutions from many countries, generating an important number of publications, documentaries, exhibitions, symposia, and research projects.

To my mind, conservation is the single most important element in this new-found interest; without an active program of conservation, future endeavors to understand the significance of this phenomenon would be severely compromised, or prevented altogether. Up to the early 1980s, the central sierras of Baja California were an unprotected wilderness. Their sparse population represented an outpost of Mexican culture and had no links to the indigenous people who created the remarkable concentration of prehistoric art. Mexican Government — federal, state, and local — had little interest in the matter, and their official indifference produced alarming results. Looting of sites by local inhabitants and visitors was widespread; official neglect was interpreted as tacit permission to vandalize, collect, deface, or otherwise destroy the rock art itself as well as associated archaeological material.

Today, a very different attitude exists among sierra folk and visitors to their mountains; both have come to realize the importance of their legacy from the past. The local inhabitants have become an effective first line of defense that protects rock art and is backed by official concern and support. As a shining example of this change in attitude, a strategy has been created for the conservation and management of the Sierra de San Francisco which is a model for the rest of the peninsula, Mexico, and the world.

During the last 20 years, an ongoing quest for knowledge and the persistence of a handful of people have brought about significant changes. The most critical and the most difficult step was to involve the government of Mexico. Appropriate agencies had to be convinced of the importance of this cultural heritage and to give it a priority within the national context. We have such extraordinary archaeological wealth in Mexico that Baja California scarcely had been noticed; official attention was firmly focused on Mesoamerica. After many years of representing the importance of Baja California's rock art to presidents, governors, officials, and basically anyone who would listen, I began to receive support and encouragement from the Instituto Nacional de Antropología e Historia (INAH) for my efforts to promote conservation and research. Among those who have been instrumental in bringing about a new awareness are Teresa Franco, Director of INAH, Alejandro Martínez Muriel, Director of Archaeology at INAH, and Jorge Amao Manríquez, Director of INAH in Baja California Sur.

In 1985 and 1986, INAH opened regional centers in Baja California Sur and Baja California respectively and began to take responsibility for the protection of some of the most accessible and most frequently visited rock art sites. A survey of the peninsula's vast archaeological heritage initiated in the early 1980s was revived. It had been plagued by numerous problems, which caused it to advance in fits and starts or grind to a halt on several occasions. In 1988, El Vizcaíno Biosphere Reserve was declared, providing additional protection for rock art sites within its boundaries. Its 5.5 million acres include the Sierra de San Francisco and the extreme northern end of the Sierra de Guadalupe. In 1989, the Fundación Amigos de Sudcalifornia, Asociación Civil (AMISUD) was founded. This Mexican nongovernmental organization based in La Paz is dedicated to the conservation and understanding of Baja California Sur's cultural heritage. It provides a link between research and conservation projects and the Mexican Government, contributes to the training of sierra folk in serving as guides and custodians, and is one of the driving forces behind the protection, conservation, and management of the state's cultural resources.

A team from the University of Barcelona undertook three seasons of investigation, 1989–1991, at Great Mural sites in the Sierra de San Francisco and Sierra de Guadalupe. Their researchers carried out archaeological excavations at Cueva del Ratón and a shelter without paintings in Arroyo de San Gregorio—which turned out to be a lithic workshop of impressive proportions. They also reported the first radiocarbon dates for Great Mural pigments at Cueva del Ratón. The black mountain lion gave a date of 4,845 B.P. ±60 years. This date created controversy in some academic circles because it pushed back the time frame considerably from previous estimates. The team has published papers and articles on its findings and conclusions.

In October of 1992, the Programa de Proyectos Arqueológicos Especiales (INAH 1992–94) chose 12 archaeological zones in Mexico for special consideration and funding. The Sierra de San Francisco was among them. The project was the greatest effort Mexico had ever undertaken regarding the archaeology of hunters and gatherers. As a result, our perception of the achievements of pre-Columbian nomadic cultures in Mexico has been irrevocably altered—and we are richer for it. A team from INAH was assigned full time to the area to complete a much delayed survey and undertake a series of excavations. Among their findings was the discovery in Cueva Pintada of a fragment of textile which proved to be 3,000 years old, the oldest yet discovered in northwest Mexico. Late in the project, human bones from a site known as Cueva del León were discovered. They show unmistakable signs of having been painted in red ochre and black pigment. This project also contained provisions to develop conservation practices at six of the most frequently visited rock art sites: Cueva del Ratón, Cueva de Las Flechas, Cueva Pintada, Cueva de La Soledad, Cueva de la Boca de San Julio, and Cueva de Los Músicos (Boca de San Julio II).

In December of 1993, UNESCO designated the Sierra de San Francisco a World Heritage Site. This gave even greater priority within Mexico to an important international effort to recognize and protect this fragile cultural treasure. A number of highly respected individuals in the field of rock art consider the Great Murals to be among the most important concentrations of prehistoric parietal art on earth. Philip Tobias of the University of Witwatersand in South Africa and Sharon Sullivan, Director of the Australian Heritage Commission, place them in the illustrious company of Australian Aboriginal art, art of South African Bushmen, Paleolithic art of Southern Europe, and art found on the Tasili N'Ajjer Plateau in Algeria.

In May of 1994, INAH, The Getty Conservation Institute, the Government of Baja California Sur, and AMISUD jointly formed and fielded the Proyecto de Conservación de Pintura Rupestre de la Sierra de San Francisco. The project's first field season began at Cueva del Ratón just as the Programa de Proyectos Arqueológicos Especiales was nearing completion. These two programs coincided in their aims to conserve and manage the area's sites. I have worked closely with both and take justifiable pride in what they have accomplished.

The Proyecto de Conservación is training conservators from Mexico, Argentina, Bolivia, and Chile in the disciplines necessary for conservation of rock art. This project also achieved a historical first for Mexico: the creation and implementation of a management plan incorporating a consensus of the interests of everyone with a stake in the area. This plan is distinguished by its simplicity, logic, and absolute reliance on local participation and input. The walkways, livestock gates, and signs installed by INAH have been welcomed by the vast majority of residents and visitors. The villages of San Francisco de la Sierra and Santa Marta have organized to serve as staging areas for visits. Villagers participate enthusiastically as guides, outfitters, and custodians in a program they helped develop and implement. This is a significant achievement which brought the people of the Sierra de San Francisco into the decision-making process. They became partners and principal beneficiaries of the rational development of their mountains and the archaeological treasure they contain.

In San Ignacio, INAH set up a museum and visitor center where trips to the cave paintings of the Sierra de San Francisco can be authorized, organized, and scheduled. Since January 1995, rules and regulations have been in effect which provide protection for the sites and the natural environment, outline the responsibilities of guides and custodians, and install a code of behavior for visitors to the area.

A change in attitude on the part of the Mexican Government, the local inhabitants, researchers, academics, and visitors alike has come slowly and not without controversy. Diverse interests and opinions yielded to compromises carefully arranged through discussions and negotiations. It has been a positive and welcome change and one which places the future of this most fragile of archaeological manifestations on firmer ground.

This book is a guide to some of the remotest and most beautiful environments on the peninsula, settings that display much more than cave paintings. The natural context is a treasury of biodiversity, the people that inhabit these mountains are a culture little-known or studied. The reader needs to be aware of the responsibility which is implicit in this work should it be used as a field guide. It not only offers an opportunity to experience the cave paintings of Baja California but also its culture and natural environment. It provides an access key to a delicate world where one must tread softly and with respect. Please help Mexico conserve its cultural and natural heritage — your actions will speak loudly of your intentions.

I have no doubt that future volumes will be written about this remarkable art form and that it will loom large in the world's cultural heritage. I also believe that the explorations described in *The Cave Paintings of Baja California* will remain a basic part of the story. It is an honor and a privilege to have been a participant.

— Enrique Hambleton, President of AMISUD

235

Appendix

Leon Diguet among the Great Murals

Leon Diguet, born in Le Havre in 1859, was a French industrial chemist brought to Baja California by a French mining concern in 1889 and installed in the company town of Santa Rosalía. Diguet took a broad interest in the naturalism of the mid-peninsula. He explored and collected in the area during his three-year stint with the company and, on his return to France in 1892, he gave extensive collections to the Museum of Natural History and the Museum of Man in Paris.

The quality of these collections and Diguet's enthusiasm attracted attention. Shortly after returning to France, he was authorized and financed to lead an expedition to observe and collect in Baja California. This proved to be the beginning of a series of five such ventures in various parts of Mexico.

Diguet's Baja California exploration of 1893–94 produced most of the data for his important paper, "Notes on the Pictographs of Baja California" (1895). Diguet's work and especially this article and its photographs and drawings entitle him to be considered the first serious student of the Great Murals. Through him, the outstanding sites of San Borjitas, Los Monos de San Juan, and Cuesta de Palmarito were disclosed to the world and, indeed, the phenomenon of rock painting on the peninsula was rediscovered.

Diguet closed his 1895 publication with "a list of localities where one can observe specimens. . . . " Of the 30 rock art sites that he enumerated, the first 18 fall in or near the Great Mural area:

1. Cave of el Zalate near the 29th parallel, about 15 leagues from Calamahi [Calmallí], near the road from Calamahi to San Borga [San Borja].

2. Cave of el Carmen, between Calamahi [Calmallí] and Santa Gertrudis.

3. Santa Gertrudis, a cave in a cañada opening into the arroyo, across from the mission.

4. Between Santa Gertrudis and Puerto Trinidad, near the highest point of the cuesta de San Juan.

5. Cave, a few leagues away from the rancho of San Pablo, near the 28th parallel.

6. Rock shelter one league from the rancho of San Pablo, on the way to Calamahi [Calmallí].

7. The sierra of San Francisco, the rock shelters of Palmarito and of Cuesta Blanca and of Cueva del Raton, at the height of the sierra and near the rancho of San Francisco.

8. Cañada del Muerto, near the 27th parallel: petroglyphs and cliff with paintings.

9. San Juan in the arroyo of San Pedro.

10. San Matillita [San Matiitas], cañada opening into the arroyo of San Adeo [San Tadeo].

11. San Adeo [San Tadeo], rock shelter near the rancho.

12. Petroglyphs in the arroyo of las Piedras Pintas, near Mulegé.

13. Paintings in a cañada, near the rancho de Trinidad, about 10 leagues from Mulegé.

14. Paintings in the sierra of Guadalupe, near the ranchos of Guadalupe, San Isabel [Santa Isabel] and of el Pozo.

15. San Borgita [San Borjitas], near the rancho de San Baltazar, 10 leagues from Mulegé.

16. Arroyo de Guajademí, a few deer painted in the caves and one stone covered with petroglyphs.

17. A cliff with paintings near the rancho of San José, in the arroyo de Guajademí.

18. Paintings in a cañada, near the rancho of la Purísima Vieja.

In 1974, in response to awakening interest in Baja California rock art, Campbell Grant published a translation of Diguet's list in his *Rock Art of Baja California,* from which I borrowed the above. Grant called Diguet's inventory vague and inaccurate and despaired of finding most of his sites. However, Grant spent very little time in the peninsular field and he passed judgment too quickly. With some fieldwork and by making a few cautious assumptions, good arguments can be made for the locations of most of Diguet's sites.

Inconsistency is the severest obstacle. While some sites are pinpointed (like #4), others are unspecific to the extent of many miles (like #2). Some specify whether paintings or petroglyphs were to be found, others do not. Most refer to single sites, but in two cases (#7 and #14), three sites are grouped which are actually miles apart. Finally, the list in general seems to start in the north and work south but there is obvious confusion of this plan in #s 5, 6, 7, as well as in #s 14 and 15. In these cases there is either a reversal or a severe doubling back.

The most probable reason for this inconsistent report was that Diguet did not personally visit all the sites he reported. He certainly employed guides, and when he found that they led him to good examples of rock art, he probably asked them about other sites. This could account for odd groupings like #7 and #14.

On the positive side, most of the place names used by Diguet demonstrably survive in the areas involved.

Allowing for a few spelling errors by Diguet and making the probable corrections (in brackets in the list above), just two out of the 30 place names used in #s 1-18 remain stubbornly obscure. These are the Caves of El Zalate and El Carmen in items #1 and #2. The former may be truly lost. A cave with a huge, spreading zalate tree issuing from its mouth would be notable. But these trees are also fairly short lived. For this reason the name has appeared, mostly ephemerally, in many parts of southern Baja California. El Carmen may simply require more research; little effort has been made to tap the memories of appropriate people.

Locating the remaining place names does not locate all the art. Items like #5 will always be open to question because of vagueness. Nevertheless, most of the remainder are feasible. The present work describes the probable sites and art for #s 4, 7, 8, 9, 13, 14, 15, 16, and 17 (see Index). In addition, it gives probable locations for #10 and #11. #12 is well-known in its region.

There may always be a bit of mystery about the travels of Leon Diguet but, by referring to the above, reading his articles, and noting what he considered important enough to describe, photograph, and draw, I believe we can locate and identify most of the Great Murals that he attempted to report.

Acknowledgments

Enrique Hambleton accompanied me on most of the explorations that led to this work. He assisted and backed me up in many ways: His presence provided invaluable companionship and enthusiasm as well as insurance against the unforeseeable problems that arise in remote parts. Latterly, Enrique has become a vital part of the planning, organization, and execution of governmental and institutional moves to study and protect Baja California's rock art even as it achieves an ever-growing public. The present edition profits immeasurably from his essay on recent events relating to the Great Murals and from his permission to use the 14 of his photographs reproduced on pages x, 22, 36, 59, 61, 67, 68, 79, 88, 89, 96, 97, 151, and 197.

Ramón Arce Agúndez accompanied Enrique and me on several of our longest expeditions. He was the perfect complement to Tacho Arce, his aging father from whom he had learned much. Ramón was tireless in executing the chores that accompany long muleback expeditions and even more diligent in pursuing the goals of our explorations. He was at all times the most observant member of our party and he developed an uncanny ability to anticipate, look for, and detect rock art. I and this work owe much to him.

Many of the people who assisted me in locating and visiting the Great Murals have become part of the story on these pages, but there were others who made significant contributions to this work:

At the outset of my adventures in Baja California, before I had ever mounted a mule or even set foot on the ground, Eve Ewing showed me her photographs of peninsular rock art and shared memories of her experiences while traveling in its wildernesses. Many valuable pointers were thus obtained. Eve has retained her interest in the Great Murals and made her own contributions to finding and describing them.

Narciso Villavicencio, a native of the heart of Guadalupe now residing in Mulegé, acted as my guide and recruited the invaluable services of members of his extended family and mountain friends to make possible my significant trip into the Sierra de Guadalupe in 1980.

Marie Christine Meynet Forester devoted herself to translating long passages of the writings of Leon Diguet with great care so that several questions could be answered which were complicated by that explorer's colloquial and imprecisely written French.

Joanne Haskell Crosby, my wife, did the composite representation of art at Cueva de la Serpiente, worked with me to create many of the small facsimiles of rock painting details, typed the original manuscript of this work, and managed our family and affairs during my necessarily extended absences. The entire project depended on her essential partnership.

Ristin Crosby Decker, our elder daughter, examined several important sites, including El Batequi. Later, working with dozens of photographs, she created the restored facsimile of the grand cavalcade on the ceiling of that site which is reproduced in this work. Since then, she has completed major commissions to create full-scale facsimiles of important groupings of Great Murals at Twin Dolphin Hotel, Cabo de San Lucas, and at Rancho La Puerta, Tecate.

➤ ➤ ➤

Diana and Lowell Lindsay, otherwise known as Sunbelt Publications, are responsible for this new edition. I am grateful to them not only for their enthusiasm and devotion to the production of a good work, but also for giving me the satisfaction of adding a few new rock art sites, including some of Enrique Hambleton's excellent photographs, and re-editing what was actually my first attempt to write. I also appreciate the invaluable production services provided by Gerald Marino, the very involved and knowledgeable supervisor of the whole project, and members of the Marino Group: Paul Slick for an apt and fresh book design, Dana Monroe for valiant copy editing of a difficult text; and Dale Stauffer at ColorType for personal attention to the reproduction of all the images that form the backbone of this work.

Glossary

In some cases the words or usages in this text are peculiar to parts of Baja California and are not found in a standard Spanish-English dictionary.

ademe, a wall of dry-laid stone to support a fill of rubble in building hillside trails

aerolito, a meteorite

ancón, a bank or shelf of level ground just above the wash of a watercourse

andariego, a wanderer; a person with no permanent place of residence

angostura, a narrows; a narrow part of an arroyo

arroyo, a major watercourse

aura, the common bald vulture (*Cathartes aura*)

bahía, a bay on ocean or gulf

batequi, a waterhole dug in the sand of the *caja* of an arroyo

bebelama, an indigenous tree (*Bumelia occidentalis*)

berrendo, the pronghorn antelope (*Antilocapra americana*)

borrado-a, erased, faded, worn away

borrego, the bighorn sheep or mountain sheep (*Ovis canadensis*)

brinco, a leap or jump; a place which forces one to jump

caja, the bed or wash of a watercourse

camino real, a principal road or trail

cañada, a watercourse tributary to an arroyo

cajón, an impressively steep-walled narrow watercourse; gorge

cantera, a volcanic agglomerate stone easily worked with hand tools

cantil, a high rock palisade; usually the broken edge of a flow of volcanic stone

cantilería, an impressive array of *cantil; cantil en masse*

cardón, the giant cactus (*Pachycereus pringlei*); vertical, usually branched and grows to over 50 feet in height

carrizo, a canelike giant grass plant, heights to ten feet

chubasco, a violent, rain-laden summer storm

cirio, a columnar plant (*Fouquiera columnaris*) of the Ocotillo family; usually a single unbranched stalk growing to 40 or more feet

Cochimí, the people inhabiting the Great Mural area during the contact and mission periods—16th to 19th centuries—and probably long before

comida, food in general; the midday meal

copalquín, the "elephant tree;" a small tree with swollen multitrunks (*Pachycormus discolor*)

cuesta, a steep trail up the slope of an arroyo or mountain side

cueva, a cave or deep rock shelter

cuevona, an unusually large cave; the largest cave in a region

dátilillo, a giant yucca (*Yucca valida*), similar to the Joshua tree

dueño, owner; proprietor; landlord; master

falda, the slope of a hill; literally, a skirt

falluquero, in former times, a mounted dry-goods salesman

garabatillo, a leguminous shrub (*Mimosa purpurescens*) with long branches, wicked thorns

gato montés, the peninsular bobcat or lynx (*Felis rufus*)

guatamote; huatamote, a tall-stemmed arroyo shrub (*Baccharis glutinosa*)

huerta, an orchard; a vegetable garden

La Jollan Culture, the human group that occupied areas west of the mountains of southern California and northern Baja California about 5,000 B.C.

león, the mountain lion or puma (*Felis concolor*)

mancha, a spot or stain

mano, a hand grindstone worked on the surface of a metate

mesa, elevated but level terrain; in central Baja California, the surviving surface of an eroded lava flow

metate, a grindstone used by prehistoric native Americans

mezcal, any of several native agaves

mezquite, a common arroyo tree (*Prosopis* species)

mono, a caricature, a drawing of a human figure

palo blanco, a slim, often multitrunked tree with white bark (*Lysiloma candida*)

palo brea, a small, green-barked leguminous tree (*Cercidium praecox*) *paraje,* a stopping place; usually selected for available water and animal fodder

picacho, a sharp mountain peak, usually somewhat solitary

pila, a reservoir, usually made of stone and mortar

pilón, pylon; sugar loaf; shaped like a pylon or sugar loaf

pinturita, a small or miniature painting

pitahaya, the organ pipe cactus (*Lemaireocereus thurberi*), a vital source of food for aboriginal man in Baja California

portezuelo, a pass, usually over a ridge between adjacent watercourses

ranchería, a settlement of Indians who lived and moved together seasonally; the headquarters of such a group

respaldo, an overhung rock face

salto, a waterfall; the site of a seasonal falls

San Dieguito Culture, the earliest human group—about 8,000 B.C.—to leave large numbers of identifiable artifacts in southern California

tajo, a man-made water catchment dug or scraped out of a natural low area

tezontle, a basaltic rock made light by inclusive gas bubbles

tinaja, a natural water catchment

torote, a small tree (*Bursera microphylla*) with swollen trunk and branches and tiny leaves

visita, a visiting station; a place outside a mission visited periodically by a priest to hold services

vivienda, a site of regular prehistoric encampments

zalate, the native fig (*Ficus palmeri*), which can become a large, spreading tree; has off-white bark; regularly extends above-ground roots up to 50 feet seeking for water.

Glossary

Bibliography

The following list contains the works I consulted during research for earlier editions of this book. I have added items suggested by Enrique Hambleton, Ken Hedges, and Anita Alvarez de Williams, and selected a few articles that I found most pertinent to this work among the many on Baja California rock art in the series published by The San Diego Museum of Man: "Rock Art Papers," vols. 1–12, included in San Diego Museum Papers, vols. 16–33 (1983–1995).

Aschmann, Homer
1959   *The Central Desert of Baja California: Demography and Ecology.* Ibero-Americana, no. 42. The University of California, Berkeley and Los Angeles, 43–44. Reprinted 1967, Riverside, California: Manessier.

Barco, Miguel del
1973   [Adiciones y correcciones a la Noticia de Miguel Venegas.] Edited by Miguel León-Portilla; published under the title *Historia natural y crónica de la Antigua California.* Universidad Nacional Autonoma de México, México, D. F.

Bayle, Constantino
1946   *Misión de la Baja California* (pp 267–68, anonymous [1790]). Madrid: Editorial Católica.

Bendímez Patterson, Julia
1991   "Proyecto de registro de sitios Arqueológicos con pictografias y petrograbados en Baja California." In *Propuesta: Programa de Investigación y Conservación de Patrimonio Arqueológico de Baja California.* Arq. Jorge Serrano González, Arq. Julia Bendímez Patterson, Centro Regional del Instituto Nacional de Antropología e Historia [INAH] en Baja California, Mexicali.

Brandt, John C., Stephen P. Maran, et al
1975   "Possible Rock Art Records of the Crab Nebula Supernova in the Western United States." In *Archaeoastronomy in Pre-Columbian America,* edited by A. F. Aveni. Austin, Texas: University of Texas Press.

Casado, María del Pilar, and Lorena Mirambell, eds.
1990   "Arte rupestre en Baja California. . . ." *El arte rupestre en México:* Antologías, Serie Arqueológica, Instituto Nacional de Antropología e Historia [INAH], 131–256.

Clavijero, Francisco Javier
1937   *The History of [Lower] California,* translated from the Spanish by Sara E. Lake and A. A. Gray. Stanford: Stanford University Press, 84–85. Reprinted 1971, Riverside, California: Manessier.

Cover, Del
1990   "Clavelitos." *Rock Art Papers,* 7, included in San Diego Museum Papers, 26. [Reports the discovery of a site in a cañada tributary to the Arroyo de Cadegomó that exhibits paintings in the styles of several of the "schools" found in the southern reaches of the Sierra de Guadalupe.]

Dahlgren de Jordán, Barbro
1954   "Las pinturas rupestres de la Baja California." *Artes de México,* 3: 22–8.

Dahlgren, Barbro, and Javier Romero
1951   "La prehistoria Baja Californiana: Redescubrimiento de pinturas rupestres." *Cuadernos Americanos,* 58: 153–78.

Diguet, Leon
1895   "Note sur la Pictographie de la Basse Californie." *Anthropologie,* 6: 160–75. 1899

"Rapport sur une Mission Scientifique dans la Basse-Californie." *Nouvelle Archives des Missions Scientifiques,* 9:1–53.

1912   *Territorio de la Baja California: Reseña Geográfica y Estadística.* Mexico, D. F.: Librería de la Viuda de C. Bouret.

Ewing, Eve
1983   "Two Rock Art Sites from the Sierra de San Juan, Central Baja California." *Rock Art Papers,* 1, in San Diego Museum Papers, 16. [Reports one of very few surveys made of rock art in the Sierra de San Juan.]

Fullola, José María, María M. Bergadá, Victoria del Castillo, María Angeles Petit, and Albert Rubio
1994a   "Comunidades pre-hispánicas de Baja California." *Investigación y Ciencia* [Spanish Edition of *Scientific American*], 211 (April 1994): 8–15.
1994b   "A propósito de la datación de las pinturas rupestres." *La Vanguardia,* Science and Technology Supplement (30 April 1994), Barcelona.

Gardner, Erle Stanley
1962a   "A Legendary Treasure Left by a Long Lost Tribe." *Life,* 53 (3): 57–64.
1962b   *The Hidden Heart of Baja.* New York: Morrow.
1967   *Off the Beaten Track in Baja.* New York: Morrow.

Grant, Campbell
1974   *Rock Art of Baja California.* Los Angeles: Dawson's Book Shop. [Includes "Notes on the Pictographs of Baja California" by Leon Diguet (1895), translated from the French by Roxanne Lapidus.]

Gutiérrez M., María de la Luz
1994   "Pintura rupestre en la Sierra de San Francisco, Baja California Sur." *Revista de Arqueología Mexicana,* 1 (6): 57–63.

Gutiérrez M., María de la Luz, Enrique Hambleton, Justin Hyland, and Nicholas P. Stanley Price

1996   "The management of World Heritage sites in remote areas: The Sierra de San Francisco, Baja California, Mexico." *Conservation and Management of Archaeological Sites,* 1 (4).

Hambleton, Enrique
1979   *La Pintura rupestre de Baja California.* México, D. F.: Fomento Cultural Banamex

Johnson, William Weber
1972   *Baja California.* Time-Life Books, *The American Wilderness* series. New York: Time Inc.

Lafferty, Christopher M.
1983   "The Correct Identification of Two Cave Paintings in Baja California." *Rock Art Papers, 1, in San Diego Museum Papers, 16. [Argues persuasively that figures at Cueva Pintada and San Gregorio, commonly assumed to represent whales, have the anatomy of pinnipeds.]*

López, Ernesto Raúl
1970   "Nuevos hallazgos de pinturas rupestres en Baja California." *Calafia,* 1 (3): 19–25. Universidad Autónoma de Baja California, Mexicali. English translation published [1972] in *Pacific Coast Archaeological Society Quarterly,* 8 (1): 10–14.

Massey, William C.
1947   "Brief Report on Archaeological Investigations in Baja California." *Southwestern Journal of Anthropology,* 3 (4): 344–59.
1949   "Tribes and Languages of Baja California." *Southwestern Journal of Anthropology,* 5 (3): 272–307.
1961   "The Cultural Distinction of Aboriginal Baja California." *In Homenaje a Pablo Martinez del Rio,* 411–422. México, D. F.

Meighan, Clement W.
1966   "Prehistoric Rock Painting in Baja California." *American Antiquity,* 31 (3): 372–92.
1969   *Indian Art and History, the Testimony of Pre-hispanic Rock Paintings in Baja California.*

Baja California Travels Series, 13. Los Angeles: Dawson's Book Shop.

Miller, William C.
1955   "Two Prehistoric Drawings of Possible Astronomical Significance." Astronomical Society of the Pacific, San Francisco, California. Leaflet no. 314 (July 1955).

Moore, Elanie A.
1984   "Aboriginal Murals, Baja California Sur: A Visual Study." Master's thesis, Art Center of Design, Pasadena, California.

Ritter, Eric W., and Anita Alvarez de Williams
1991   "Baja California Rock Art Bibliography." An extensive list of major and minor publications, on file at Museo Universitario, Universidad Autónoma de Baja California/Mexicali.

Rubio, Albert, Victoria del Castillo, José María Fullola, and María Angeles Petit
1994   "The first rock art datings in Lower California (Mexico)." *International Newsletter on Rock Art.* Comitç Internacional D'Art Rupestre, Foix, 9:1–4.

Stanley Price, Nicholas P.
1995   "Conservation of Rock Art in Baja California, Mexico. Report on the first two field campaigns, 1994 1995" (unpublished). The Getty Conservation Institute, Marina Del Rey, California.
1996   "The Great Murals: Conserving the Rock Art of Baja California." The Getty Conservation Institute Newsletter, 11 (2): 4–9.

Uriarte, María Teresa
1981   *Pintura rupestre en Baja California: Algunos métodos para su apreciación artística.* Cuadernos del México Prehispánico, Colección Científica no. 106, Instituto Nacional de Antropología e Historia [INAH], México, D. F.

Viñas, Ramón
1991   "Observaciones astronómicas en las pinturas rupestres de Baja California Sur." *Revista Panorama,* Editorial Universidad Autónoma de Baja California Sur, La Paz.

Viñas, R., E. Sarriá, A. Rubio, and V. del Castillo
1990   "Repertorio temático de la pintura rupestre de la Sierra de San Francisco, Baja California." *El Arte Rupestre de México,* María del Pilar Casado and Lorena Mirambell, Antologías, Serie Arqueológica, Instituto Nacional de Antropología e Historia [INAH], México, D. F.

Viñas, Ramón, and Enrique Hambleton
1991   "Los grandes murales de Baja California Sur." *Revista de Arqueología.* Instituto Nacional de Antropología e Historia [INAH], México, D. F.

Williams, Anita Alvarez de
1975   *Primeros pobladores de la Baja California: Introducción a la antropología de la Peninsula.* Mexicali: Talleres Gráficos del Gobierno del Estado de Baja California.

Index

- For items that pertain directly to rock paintings, consult first the heading "Great Mural art" in this index.
- The symbol ▲ indicates a rock art site or sites located at or in the immediate area of the indexed item.
- Italic numerals indicate illustrations of indexed items. Most italicized pages also contain textual references to the indexed items.
- Geographic items are marked [G] for Guadalupe, [SB] for San Borja, [SF] for San Francisco, or [SJ] for San Juan in cases where placenames are duplicated in the different sierras.

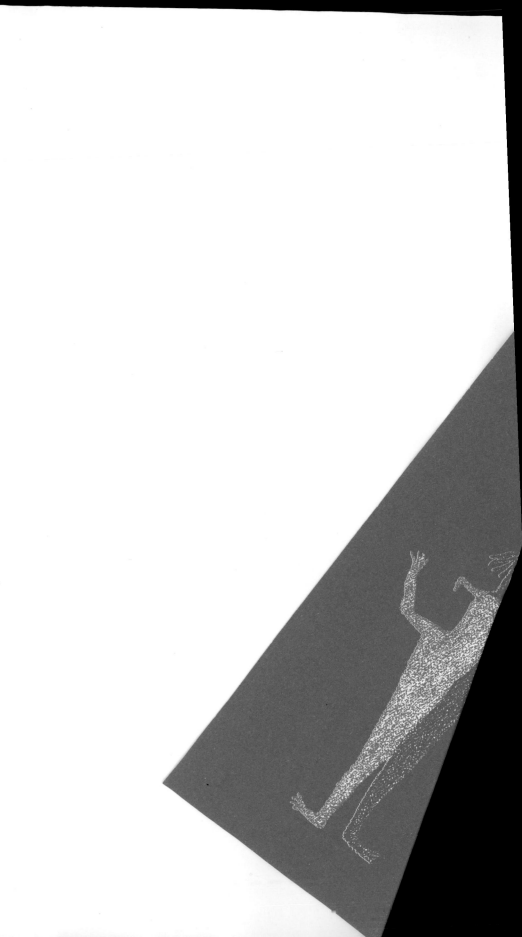